Fiscal Policy and Social Welfare

Fiscal Policy and Social Welfare

An Analysis of Alternative Tax
and Transfer Systems

John Creedy

The Truby Williams Professor of Economics
University of Melbourne, Australia

Edward Elgar
Cheltenham, UK • Lyme, US

Published by
Edward Elgar Publishing Limited
8 Lansdown Place
Cheltenham
Glos GL50 2HU
UK

Edward Elgar Publishing, Inc.
1 Pinnacle Hill Road
Lyme
NH 03768
US

Reprinted 1997

British Library Cataloguing in Publication Data
Creedy, John
    Fiscal Policy and Social Welfare:
    An Analysis of Alternative Tax and Transfer
    Systems
    I. Title
    336

Library of Congress Cataloguing in Publication Data
Creedy, John, 1949–
    Fiscal policy and social welfare: an analysis of alternative tax
and transfer systems / John Creedy.
    Includes index.
    1. Tax incidence—Mathematical models. 2. Taxation—Mathematical
models. 3. Income distribution—Mathematical models. 4. Transfer
payments—Mathematical models. I. Title
HJ2321.C73 1996
336.2—dc20   95–36558
                                                              CIP

ISBN 978 1 85898 246 5

Printed and bound by CPI Group (UK) Ltd, Croydon, CR0 4YY

Contents

Figures

Tables

Acknowledgements

This book represents an attempt to present a systematic treatment of the modelling of tax and transfer systems, and their redistributive effects, moving gradually from the context of fixed pre-tax income distributions, through the case of fixed wage rate distributions, and finally to the general equilibrium framework. Parts of the book draw on, or use insights from, work previously carried out with joint authors. This includes work on pensions with Richard Disney (1992) and Margaret Morgan (1993); on value added taxes with Norman Gemmell (1982, 1984); on majority voting with Patrick Francois (1993); on lifetime redistribution with Lisa Cameron (1995); and on income distribution in general equilibrium with Guay Lim (1995). I have learnt much from collaborating with these authors. Other parts of the book draw on results in Creedy (1982; 1992; 1993 a, b; 1994 a, b; 1995). I should like to thank the relevant journals for permission to make use of parts of these papers.

In planning and preparing the book I have benefited from the suggestions of Peter Lambert, whose own work continues to provide much stimulus. His book (Lambert, 1993a) was particularly useful in planning the first two substantive chapters of the present book. I should also like to thank Swee Teen Chua and Rajat Sood for their detailed and very helpful comments on an earlier draft. I only wish I could satisfy all their requests for improvements.

The huge burden of word processing was borne with skill and humour (both very important) by Julie Carter and Karen Bennett. My original diagrams were computer scanned, and the camera-ready copy was then produced by Anthony Draga.

1. Introduction

The aim of this book is to provide a consistent treatment of tax and transfer systems and their redistributive effects. The emphasis is very much on the modelling of alternative structures; the more detailed theoretical public finance treatment of taxes and the conceptual issues relating to income redistribution have been dealt with at length by other authors. The discussion moves systematically from the context of fixed labour supplies, so that the pre-tax income distribution is fixed, to that of endogenous labour supplies, assuming instead that the distribution of wage rates is fixed. Finally, the analysis is extended to a general equilibrium framework, so that wage rates too are endogenous. Significant attention is given to the analysis of taxes and redistribution in a multi-period framework, including the treatment of pension schemes. Consistent with the emphasis on modelling, many numerical examples are given using tables and diagrams. These examples were all produced using computer programs written by the author. Copies of the programs, along with documentation, are available on request; see Creedy (1995b).

1.1. OUTLINE OF FUTURE CHAPTERS

The substance of the book is divided into three major parts, dealing respectively with fixed labour supplies, variable labour supplies, and general equilibrium. Before starting the analysis of taxes, however, Chapter 2 introduces some preliminaries. The purpose of this is to present some basic tools of analysis that are used in later chapters. Hence it discusses the representation of income distributions, the measurement of inequality and the associated social welfare functions. Alternative schemes are examined in later chapters in terms of their effects on inequality and social welfare. Much use is made of the lognormal distribution as a description of income and wage rate distributions, and for this reason its basic properties are given in an appendix to Chapter 2.

Part I, on fixed labour supplies, begins with another chapter that is largely of an introductory nature. Chapter 3 describes some basic measures of progressivity and discusses the relationship between social welfare and tax and income distribution changes. The treatment of particular tax structures begins in Chapter 4 with the analysis of income taxation on its own. Alternative functional forms used for the specification of income tax structures are considered. Emphasis is given to the problem of deriving the form of the government's budget constraint, which imposes a restriction on the extent to which tax parameters can be varied. The results are used extensively in later chapters.

Chapter 5 combines income taxation with transfer payments and consumption taxes. Alternative forms of transfer payment systems are modelled, with emphasis on the linear income tax and various forms of minimum income guarantee. Chapter 6 then shifts the framework of analysis to the multi-period or life-cycle context. Examples of the effects of a tax change, namely a partial shift from an income tax towards a general consumption tax (with some exemptions), are given in both cross-sectional and lifetime frameworks. One issue that arises in examining taxes over a longer period is that of the income concept to use; that is, should present values or annual averages or other measures based on annuities be used? This chapter presents alternatives and provides an evaluation of the effects of using different concepts to evaluate tax structure changes.

A special issue in the multi-period context, that of government pension systems, is examined in Chapter 7. This chapter shows how pensions can be modelled and, as with earlier chapters, pays particular attention to the government's budget constraint. The problem of financing pensions in a pay-as-you-go system, where current pensions are financed from current contributions, is considered in detail. The special problem of financing pensions within a single cohort is then examined.

A long-standing issue in the evaluation of alternative transfer systems concerns the choice of universal benefits as in the linear income tax, compared with the use of means-testing, as in the minimum income guarantee. One aspect is that the choice obviously depends on the social evaluation approach used. Hence, the value judgement that transfers should aim only to relieve poverty leads to the adoption of means-testing, whereas a concern for wider income redistribution often leads to support for universal benefits. These issues are examined in Chapter 8.

Part II relaxes the assumption of fixed labour supplies and so begins with the basic analysis of labour supply. Chapter 9 examines labour supply variations with alternative tax and transfer systems. Given the difficulty of establishing general results, the chapter concentrates on the use of Cobb–Douglas utility functions although the alternative case of CES functions is treated in an appendix.

The special problem of deriving the government's budget constraint in the face of labour supply variations is examined in Chapter 10, for alternative tax structures. The earlier methods obtained in Part I are suitably extended. The analysis of the budget constraint is substantially simplified in the case of Cobb–Douglas utility functions because of the linear relationship between earnings and wage rates.

The various results are then brought together in Chapter 11, which examines the relationship between equity and efficiency. The standard 'optimal tax' problem, of maximizing a social welfare function, is examined. The chapter turns again to the debate concerning means-testing versus universal benefits, first raised in Chapter 8.

As in Part I, the analysis then shifts from the single-period to the multi-period context. Chapter 12 concentrates on two-period models involving income taxation and commodity taxes, with variable labour supplies. A special feature of this chapter is the introduction of heterogeneity, such that individuals have different tastes which may be correlated with wage rates. Finally, the chapter examines income redistribution resulting from alternative pension systems. It is seen that there are similarities between the properties of two-tier pension schemes and the modified minimum income guarantee scheme considered earlier.

The two-period framework is continued in Chapter 13, which is concerned with the special problem of voting over tax schemes. Voting in the context of a fixed income distribution, discussed briefly in several earlier chapters, is particularly straightforward, but special problems arise when there are labour supply variations. Such variations give rise to double-peaked preferences, although a majority voting equilibrium can be shown to exist in the single-period framework, so long as the ranking of individuals by pre-tax income is unchanged. Chapter 13 demonstrates that in a two-period framework a majority voting equilibrium may not exist when there is a tax-free threshold in the income tax.

Part III turns to the general equilibrium framework, concentrating on two-sector models. Chapter 14 concentrates on the basic structure of two-sector models using diagrams, while Chapter 15 sets out the formal analytics. This chapter also examines alternative tax structures in general equilibrium. The discussion is in terms of Cobb–Douglas production and utility functions, but the CES case is presented in an appendix. Finally, Chapter 16 extends the two-person general equilibrium model to the many-person case. This makes it possible to generate a personal distribution of income and to examine the effects of tax changes on the distribution.

It must be stressed that this book makes no attempt to be comprehensive, and many issues that are both interesting and important have been excluded. Thus there is no discussion of risk-taking and taxation or of administrative issues, for example. The treatment concentrates on individuals, yet important issues arise when attempting to allow for non-income differences between individuals which may be regarded as relevant from the point of view of social evaluation. However, it is hoped that the book can provide an introduction to some of the issues and techniques involved in modelling alternative tax and transfer systems.

2. Some preliminaries

The emphasis of this book is on modelling income tax and transfer systems and evaluating the effects of alternative systems on income distribution in a variety of contexts. It is not primarily concerned with the fundamental issues relating to the measurement of inequality or progressivity, or with comparisons between distributions which do not involve the use of single summary statistics. In most cases, tax structures will be compared using a number of well-known inequality and progressivity measures and social welfare functions. Such welfare functions involve explicit and quite specific cardinal interpersonal comparisons. The present chapter, along with the following chapter on tax progression, aims to provide a very brief summary of some of the basic mechanics involved. Section 2.1 describes the famous Lorenz curve and the lognormal distribution which is used in many places below. The two most commonly used inequality measures, due to Gini (1912) and to Atkinson (1970), are described in section 2.2. The properties of alternative social welfare functions are discussed in section 2.3.

2.1 INCOME DISTRIBUTION

Lorenz Curves

Suppose there are N individuals whose incomes are denoted y_i, $i = 1, ..., N$. Furthermore, these incomes are assumed to be ranked in ascending order such that $y_1 < y_2 < ... < y_N$. A very useful way of representing the variation in incomes among individuals is to construct a Lorenz curve. This shows diagrammatically the relationship between the proportion of *people*, with income less than or equal to a specified amount, and the proportion of *income* obtained by those individuals. The proportion of people is given, for say the kth income in the list, by k/N. The corresponding proportion of income is expressed as $(\sum_{i=1}^{k} y_i)/(\sum_{i=1}^{N} y_i)$. For example, when $k = 1$ the associated proportion of people is $1/N$ while the proportion of total income is $y_1/(N\bar{y})$ where $\bar{y}$ denotes the arithmetic mean income level. If everyone has the same income, $y_i = \bar{y}$, then for all k the proportion of total income is $k\bar{y}/N\bar{y} = k/N$ and is equal to the proportion of people.

When incomes are unequal, the fact that they are ranked in ascending order means that the proportion of people will be less than the proportion of total income, except when $k = N$. Typically the Lorenz curve looks like the curve shown in

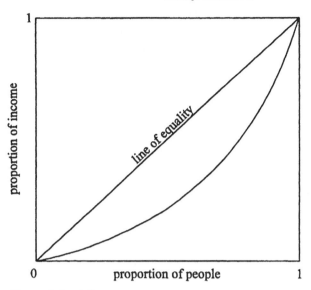

proportion of income

line of equality

0   proportion of people   1

Figure 2.1   A Lorenz curve

Figure 2.1. If everyone except person N has a zero income, then $\sum_{i=1}^{k} y_i$ is zero for all $k < N$. This case of extreme inequality therefore produces a curve which follows the bottom and right-hand edge of the box. Any distribution which has a Lorenz curve that is unambiguously closer to the diagonal of equal incomes than another distribution can therefore be said to be more equal. This basic idea is given a welfare interpretation in Chapter 3. The Lorenz curve is thus a very basic and powerful device for describing a distribution. If two Lorenz curves intersect, there is an obvious problem in making an unequivocal ranking of the two distributions in terms of their inequality. Further criteria need to be brought to bear on the comparison in such a case.

Table 2.1   Individual incomes

Person i	y_i	$F(y_i) = \dfrac{i}{N}$	$\sum_{j=1}^{i} y_j$	$\sum_{j=1}^{i} y_j / \sum_{j=1}^{5} y_j = F_1(y_i)$
1	10	0.2	10	0.056
2	20	0.4	30	0.167
3	30	0.6	60	0.333
4	50	0.8	110	0.611
5	70	1.0	180	1.000

$\bar{y} = \sum y_i / 5 = 36$

An example of the calculations involved in producing a Lorenz curve is shown in Table 2.1 for the simple case where there are just five individuals, whose incomes are given in the second column. The proportion of people with incomes less than or equal to y_i is denoted $F(y_i)$ and in this case is simply $i/5$, since the individuals are ranked in ascending order and the index, i, represents the rank. The total income obtained by those with incomes less than or equal to y_i is given by $\sum_{j=1}^{i} y_j$, and is shown in the fourth column of Table 2.1. The fifth column translates the total income values, in column 4, into values which represent the proportion of total income. These proportions are denoted $F_1(y_i)$. Such proportions of total income play a large role in later chapters of this book, so the notation $F_1(y)$ is used extensively. The Lorenz curve is obtained by plotting the values in column 5 on the vertical axis with the corresponding values given in the third column on the horizontal axis; hence it represents $F_1(y)$ plotted against $F(y)$.

Individual income distribution data are not always available, and most published data give grouped frequency distributions. An example is given in Table 2.2 where the individual data are grouped into six classes, as shown in the second column of the table. The midpoint of each class is given in the third column, and the assumption is usually made that all the individuals in each class are concentrated at the class midpoint; in this way the process of grouping involves a loss of information. The midpoints are denoted y_i, where the i subscript represents the ith class rather than the ith individual. The number of individuals in each class is denoted N_i and is shown in the fourth column. These values are converted into relative frequencies, f_i, in column 5, so that $f_i = N_i/N$. The proportion of people with incomes less than or equal to the *upper value* of each class is given in the sixth column; hence, if the upper value of the ith class is y_i^u, then $F(y_i^u) = \sum_{j=1}^{i} f_j$. The steps involved in producing the proportions of total income, $F_1(y_i^u)$, are shown in the last three columns of Table 2.2. The proportions are given by $F_1(y_i^u) = \sum_{j=1}^{i} y_j f_j/\bar{y}$, where $\bar{y}$ is the arithmetic mean value of income. Notice that $\bar{y}$ is equal to $\sum_{i=1}^{6} y_i f_i = 13.5$. In the case where individual data are available, the equivalent of f_i is of course $1/N$, so $\bar{y} = \sum y_i (1/N)$.

Much of the analysis of changes in income distribution, resulting from tax structure changes, is carried out using a continuous distribution of income instead of the discrete forms used above. In other words, income is assumed to vary continuously. The corresponding concepts used in the production of the Lorenz curve are identical, but a slight change of notation is required. The essential difference is that summation signs need to be replaced by integral signs. For a continuous distribution of income, where $0 < y \leq \infty$, the proportion of people with incomes less than or equal to a specified amount is, as before, given by $F(y)$. The relative frequency is now $f(y)$, so that $F(y) = \int_0^y f(u)du$. Notice that it is necessary to introduce the artificial variable, u, in the integral. This corresponds to introducing the index, j, in the discrete case of the grouped distribution

Table 2.2   A grouped income distribution

Class	Range	Midpoint	Number	Relative frequency	$F(y_i^u) = \sum_{j=1}^{i} f_j$	$y_i f_i$	$\sum_{j=1}^{i} y_j f_j$	$F_1(y_i^u) = \sum_{j=1}^{i} y_j f_j / \bar{y}$
i		y_i	N_i	$N_i/N = f_i$				
1	1–5	3	4	0.100	0.100	0.30	0.30	0.022
2	6–10	8	12	0.300	0.400	2.40	2.70	0.200
3	11–15	13	10	0.250	0.650	3.25	5.96	0.441
4	16–20	18	7	0.175	0.825	3.15	9.10	0.674
5	21–25	23	4	0.100	0.925	2.30	11.40	0.844
6	26–30	28	3	0.075	1.000	2.10	13.50	1.000

$N = \sum_{i=1}^{6} N_i = 40$; $\bar{y} = \sum_{i=1}^{6} y_i f_i = 13.5$

where $F(y_i) = \sum_{j=1}^{i} f_j$. Hence $dF(y) / dy = f(y)$, which indicates directly the distinction between the $f(y)$ density shown in Figure 2.2 and the area to the left of any income represented by the integral $F(y)$.

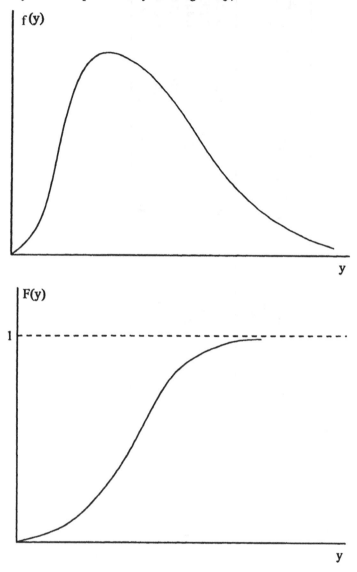

Figure 2.2   Density and distribution functions

The proportion of total income obtained by those with incomes less than or equal to y is, as before, denoted by $F_1(y)$ and is now expressed as:

$$F_1(y) = (1/\bar{y}) \int_0^y uf(u)du \qquad (2.1)$$

The arithmetic mean income, $\bar{y}$, is given by $\bar{y} = \int_0^\infty yf(y)dy$. In this type of expression it is convenient to substitute the more succinct $dF(y)$ for $f(y)dy$. Hence $\bar{y} = \int_0^\infty ydF(y)$ and $F_1(y) = (1/\bar{y}) \int_0^y udF(u)$. The function $f(y)$ is known as the *density function*, and $F(y)$ is known as the *distribution function*. The mean is also known as the first moment of the distribution, and for this reason $F_1(y)$ is called the *first moment distribution function* of y. Technically, the Lorenz curve can therefore be described as the relationship between the distribution function and the first moment distribution function. This way of describing the Lorenz curve and associated characteristics of the income distribution may at this stage appear rather cumbersome, but will be found to be extremely useful in later chapters of this book. In view of the fact that the Lorenz curve is obtained by plotting the first moment distribution against the distribution function, the slope at any point is given by $dF_1(y) / dF(y)$. From (2.1) this slope is obtained as $y/\bar{y}$. Hence, the point on the Lorenz curve that has a slope of $45°$, that is where $dF_1/dF = 1$, corresponds to the arithmetic mean of the distribution.

The Lognormal Distribution

For many purposes there is no need to make any specific assumptions about the form of the income distribution. However, it is often very useful to introduce a fully specified functional form for the distribution. This is particularly important where simulations or other numerical exercises are required. The most frequently used distribution for such purposes is known as the lognormal distribution. A variable is said to be lognormally distributed if its logarithm follows a normal distribution. If $\log(y)$ is $N(\mu, \sigma^2)$ where μ and σ^2 are the mean and variance of log-incomes, then it is said that y is $\Lambda(\mu, \sigma^2)$. This form is popular because it provides a good approximation to empirical income distributions, is very flexible and has some convenient analytical properties. These properties are not derived here, but some may be stated without proof. In particular, the mean is given by:

$$\bar{y} = \exp(\mu + \sigma^2/2) \qquad (2.2)$$

and the median is $\exp(\mu)$, while the mode is equal to $\exp(\mu - \sigma^2)$. The variance is given by:

$$V(y) = \bar{y}^2 \{\exp(\sigma^2) - 1\} \qquad (2.3)$$

Some further properties are described in Appendix 2.1 and introduced in later chapters when required.

2.2   INEQUALITY MEASURES

It has been suggested that the Lorenz curve allows an unambiguous inequality comparison of income distributions only if the curve for one distribution lies entirely outside that of another distribution. It is nevertheless often required to rank distributions when their Lorenz curves intersect. Even when they do not cross, some measure of the extent of the difference is required in addition to the straightforward ranking. For such purposes it is necessary to produce a single summary statistic which measures inequality. Many measures have been devised, but the discussion in this book makes most use of two measures, the Gini and Atkinson measures.

The Gini Measure

The Gini inequality measure, G, is related directly to the Lorenz curve and reflects the extent to which the curve departs from the 45° line of equality. The Gini measure is defined as the ratio of the area enclosed by the diagonal and the Lorenz curve, divided by the area below the diagonal. This approach ensures that the Gini coefficient lies between zero (for complete equality) and one (for extreme inequality). The area below the diagonal is equal to 1/2, given that the height and base are both unity. Therefore G is twice the area enclosed by the Lorenz curve and the diagonal. This geometric measure needs, however, to be converted into a more directly applicable algebraic expression. Several alternatives are available, but a very useful way of expressing this area is the following:

$$G = 1 + 1/N - (2/N^2)\sum_i (N + 1 - i)\,(y_i/\bar{y}) \qquad (2.4)$$

Using the incomes of Table 2.1, it can be found that G = 0.333. This expression shows that the Gini measure depends on the ranking of individuals' incomes, as well as their size, because of the term in $(N + 1 - i)$. Yet another way of writing the Gini measure arises from the result that it is half the relative mean difference, D, which depends on the absolute differences between all pairs of incomes such that:

$$D = \left(1/\bar{y}N^2\right)\sum_{j=1}^{N}\sum_{i=1}^{N}\left|y_i - y_j\right| \qquad (2.5)$$

The link between (2.5) and (2.4) is achieved using the fact that $|y_i - y_j| = y_i + y_j - 2 \min(y_i, y_j)$. Yet another way of expressing the Gini measure, along with an extension, is presented in Appendix 2.2.

Atkinson's Measure

Atkinson's (1970) measure of inequality is not related directly to the Lorenz curve. An important feature is that it is directly related to a social welfare function, W, expressed as the following function of individual incomes y_i (for $i = 1, ..., N$):

$$W = \frac{1}{N} \sum_i U(y_i) \tag{2.6}$$

where $U(y_i)$ represents the social value attached to individual i's income. This should not be confused with i's own utility function. The form of the function U reflects the inequality aversion of the decision-taker or individual making the judgements. Atkinson concentrated on the implications of assuming:

$$U(y) = \frac{1}{1-\varepsilon} y^{1-\varepsilon} \qquad \varepsilon \neq 1, \varepsilon > 0$$

$$= \log y \qquad \varepsilon = 1 \tag{2.7}$$

In the context of risk aversion, this function has constant relative risk aversion, $-yU''(y)/U'(y)$, equal to the parameter ε. In the present context, ε is a measure of relative inequality aversion. If $\varepsilon = 0$, then social welfare is measured by arithmetic mean income and the distribution of income is irrelevant. This indicates the absence of any aversion to inequality. As ε increases, increases in the higher incomes are given relatively less weight in producing social welfare compared with increases in the lower incomes. In view of the fact that the choice of ε reflects a value judgement, it is usual in investigating income distributions to report results for a range of values of ε. In theoretical studies, such as the analysis of optimal taxation, the aim has been to try to understand the structure of models and the implications of different attitudes towards inequality.

A cornerstone of Atkinson's approach to the measurement of inequality is the concept of the equally distributed equivalent level of income, y_e. This is defined as the level of income which, if obtained by everyone, produces the same social welfare as the actual distribution. Hence y_e is defined by:

$$W = \frac{1}{N} \sum U(y_i) = U(y_e) \qquad (2.8)$$

The inequality measure, $A(\varepsilon)$, is defined in terms of the proportional difference between arithmetic mean income and the equally distributed equivalent level. Hence Atkinson's measure is defined as:

$$A(\varepsilon) = (\bar{y} - y_e)/\bar{y} = 1 - y_e/\bar{y} \qquad (2.9)$$

Using (2.7) and (2.8), the equally distributed equivalent is:

$$y_e = \left(\frac{1}{N} \sum_{i=1}^{N} y_i^{1-\varepsilon} \right)^{1/(1-\varepsilon)} \qquad (2.10)$$

The value of y_e can therefore easily be calculated given a set of incomes. For example, using the incomes in Table 2.1, it can be found that $y_e = 34.6631$ when $\varepsilon = 0.20$. This means that if everyone has this income level, social welfare is the same as with the actual distribution, which has an arithmetic mean of 36. The corresponding Atkinson measure is thus equal to 0.0371. If ε is higher, say at 0.5, the equally distributed equivalent is 32.6025 and the measure of inequality is increased to 0.0944. For values of ε of 2 and 3 respectively, y_e drops to 22.9759 and 18.7546, implying inequality measures of 0.3618 and 0.4790. Substitution shows that $A(0) = 0$ and $A(\infty) = 1$.

It may be noted that Atkinson's measure is not decomposable. This means that if the population is divided into a number of different groups, the overall measure cannot be expressed conveniently in terms of the measures for each group separately (the within-group components) and a term reflecting the variation between groups (assuming equality within groups). However, the transformation, $J(\varepsilon) = \{1 - A(\varepsilon)\}^{1-\varepsilon} - 1$, belongs to what has been called the class of 'generalized entropy' measures and is thus decomposable; for use of this transformation, see Coulter *et al.* (1994). It can be seen that $J(\varepsilon)$ does not lie between 0 and 1; for example, when ε takes the values 0.2, 0.5, 2 and 3, $J(\varepsilon)$ is respectively -0.0298, -0.0484, 0.5669 and 2.6846.

Very few attempts have been made to examine individuals' views about inequality aversion, and those using the function (2.7) have not usually suggested that it represents widely held views, implicit or otherwise, about social values. Studies which have attempted to estimate the value of ε implied by government policies include Christiansen and Jansen (1978) for Norway, and Stern (1977) for the UK. They obtain values of ε between 2 and 3, but do not compare alternative welfare functions. In discussing alternative values to use in measuring inequality, Lambert (1993a, p. 229) suggests using the range 1, 1.5, 2, 3 and 4.

Atkinson (ed., 1973, p. 5) suggested that, 'we must recognise that it is not easy to form a judgement about appropriate values of ε'. It is necessary to make some kind of translation to orders of magnitude about which people might be able to have a much more direct, or intuitive, grasp. Atkinson described a mental experiment in order to give some idea of the implications of different values. For example:

> Suppose that there are two people, one with twice the income of the other, and that we are considering taking £1.00 from the richer man and giving £x to the poorer (the remaining £1 – £x being lost in the process – e.g. in administering the transfer). How far can £x fall below £1.00 before we cease to regard the redistribution as desirable? (Clearly if we are at all concerned with inequality £x = £1.00 is considered desirable.) The answer to this question determines the value of ε.

A similar, but slightly more complex, type of mental experiment was discussed by Okun (1975, pp. 91–5), who used the term 'leaky bucket' experiment. Section 2.3 returns to this aspect of Atkinson's approach.

2.3   SOCIAL WELFARE FUNCTIONS

The Atkinson-based Welfare Function

A further feature of Atkinson's approach is that it is possible to express social welfare in terms of arithmetic mean, $\bar{y}$, and inequality $A(\varepsilon)$. This is particularly useful because it enables the implied trade-off between the two objectives of raising average income and reducing its inequality to be expressed directly. To see this, rearrange (2.9), giving:

$$y_e = \bar{y}(1 - A(\varepsilon)) \tag{2.11}$$

so that welfare per person can be expressed in terms of $\bar{y}$ and $A(\varepsilon)$, using (2.8), as:

$$W = U\{\bar{y}(1 - A(\varepsilon))\} \tag{2.12}$$

It is however usual to write W as $\bar{y}\{1 - A(\varepsilon)\}$ rather than (2.12), because it is simpler and has the same properties, particularly regarding policy trade-offs. This way of writing the welfare function is called the *abbreviated welfare function*. The nature of the trade-off between 'equity and efficiency' is the same for both forms, and is:

$$\left.\frac{d\bar{y}}{dA(\varepsilon)}\right|_W = \frac{\bar{y}}{1 - A(\varepsilon)} \qquad (2.13)$$

These results apply to any form of U but, as already noted, Atkinson concentrated on the constant relative inequality aversion case. The parameter ε reflects the concavity of the function U. It also reflects the convexity of the social indifference curve showing combinations of y_i and y_j for persons i and j for which W is constant. Substituting (2.7) into (2.6) and totally differentiating gives:

$$\left.\frac{dy_i}{dy_j}\right|_W = -\left(\frac{y_j}{y_i}\right)^{-\varepsilon} \qquad (2.14)$$

The marginal rate of substitution between y_i and y_j therefore depends only on the ratio of incomes and not on their absolute levels. Furthermore, (2.14) holds for any two individuals in a population and does not depend on their ranks in the distribution or on the incomes of other individuals. An indifference curve is shown in Figure 2.3, where B is the point representing the incomes y_1 and y_2. This curve is symmetrical about the 45° line through the origin. A value of $\varepsilon = 0$ gives an indifference curve through B which coincides with the 45° line through B and C. This reflects the absence of any aversion to inequality. An infinitely high value of ε would give an L-shaped indifference curve, which reflects extreme aversion. The extent of aversion to inequality is therefore reflected by the shape of the indifference curve in relation to these two extremes. For the two-person case the equally distributed equivalent income is obtained from point A, so that the Atkinson inequality measure is the ratio AC/OC.

However, in practice it is necessary to ask people about a variety of discrete transfers, rather than to restrict attention simply to the slope of an indifference curve, so that (2.14) will no longer apply. Consider a transfer such that γ is taken from person 2 and θ is given to person 1, so that $\gamma - \theta$ is lost in the process. After the transfer, social welfare is W' and, writing $\delta = y_2/y_1$ with $y = y_1$, it is given by:

$$W' = \frac{1}{1 - \varepsilon}\left\{(y + \theta)^{1-\varepsilon} + (\delta y - \gamma)^{1-\varepsilon}\right\} \qquad (2.15)$$

Equating pre- and post-transfer social welfare and solving for θ, gives:

$$\theta = y[\{1 + \delta^{1-\varepsilon} - (\delta - \gamma/y)^{1-\varepsilon}\}^{1/(1-\varepsilon)} - 1] \qquad (2.16)$$

Given a set of questions with various values of y, δ and γ, this result can be used to estimate a value of ε for each respondent. Using such a questionnaire approach, Amiel and Creedy (1994) found implied values of ε that typically were substantially below 1.

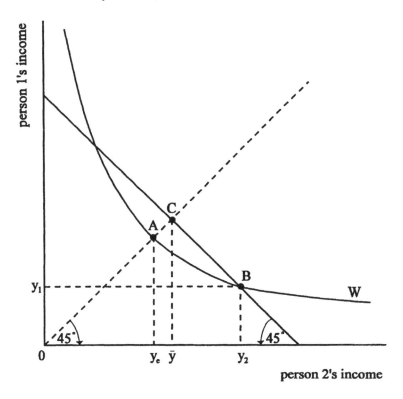

Figure 2.3   Constant relative inequality aversion

A Gini-based Welfare Function

The Atkinson measure and its associated abbreviated social welfare function are based on the use of a welfare function such as that in (2.6). The Gini is not consistent with an individualistic social welfare function which is increasing, symmetric and differentiable, such as that in (2.6). Nevertheless, social welfare functions have been proposed which are consistent with the use of the Gini measure. These are discussed in the present section in relation to their implications for inequality aversion. First, Sen (1973) proposed a 'pairwise maximin' criterion according to which the welfare level of any pair of individuals is equal to the income of the poorest of the two. He then showed that average welfare across all pairs is equal to $\bar{y}$ (1–G). This result essentially arises from the mean-difference basis of the Gini measure.

An alternative approach was suggested by Lambert (1993a), whereby each individual's utility depends on income and the income distribution, so that in general terms utility is U(y, F). Lambert showed that, in considering the class of welfare functions, W = ∫ U(y, F) dF(y), two separate cases give rise to an abbreviated welfare function involving the Gini measure. One case involves U reflecting relative deprivation while in the other case U is specified in terms of the rank position of each individual in the income distribution. For both specifications, welfare (average utility) can be written as $\bar{y}$ (1 – kG), where the parameter, k, is restricted to the range $0 < k \leq 1$. In later chapters, attention is restricted mainly to the case where $k = 1$ when reporting numerical results, but for present purposes it is useful to consider the more general case. Substituting the expression for G in (2.4) and considering a reduction in j's income of γ with an increase in i's income of θ for which W is unchanged, gives:

$$\theta = \gamma \left\{ \frac{k(N+1-2j)+N}{k(N+1-2i)+N} \right\} \tag{2.17}$$

Thus the ratio of θ/γ is constant and depends on k,N and the rankings of the two relevant individuals. This contrasts with the results for the Atkinson inequality measure, reflecting the different perspectives of the two measures. The Atkinson measure is said to reflect the 'wastefulness' of inequality (so that the rankings of the two individuals in the distribution do not matter) whereas the Gini measure is said to reflect the 'unfairness' of inequality.

In producing (2.17), it is assumed that the transfer does not affect the rankings of individuals. In the case of just two persons, so that $j = N = 2$ and $i = 1$, it reduces to:

$$\theta = \gamma \left\{ \frac{2-k}{2+k} \right\} \tag{2.18}$$

Furthermore, substitution into (2.4) gives:

$$G = \frac{1}{2} - \left(\frac{y_1}{y_1 + y_2} \right) = \frac{1}{2} \left(\frac{\bar{y} - y_1}{\bar{y}} \right) \tag{2.19}$$

The situation corresponding to the two-person Gini-related welfare function is shown in Figure 2.4, for comparison with Figure 2.3. Using (2.19) the Gini measure is (EC/OC)/2. When $k = 1$ the line AB has the slope of 1/3, obtained by substituting into (2.18). An individual with such a welfare function would tolerate a leaky bucket which always loses 2/3 of the amount taken from the richer person.

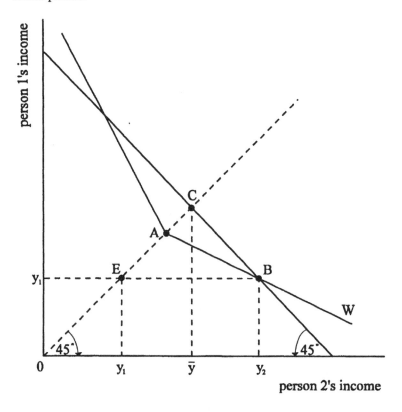

Figure 2.4   Gini-based social indifference curves

In general, the leak tolerated depends on the population size and the ranks of the two individuals. For example, with $k = 1$, suppose that $j = N$ and $i = 1$. This implies that $-dy_1/dy_N|_W = \theta/\gamma = 1/(2N - 1)$ and for large N simply confiscating the richest person's income, until it reaches the level of the next richest person, is tolerated. For $j = N/2$ (a transfer from the median person) and $i = 1$, $\theta/\gamma = (1 + N)/(2N - 1)$ and for large N a leak of 1/2 the transfer is tolerated. Other abbreviated welfare functions involving the Gini measure have been proposed, for example by Kakwani (1980) and Dagum (1990), but they are not considered here.

The Cost of Inequality

The abbreviated social welfare functions involving Atkinson's inequality measure and Sen's maximin criterion take the same general form whereby welfare per person is expressed as $\bar{y}(1 - I_y)$, where I represents the inequality measure (either $A(\varepsilon)$ or G). Another way of looking at this is to rewrite social welfare as $\bar{y} - (\bar{y}I_y)$, which can be seen as average income less a term that can be said to reflect the cost of inequality.

This way of viewing social welfare emphasizes mean income and its inequality, which is often related to the issue of 'equity versus efficiency'. It does not allow for a separate concept of poverty. However, some people attach a great deal of importance to a threshold income level and argue that those people below such a level suffer in a substantially different way from 'simply' having a relatively low income. A variety of poverty measures have accordingly been produced, and each depends on an exogenously imposed poverty level or threshold income. It is tempting to ask if social welfare can be decomposed into three terms; that is, can welfare be written as mean income less a cost of inequality, less a cost of poverty? The cost of poverty might thus depend on a measure of poverty in the way that the cost of inequality is written above in terms of an inequality measure. This difficult question has been discussed by Atkinson (1987a), and is considered again in Chapters 6 and 11 below, when evaluating alternative tax and transfer schemes.

This chapter has aimed to introduce a number of analytical tools which will be used extensively in later chapters. The representation of income distributions was examined, stressing the famous Lorenz curve. Two of the most frequently used inequality measures, the Gini and Atkinson measures, were introduced. Then, the relationship between the measures and the succinct expression of value judgements in a social welfare function were discussed. In evaluating income distributions and the effects of tax and transfer schemes, it is not possible to avoid making value judgements. For this reason it is most important to make such judgements explicit. The implications of adopting alternative value judgements can then be examined, and this type of exercise will be important in later chapters of this book.

APPENDIX 2.1   THE LOGNORMAL DISTRIBUTION

In addition to providing a good approximation to empirical distributions of income, the lognormal distribution is very tractable in economic models. Many useful properties of the lognormal $\Lambda(\mu, \sigma^2)$ stem from its close relationship with the normal distribution $N(\mu, \sigma^2)$. Further properties are stated here without proof;

the standard work is Aitchison and Brown (1957). For example, if v_q denotes the qth percentile of the $N(0,1)$ distribution, the corresponding percentile of the lognormal distribution, y_q, is given by:

$$y_q = \exp (\mu + v_q \sigma) \tag{2.20}$$

The additive property of normal variables, such that if x is $N(\mu, \sigma^2)$ then $a + bx$ is $N(a + b\mu, b^2\sigma^2)$, translates into a multiplicative property of lognormal variables. Hence if y is $\Lambda(\mu, \sigma)$, ay^b is lognormally distributed as:

$$\Lambda(\log a + b\mu, b^2 \sigma^2) \tag{2.21}$$

The above discussion of the Lorenz curve introduced the concept of the first moment distribution, $F_1(y)$, corresponding to the distribution function $F(y)$. In later chapters, use will be made of higher-order moment distributions, defined in an analagous manner. Hence the jth moment distribution $F_j(y)$ is defined as:

$$F_j(y) = \frac{\int_0^y u^j dF(u)}{\int_0^\infty u^j dF(u)} \tag{2.22}$$

This also applies to fractional rather than just integer moment distributions. The following very convenient result holds for the lognormal distribution, concerning the relationship between the various distribution functions:

$$\Lambda_j(\mu, \sigma^2) = \Lambda (\mu + j\sigma, \sigma^2) \tag{2.23}$$

For example, the first moment distribution function of y has a mean of logarithms of $\mu + \sigma$, and a variance of logarithms of σ^2.

The Atkinson and Gini inequality measures reduce to convenient expressions for a lognormal distribution. It can be shown that:

$$A(\varepsilon) = 1 - \exp\left(-\frac{\varepsilon\sigma^2}{2}\right) \tag{2.24}$$

$$G = 2N\left(\frac{\sigma}{\sqrt{2}}|0,1\right) - 1 \tag{2.25}$$

The normal integral N(z| 0,1) does not have an explicit solution, so that it is often necessary to use published tables of the normal distribution. When numerical results are obtained below, the integrals are evaluated using a polynomial approximation to the integral given by Aitchison and Brown (1957).

APPENDIX 2.2   THE EXTENDED GINI MEASURE

The formula for the Gini coefficient is given in equation (2.4). Another very convenient way of writing this is:

$$G = (2/\bar{y}) \, \text{Cov}\{y, F(y)\} \qquad (2.26)$$

The equivalence of the two expressions can be seen as follows. If $y_1 < y_2 < \ldots < y_N$, then $F(y_j) = j/N$ and:

$$\text{Cov}\{y, F(y)\} = \frac{1}{N} \sum \frac{j y_j}{N} - \frac{\bar{y}}{N} \sum \frac{j}{N} \qquad (2.27)$$

which uses the standard definition of the covariance, whereby $\text{Cov}(x,y) = E(xy) - E(x)E(y)$. Using the fact that $\sum j = (N/2)(N+1)$, the substitution of (2.27) into (2.26) gives:

$$G = \frac{2}{\bar{y} N^2} \sum j y_j - \left(1 + \frac{1}{N}\right) \qquad (2.28)$$

To get the expression in (2.4), it is necessary to use the result that:

$$\frac{2}{\bar{y} N^2} \sum (N + 1 - j) y_j = 2\left(1 + \frac{1}{N}\right) - \frac{2}{\bar{y} N^2} \sum j y_j \qquad (2.29)$$

The form in (2.26) is useful for numerical work, and it also suggests an extension of the Gini measure which allows for a parameter, v, that reflects different views about inequality. Following Yitzhaki (1983), the extended Gini, $G(v)$, for $v > 1$, takes the form:

$$G(v) = -\frac{v}{\bar{y}} \text{Cov}\left\{y, (1 - F(y))^{v-1}\right\} \qquad (2.30)$$

Substitution shows that G(2) = G. In this extension, v has a similar role to that of ε in Atkinson's measure. Thus $G(1) = A(0) = 0$ and $G(\infty) = A(\infty) = 1 - y_1/\bar{y}$, where y_1 is the minimum income. The behaviour of the two measures is illustrated in Figure 2.5. The measures were obtained for a population of 1000 individuals drawn at random from a lognormal distribution having a variance of logarithms of 0.5.

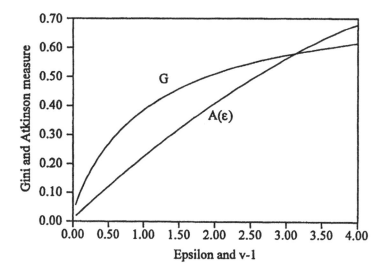

Figure 2.5   The extended Gini and Atkinson measures

Social Welfare and the Extended Gini

The extended Gini measure can be used in evaluating social welfare by using the abbreviated form of the welfare function based on $G(v)$ so that $W = \bar{y}\{1 - G(v)\}$. Substituting for $G(v)$ using (2.30) gives:

$$W = \bar{y} + v \, \text{Cov}\{y, (1 - F(y))^{v-1}\} \qquad (2.31)$$

Since $y_1 < y_2 < \ldots < y_N$, the required covariance, Cov{ }, can be expressed as:

$$\text{Cov}\{ \ \} = \frac{1}{N}\sum_i y_i(1 - i/N)^{v-1} - (\bar{y}/N)\sum_i (1 - i/N)^{v-1} \qquad (2.32)$$

Substitution of (2.32) into (2.31) and differentiating, gives:

$$
-\left.\frac{dy_j}{dy_k}\right|_w = \frac{1 + v\left\{(1 - k / N)^{v-1} - \frac{1}{N}\sum(1 - i / N)^{v-1}\right\}}{1 + v\left\{(1 - j / N)^{v-1} - \frac{1}{N}\sum(1 - i / N)^{v-1}\right\}} \tag{2.33}
$$

This result may be compared with the corresponding results in (2.16) and (2.17). For the standard Gini, where $v = 2$, (2.33) reduces to the result, using $\sum i = (N/2)(N + 1)$, that:

$$
-\left.\frac{dy_j}{dy_k}\right|_w = \frac{1 + 2\left\{(1 - k / N - (1 - \frac{1}{N})/2\right\}}{1 + 2\left\{(1 - j / N - (1 - \frac{1}{N})/2\right\}} \tag{2.34}
$$

and where $N = 2 = k$, this becomes 1/3.

It has been shown by Muliere and Scarsini (1989) that a rationale for the use of $\bar{y}\{1 - G(v)\}$ involves an extension of Sen's 'pairwise maximin' criterion. If the welfare of any v-tuple of individuals is the income of the poorest person, then the average of the welfare of all v-tuples is equal to $\bar{y}\{1 - G(v)\}$. Remember that $v = 2$ gives the standard Gini. When v is infinitely large, welfare becomes equal to the poorest income.

PART I

Fixed Labour Supplies

3. Redistribution and progressivity

The previous chapter presented two extensively used measures of inequality, the Gini and Atkinson measures, and introduced the concept of an abbreviated social welfare function, whereby welfare is expressed in terms of arithmetic mean income and its inequality. Social welfare does not necessarily increase when a tax change reduces inequality, even if there is a strong aversion to inequality built into the welfare function, because of the possible effect on mean income. Arithmetic mean net income may fall if total tax revenue increases or if there are incentive effects that lead people to work less. Tax structures can be evaluated in terms of social welfare, as shown in later chapters. Another important concept is that of tax progressivity. The present chapter briefly discusses this concept and presents alternative measures. A tax structure is generally said to be progressive if the marginal tax rate exceeds the average tax rate, so that the average rate is increasing. However, the variations in the average and marginal tax rates provide only partial information about the effects of a tax structure. It is important to be able to evaluate the precise effects of a tax structure, or a change in the structure, on the income distribution. These effects depend on the form of the distribution itself; for example, high marginal rates are irrelevant if no individuals have incomes in the relevant range. It is necessary to have precise measures of the degree of progressivity. It might be tempting to think that an increase in the progressivity of a tax system automatically involves a reduction in inequality, but this chapter will show how the relationship between the two concepts is not so straightforward.

Before introducing specific measures, section 3.1 briefly discusses some general results relating the various concepts; in particular, the general relationship between changes in social welfare and changes in Lorenz curves is examined. Precise measures of progressivity are presented in section 3.2. This is followed in section 3.3 by an examination of the idea of the welfare premium arising from progressivity, in terms of a comparison between social welfare with the progressive tax structure and the level of social welfare that would result from a proportional tax generating the same revenue.

3.1 SOCIAL WELFARE AND LORENZ CURVES

The previous chapter introduced the Lorenz curve as a way of representing income distributions diagrammatically. It was suggested that two distributions can be compared in terms of their inequality if one distribution has a Lorenz curve that lies entirely inside that of the other distribution; that is, it is closer to the diagonal line of equality. This idea is also reinforced by the result that an income transfer from a richer to a poorer person that does not change their ranking will shift the Lorenz curve inwards towards the line of equality. The idea that inequality is reduced by such rich-to-poor transfers is widely accepted. Where Lorenz curves intersect, and unequivocal comparisons cannot be made, particular summary measures of inequality can be used, such as the Gini measure which is linked to areas of the Lorenz diagram, or alternatives such as Atkinson's measure. These measures were shown to be linked to explicit social welfare functions which in each case have an abbreviated form given by the product of arithmetic mean income and equality (equal to one minus inequality, given that the maximum inequality is unity in each case, at least for large populations). This form can be used to compare alternative tax structures directly. For example, different tax structures that give rise to different combinations of $\bar{y}$ and $A(\varepsilon)$ can be compared in terms of their total welfare.

In introducing his measure, Atkinson (1970) also obtained a more general result concerning welfare and the Lorenz curve that has formed the starting point of many investigations. Consider the class of welfare functions examined by Atkinson, which take the form $W = (1/N) \sum_i U(y_i)$, where U, reflecting the decision maker's value judgements, is increasing and concave. The fact that U is increasing means that this class represents 'Paretian' welfare functions, since an increase in any y_i, with all other values unchanged, increases total welfare. Furthermore, the concave property implies that a transfer of \$1 from a richer to a poorer person increases social welfare. The idea that such transfers increase social welfare is referred to as the *principle of transfers*. The role of transfers in affecting the Lorenz curve was mentioned at the beginning of this section. The two results can be combined to obtain a simple but powerful result linking Lorenz curves to the broad class of welfare functions. Atkinson showed formally that for distributions with equal arithmetic means, Lorenz dominance, such that the Lorenz curve of distribution A lies entirely inside that of distribution B, implies that social welfare under A exceeds that under B, and vice versa, for all welfare functions in the above class. This result provides the welfare interpretation of Lorenz dominance which was mentioned briefly in the previous chapter. If distribution A, the Lorenz dominating distribution, also has a higher arithmetic mean than distribution B, then it is clear that the welfare comparison must continue to hold.

In the present context this important result applies to comparisons between tax structures which are revenue neutral. This is because revenue-neutral structures produce after-tax distributions of income which have the same arithmetic mean net income. Lorenz dominance in terms of the post-tax income distributions for two tax structures implies a clear welfare ranking, without imposing further restrictions on the form of U.

When the arithmetic means of the distributions being compared differ, Shorrocks (1983) has shown that the appropriate concept is that of the *generalized Lorenz curve*. This relates the cumulative *amount* of income, rather than its proportion, to the corresponding proportion of people. Hence the generalized Lorenz curve relates $\bar{y}F_1(y)$ to $F(y)$, rather than relating $F_1(y)$ to $F(y)$. When arithmetic means differ, Atkinson's result stated above can be translated directly in terms of generalized Lorenz curves. In addition, generalized Lorenz dominance can be used to establish welfare rankings in some cases where the Lorenz dominating distribution has the relatively smaller arithmetic mean. Furthermore, there may be cases where distributions with equal arithmetic means produce Lorenz curves which intersect, so that Atkinson's result cannot be used, but the generalized Lorenz curves do not intersect, so that an unequivocal comparison can be made without imposing further restrictions on the welfare function.

When Lorenz curves and generalized Lorenz curves intersect, further restrictions need to be imposed on the welfare functions in order to make unequivocal comparisons. It is not always necessary, however, to make assumptions about the precise form of U, depending on the nature of the distributions being compared. Various conditions have been established for the class of welfare functions which, in addition to being increasing and concave, reflect what is called the *principle of diminishing transfers*. This is more specific than the principle of transfers, and requires that transfers at the lower end of the income distribution are valued more highly than those in the higher ranges. Technically this requires that the third derivative of U is positive, whereas the principle of transfers concerns only the second derivative, to give concavity. For a complete summary of the results, see Lambert (1993a). It may be mentioned that the constant relative inequality aversion form of U used in developing the Atkinson inequality measure, where $U = y^{1-\varepsilon}/(1-\varepsilon)$, is itself a special case of a function displaying the principles of diminishing transfers, since $d^3U/dy^3 = (1+\varepsilon)\varepsilon y^{-(2+\varepsilon)}$ and is always positive.

Finally, the idea of progressivity itself can be related to Lorenz curves. A given tax yield can be considered as being obtained using a proportional tax, which leaves the Lorenz curve unchanged. Then a revenue-neutral progressive change in the tax structure can be considered. The system is progressive if the post-tax Lorenz curve dominates (lies inside) that of the pre-tax distribution. The links between Lorenz dominance, reductions in inequality and increases in social welfare can thus be made.

Such general results are important in appreciating the relationships among the various concepts and in understanding the types of overall comparison which may be made using a minimum of assumptions about the social welfare function. They can be used to establish results which are very robust. However, the approach followed in later chapters is to evaluate changes in terms of explicit social welfare functions, inequality and progressivity measures. Alternative measures are therefore described in the next section.

3.2   ALTERNATIVE PROGRESSIVITY MEASURES

First, it is useful, following Lambert (1993a, p. 160), to distinguish between the two separate but related concepts of *progression* in the tax rate structure and of *progressivity*. The first relates to the nature of the tax structure alone and, as stated earlier, a structure is said to be progressive if the marginal rate exceeds the average rate at all income levels. The second concept refers to the effectiveness of the tax structure when applied to a given income distribution. The effectiveness of a given tax function can vary substantially depending on the form of income distribution.

Consider a general tax structure, $T(y)$, where $T(y)$ is the tax paid on an income of y. The marginal and average rates are respectively defined as $dT(y)/dy = m(y)$ and $T(y)/y = a(y)$. A variety of measures of progression have been proposed to reflect the extent to which $m(y) > a(y)$ for a progressive system. Musgrave and Thin (1948) suggested using the extent to which average and marginal rates increase with pre-tax income, given by $da(y)/dy = \{m(y) - a(y)\}/y > 0$ and $dm(y)/dy = m'(y) \geq 0$ respectively, along with two elasticity measures. Liability progression is the elasticity of $T(y)$ with respect to y, $m(y)/a(y) > 1$, while residual progression is the elasticity of net income $y - T(y)$ with respect to y, $\{1 - m(y)\}/\{1 - a(y)\} < 1$.

Average rate progression ensures disproportionality in tax payments and a reduction in inequality as a result of the tax system, but marginal rate progression is not required since a linear but non-proportional tax function can be progressive, as shown in later chapters. A comprehensive analysis of these measures and the relevant general results can be found in Lambert (1993a). Given the focus of the present book, emphasis is placed instead on examining the progressivity of alternative structures, using several measures defined in this section. These measures are related to the use of the Gini inequality measure and thereby directly to the Lorenz curve. In defining progressivity measures, it will be necessary to introduce a curve, called the concentration curve, that is very closely related to the Lorenz curve, and an associated concentration measure.

Gini and Concentration Measures

For notational convenience, suppose that y_i is a measure of individual i's pre-tax income, and this is transformed into post-tax income z_i. Individuals can be ranked in ascending order so that $y_1 < y_2 < ... < y_N$. The Gini measure of inequality was discussed in Chapter 2 in terms of an area of the associated Lorenz curve and in terms of the mean difference measure. It was shown that yet another way of expressing the Gini measure is in terms of a covariance. If G_y denotes the inequality of gross income, it can be written as:

$$G_y = \left(\frac{2}{\bar{y}}\right) \mathrm{Cov}(y, F(y)) \qquad (3.1)$$

where $\bar{y}$ is the arithmetic mean gross income and $F(y)$ is the distribution function of income. In the present case individuals are arranged in ascending order, rather than grouped into income classes, so that $F(y)$ takes the simple form whereby $F(y_i) = i/N$. This form of writing the measure is often useful for computational purposes; on the use of covariance expressions in this context, see Jenkins (1988). Based on this covariance expression of the Gini measure, Yitzhaki (1983) has suggested an extension involving an additional parameter, $v \geq 1$, whereby $G_y(v) = - (v/\bar{y}) \mathrm{Cov}[y, \{1 - F(y)\}^{v-1}]$. When $v = 2$, the expression reduces to (3.1). Hence the parameter v has a similar role to inequality aversion, ε, in the Atkinson inequality measure; $G_y(1) = 0$ and $G_y(\infty)$ depends only on the income share of the poorest person (see Appendix 2.2). In what follows, however, attention is restricted to the standard form of the Gini.

Pre-tax income y is transformed to z using the tax system $z = y - T(y)$, and the corresponding Gini measure of net income, G_z, may be obtained in the same way, after re-ranking individuals according to z. If, however, the ranking by y is maintained, an alternative measure of the distribution of net income, called the concentration index, C_z, is given by:

$$C_z = \left(\frac{2}{\bar{z}}\right) \mathrm{Cov}(z, F(y)) \qquad (3.2)$$

This concentration measure has a direct relationship with a corresponding type of Lorenz curve. If the proportion of total post-tax income (retaining the ranking of individuals by pre-tax incomes) is related to the proportion of individuals, $F(y)$, the resulting curve is called a *concentration curve*. The concentration measure is the corresponding Gini measure; that is, C_z is the ratio of the area enclosed by the concentration curve and the diagonal of equality, to the area below the diagonal. Similarly, a tax concentration curve can be obtained by plotting the proportion of total tax paid against the proportion of income, with the ranking in each case according to gross incomes. A similar concentration index, C_t, of tax paid, $t(y)$, may be obtained in the same way by substituting $\bar{t}$ for $\bar{z}$ and $t(y)$ for z in equation (3.2).

Kakwani's Measure

Kakwani's (1977) index of progressivity is based on the disproportionality in tax payments, K, defined as the difference between the tax concentration index and the Gini measure of y:

$$K = C_t - G_y \qquad (3.3)$$

If the tax is proportional, the tax concentration curve coincides with the Lorenz curve of gross income and $K = 0$. If those with relatively higher incomes pay proportionately more of their income in taxation (the average tax rate increases with income), the tax concentration curve lies outside the Lorenz curve of gross income.

The redistributive effect of a tax system can be measured in terms of the reduction in a measure of inequality from the pre-tax to the post-tax distributions of income. Any inequality measure could be used, but there is a particular role for the Gini measure, given its use in defining the Kakwani progressivity measure. The Reynolds–Smolensky measure of redistributive effect, L, is the difference between the two Gini measures of y and z, so that:

$$L = G_y - G_z \qquad (3.4)$$

Re-ranking and Horizontal Equity

In producing the various measures above, care has been taken to distinguish which ranking of individuals is appropriate. This is because it is not necessarily the case that individuals are placed in the same order when ranked according to pre-tax and post-tax incomes. In practice the ranking may change because a different tax formula is applied to different people, if they are judged to have different non-income characteristics which are relevant. This obviously involves a value judgement. But if individuals have similar non-income characteristics, any change in their ranking as a result of a tax structure can be regarded as an indication of horizontal inequity; that is, the unequal treatment of equals. The Atkinson–Plotnick index of horizontal inequity (re-ranking), P, may be defined as:

$$P = \frac{G_z - C_z}{2G_z} \qquad (3.5)$$

This expression differs slightly from that suggested by Plotnick (1981), who uses just the numerator, but follows that given by Jenkins (1988). If only a single time period is being considered and all individuals face the same tax function, it is unlikely (unless the tax function is rather unusual) that there will be any re-ranking. However, in a multi-period context where individuals' earnings fluctuate over time, it is possible for the rankings to change. An individual with a fluctuating income stream will pay more tax if there are increasing marginal tax rates, compared with someone who has the same total income but in the form of a steady income stream.

The Suits Progressivity Measure

Another progressivity measure was proposed by Suits (1977). Jenkins (1988) has shown that the Suits measure of progressivity, S, can be expressed as:

$$S = \left(\frac{2}{\bar{t}}\right) \mathrm{Cov}\big(t(y), F_1(y)\big) - G_y \tag{3.6}$$

where $F_1(y)$ has been defined in Chapter 2 as the proportion of total income obtained by those with incomes less than or equal to z. The function $F_1(y)$ is known as the first moment distribution of y.

Progressivity and Inequality

Define the aggregate tax ratio, g, as total tax revenue divided by total income. There is an important relationship between some of the various measures defined above. This was obtained by Kakwani (1984) and is as follows:

$$L = K \{g/(1-g)\} - 2G_z P \tag{3.7}$$

This shows that if there is no re-ranking, the reduction in the Gini inequality coefficient arising from the tax structure is proportional to the Kakwani progressivity measure. However, a change in the tax system which, for example, increases the Kakwani progressivity measure, that is the disproportionality of tax payments, need not necessarily reduce the Gini inequality of net income. This is because the net effect depends on what happens to the aggregate tax ratio. The possibilities are greater when re-ranking can occur. The relationship in (3.7) can, if required, be rewritten for the extended form of the Gini measure and corresponding concentration measures, involving the additional parameter reflecting attitudes towards inequality.

Numerical Examples

In order to illustrate these measures, consider just ten individuals whose pre-tax incomes are independent of the tax structure. Suppose that they face a tax function such that $t(y) = 0$ if y is less than or equal to a threshold, a, but $t(y) = t(y - a)$ when $y > a$. This type of system, having a single marginal rate applied to income measured in excess of a tax-free threshold, is frequently used in economic models and is examined in detail in the following chapters. The hypothetical incomes are shown in Table 3.1 in ascending order, along with the corresponding values of $F(y)$ and $F_1(y)$. The last two columns could be used to draw a Lorenz curve.

Table 3.1   Pre-tax incomes

Individual number	Pre-tax income, y	$F(y)$	$F_1(y)$
1	103.93	0.100	0.053
2	109.27	0.200	0.109
3	116.92	0.300	0.169
4	119.93	0.400	0.230
5	128.99	0.500	0.297
6	218.49	0.600	0.408
7	221.51	0.700	0.522
8	251.92	0.800	0.651
9	254.69	0.900	0.781
10	427.13	1.000	1.000
Arithmetic mean	195.28		

The values of y were actually generated by taking random drawings from a lognormal distribution with mean and variance of logarithms of 5 and 0.5 respectively. The effects of applying three tax functions to the pre-tax incomes are shown in Table 3.2. In each case $t = 0.30$, and comparisons are made for values of the tax-free threshold, a, of 60, 80 and 110. As the threshold increases, it can be seen that the average amount of tax falls, as expected. In the third structure, the threshold exceeds the pre-tax incomes of the poorest two individuals so they pay no tax. The various summary measures of inequality and progressivity are shown in Table 3.3. The Atkinson inequality measure is shown for four values of inequality aversion, ε, ranging from 0.2 to 0.8.

Table 3.2   Alternative tax-free thresholds

a = 60		a = 80		a = 110	
z	t(y)	z	t(y)	z	t(y)
90.75	13.18	96.75	7.18	103.93	0.00
94.49	14.78	100.49	8.78	109.27	0.00
99.84	17.07	105.84	11.07	114.84	2.07
101.95	17.98	107.95	11.98	116.95	2.98
108.29	20.70	114.29	14.70	123.29	5.70
170.94	47.55	176.94	41.55	185.94	32.55
173.06	48.45	179.06	42.45	188.06	33.45
194.35	57.58	200.35	51.58	209.35	42.58
196.28	58.41	202.28	52.41	211.28	43.41
316.99	110.14	322.99	104.14	331.99	95.14
$\bar{z} = 154.69$	$\bar{t} = 40.58$	$\bar{z} = 160.69$	$\bar{t} = 34.58$	$\bar{z} = 169.49$	$\bar{t} = 25.79$
	$g = 0.2078$		$g = 0.1771$		$g = 0.1321$

Table 3.3   Alternative summary measures

Measure	a = 60	a = 80	a = 110
Inequality of net income			
G_z	0.2261	0.2176	0.2074
A (0.2)	0.0172	0.0160	0.0145
A (0.4)	0.0341	0.0315	0.0286
A (0.6)	0.0502	0.0466	0.0423
A (0.8)	0.0658	0.0611	0.0555
Cov $(z, F(y))$	17.4860	17.4860	17.5755
Cov $(t, F(y))$	7.4940	7.4940	7.4044
Cov $(t, F_1(y))$	8.2135	8.2135	8.1396
C_z	0.2261	0.2176	0.2074
C_t	0.3693	0.4334	0.5743
K	0.1135	0.1775	0.3184
L	0.0298	0.0382	0.0484
S	0.1489	0.2192	0.3754

Note: The Gini measure of pre-tax inequality is 0.2558. The Atkinson measures, for $\varepsilon = 0.2, 0.4, 0.6$ and 0.8 respectively, of pre-tax income are 0.0220, 0.0434, 0.0640 and 0.0838.

The effect of increasing the tax-free threshold can be seen from these results. All measures of inequality of net income fall and all measures of progressivity rise. However, this is not a general result, as is shown in the next chapter where inequality is eventually found to rise as the threshold is increased further. A result in Table 3.3 that may not be anticipated is the finding that the various covariance terms are identical for the thresholds of 60 and 80. The explanation of this result is that for these thresholds all individuals pay tax and the tax structure is linear. Thus if the threshold is less than the lowest income, the tax function is simply $t(y) = t(y - a)$ and post-tax income, z, can be written:

$$z = \alpha + \beta y \tag{3.8}$$

where $\alpha = at$ and $\beta = (1 - t)$. The covariance between z and $F(y)$, for example, is then:

$$\text{Cov}(z, F(y)) = \frac{\sum i z_i}{N^2} - \left(\frac{\sum z_i}{N}\right)\left(\frac{\sum i}{N^2}\right) \tag{3.9}$$

This can be rearranged, after substituting for z using (3.8), to give:

$$N^2 \text{Cov}(z, F(y)) = \beta\left\{\sum i y_i - \left(\sum y_i\right)\left(\sum i\right)/N\right\} \tag{3.10}$$

and the term α, which contains the tax-free threshold, a, is eliminated from the expression for the covariance, and t is fixed at 0.3 in the above examples. As soon as some individuals are affected by the threshold, as when $a = 110$, there is no longer a convenient linear transformation for all incomes.

Different Treatment of Individuals

In the above examples the concentration measure of z, C_z, is always equal to the Gini measure, G_z, because the ranking of individuals by pre-tax incomes is identical. Hence there is no horizontal inequity. In order to illustrate the result of re-ranking, suppose that each individual faces a different value of the threshold, a, while everyone faces the same marginal rate, t. Table 3.4 shows, for the same pre-tax incomes as in Table 3.1, the effects of applying different thresholds. In generating the values shown in Table 3.4, each value of the threshold was a random drawing from a lognormal distribution having an arithmetic mean of 80 and a variance of logarithms of 0.2 (so that the mean of logarithms is log $80 - 0.2/2$); in practice the differences arise from different non-income characteristics.

Table 3.4   Varying thresholds

Individual number	Tax-free threshold	Tax paid	Net income
1	113.27	0.00	103.93
2	69.08	12.06	97.22
3	68.11	14.64	102.27
4	111.71	2.47	117.46
5	75.80	15.96	113.03
6	109.55	32.68	185.81
7	164.47	17.11	204.40
8	56.40	58.66	193.27
9	72.15	54.76	199.93
10	77.44	104.91	322.22
		$\bar{t} = 31.32$	$\bar{z} = 163.95$
		$g = 0.1602$	

In this example, the concentration measure, C_z, is 0.2118 whereas the Gini measure, G_z is 0.2152. This difference arises because of the re-ranking observed in Table 3.4; ranking of individuals by net income would place them in a different order (given by 2, 3, 1, 5, 4, 6, 8, 9, 7, 10). The Atkinson–Plotnick inequity measure is therefore equal to 0.0081.

3.3   THE SOCIAL WELFARE PREMIUM

Tax Structure Comparisons

In some circumstances it is possible to identify a broad range of tax structure changes which increase social welfare, using only information about the tax functions. Any tax structure can be expressed as a function of pre-tax income, $T(y)$, where $T(y)$ represents the total tax paid by an individual with an income of y. For example, Lambert (1993b) reports that for a tax change which involves a single crossing of the tax functions, when $T(y)$ is plotted against y, such that tax on the lower incomes is reduced, two cases can be distinguished. If the change is revenue-neutral or revenue-reducing, all Paretian welfare functions satisfying the principle of transfers judge the change to increase social welfare. However, if it is revenue-increasing, the change is favoured by welfare functions displaying the principle of diminishing transfers, so long as there is a 'sufficient' reduction in the variance of income and inequality aversion is not 'too low'. If tax functions intersect twice, such that there are tax reductions for the low and the high incomes, revenue-neutral changes are favoured by all welfare functions displaying diminishing transfers so long as there is a sufficient reduction in the variance of incomes. If such a change is revenue-increasing, the inequality aversion must not be too low.

The Welfare Premium

As suggested earlier, it is of interest to evaluate changes in the tax structure using a precise measure of social welfare. It is possible to make a direct link between welfare changes and inequality changes when the abbreviated form of a welfare function is used, as introduced in Chapter 2. It should be remembered that different welfare rationales are available for the Atkinson and Gini measures of inequality. The rationales differ significantly, but both give rise to an abbreviated social welfare function defined in terms of only arithmetic mean income and inequality. In general terms, the abbreviated social welfare function based on the inequality measure, I_z, and arithmetic mean, $\bar{z}$, is, as shown in Chapter 2, expressed as:

$$W = \bar{z}(1 - I_z) \tag{3.11}$$

One way of expressing the social welfare resulting from a tax system is to measure the welfare in excess of that which would arise from a proportional tax which raises the same revenue. This is referred to as the *welfare premium*, and can be obtained, for a fixed pre-tax distribution of income, as follows. Arithmetic mean income after tax, $\bar{z}$, is given by $\bar{y}(1 - g)$, where g has been defined as the overall tax ratio, and in a proportional tax system, pre- and post-tax incomes have the same relative inequality $I_y = I_z$. Hence social welfare, W_p, for a proportional tax which raises the same net revenue as the actual tax, can be expressed as:

$$W_p = (1 - g)\,\bar{y}\,(1 - I_y) \tag{3.12}$$

The social welfare from the progressive tax, W_z, is given by:

$$W_z = (1 - g)\,\bar{y}\,(1 - I_z) \tag{3.13}$$

Hence the welfare premium, Π, from progressive tax is obtained by subtracting W_p from W_z. After rearrangement, this becomes:

$$\Pi = (1 - g)\,\bar{y}\,(I_y - I_z) \tag{3.14}$$

Alternative measures of the welfare premium, for the alternative tax structures considered above, are illustrated in Table 3.5, where in each case $t = 0.3$.

Table 3.5   Measures of the welfare premium from progression

Inequality measure used	$a = 60$	$a = 80$	$a = 110$	Varying thresholds as in Table 3.4
Gini	4.0651	6.1402	8.2114	6.6559
A (0.2)	0.7368	0.9648	1.2697	1.0385
A (0.4)	1.4525	1.9017	2.5008	2.0324
A (0.6)	2.1409	2.8028	3.6839	2.9746
A (0.8)	2.7969	3.6616	4.8107	3.8597

If pre-tax incomes depend on the tax structure because of labour supply incentive effects, then the above convenient expression in (3.14) no longer holds, as shown in Part II, Chapter 11, section 2.

This chapter began by providing a brief summary of the link between Lorenz curves and social welfare, for a broad class of welfare functions. Starting with functions of the form $W = (1/N) \sum U(z)$, it was seen that, assuming only that U is Paretian and satisfies the principle of transfers (has a positive first and negative second derivatives), a distribution having a Lorenz curve entirely 'inside' that of a second distribution can be said immediately to imply a higher welfare if the arithmetic mean of the first distribution is at least as large as that of the second. The role of generalized Lorenz curves was also discussed. Where such 'dominance' results cannot be applied, more restrictions have to be placed on the form of U.

Alternative tax progressivity measures were then introduced. These measures will be used in later chapters. It was shown that there are several dimensions which need to be examined when investigating the effects of changes in taxation. Although there are interdependencies between various measures of inequality and tax progressivity, it must be remembered that they do not always move in the same direction. An empirical study which concentrates, for example, only on a summary measure of inequality of net income may omit changes that are important in an overall evaluation. Finally, the concept of the social welfare premium arising from progression was discussed. It is again worth stressing that the approaches described here apply to cases where the distribution of pre-tax income is fixed. For this reason the various measures are often described as measuring the 'impact' effect of tax and transfers.

4. Income taxation

This chapter examines a variety of income tax schedules, paying particular attention to their implications for total tax revenue. The method used to derive tax revenue, for a specified distribution of pre-tax income, will be used many times throughout this book. Section 4.1 begins with the simplest case, that of a proportional tax. Section 4.2 examines a tax function with a single tax-free threshold, and provides the basic approach to the derivation of total revenue. It will be seen in Part II that the methods continue to be very useful even when incomes are endogenous. The extension to a multi-step function is placed in Appendix 4.1. It is sometimes useful to model non-linear functions involving a small number of parameters. Two examples are presented in sections 4.3 and 4.4. A method of deriving a measure of the dispersion of post-tax income for a multi-step function is given in Appendix 4.2. The primary purpose of the chapter is therefore to introduce a number of income tax functions and techniques of analysis that will be useful in later analyses.

4.1   THE PROPORTIONAL TAX

The simplest kind of income tax to examine is the proportional tax where the tax paid, $T(y)$, by an individual with income, y, is a fixed proportion, t, of income. Hence:

$$T(y) = ty \qquad (4.1)$$

The average tax rate, $T(y)/y$, and the marginal tax rate, $dT(y)/dy$, are both constant at t. Net income, z, is $(1 - t)y$. This function is often used in economic models because of its simplicity. In a diagram with z on the vertical axis and y on the horizontal axis, the relationship between z and y is a straight line through the origin, inclined at a slope of $(1 - t)$, as shown in Figure 4.1.

A very convenient feature of the proportional tax is the fact that the tax base is the total gross income. This means that the tax revenue can be calculated without any information about the distribution of income. If $\bar{y}$ denotes arithmetic mean income, then total revenue per person, R, is simply:

$$R = t\bar{y} \qquad (4.2)$$

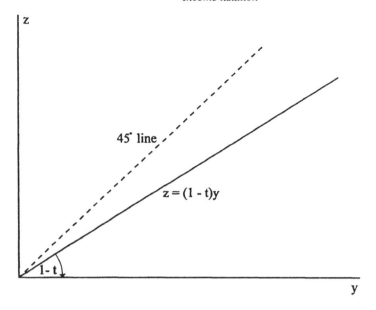

Figure 4.1 A proportional income tax

For a discrete distribution, with N individuals having incomes of y_i ($i = 1,...,N$), then $\bar{y} = (\sum_i y_i)/N$. However, it is usually more convenient to work in terms of a continuous distribution. As described in Chapter 2, let $F(y)$ denote the distribution function of income; that is, $F(y)$ is the   of individuals with income not exceeding y. The corresponding density function, $f(y)$, is given by $f(y) = dF(y)/dy$. The arithmetic mean income can thus be written:

$$\bar{y} = \int y dF(y)$$
$$= \int y f(y) dy \qquad (4.3)$$

where integration is over the whole range of incomes. Many useful analytical results can be obtained without specifying a precise functional form for $F(y)$. If a functional form is required, particularly in numerical work, the assumption will be made that incomes follow the lognormal form; that is, the logarithms of income follow the normal distribution. This convenient distribution, which provides a good description of many empirical distributions, was introduced in Chapter 2.

With the tax function (4.1), any measure of the relative dispersion of incomes will give the same value for the dispersion of y and z, since everyone's income changes by the same proportion. A corresponding result is that the elasticity of post-tax income with respect to gross or pre-tax income is unity. This elasticity was defined in Chapter 3 as measuring residual progression. Denoting the elasticity as ξ, then in general:

$$\xi = \frac{y}{z}\frac{dz}{dy} \qquad (4.4)$$

Appropriate substitution therefore gives $\xi = 1$ for the proportional tax.

Income and Consumption Taxes

Although this chapter concentrates on income taxes, it is useful to introduce consumption taxation, given the link with income. Suppose that the proportional income tax is combined with a proportional indirect tax applied at the same rate to all consumption. It is necessary to distinguish between the value of consumption goods before and after taxation has been imposed. If the value of consumption is c before tax, and a proportional tax at the rate, v, is imposed, then the post-tax value of consumption is $(1 + v)c$. Hence applying a rate of v to c gives the same tax revenue as applying the rate of $v/(1 + v)$ to the post-tax value of consumption. This gives rise to the concepts of the *tax-exclusive* rate of indirect taxation, v, and the *tax-inclusive* rate of $v/(1 + v)$. On the further simplifying assumption that all net income is consumed, the tax-inclusive rate must be applied to post-income-tax income, z, to obtain the amount of consumption tax paid, $V(y)$. Thus:

$$V(y) = \frac{v}{1+v}(1-t)y \qquad (4.5)$$

The consumption tax has therefore been expressed as a proportion of income. The total tax paid by any individual from income and consumption is obtained by adding $T(y)$ and $V(y)$ as given by (4.1) and (4.5). The overall effective tax rate, τ, is defined as $\{T(y) + V(y)\}/y$ and becomes:

$$\tau = (t + v)/(1 + v) \qquad (4.6)$$

The tax schedule facing each individual is therefore also directly proportional. However, the effective tax rate is not simply the sum of the two separate rates. If the individual saves a proportion, s, of disposable income, it can be shown that the overall effective tax rate becomes $[t + v \{1 - s (1 - t)\}] / (1 + v)$ instead of the value in (4.6); this is because the tax-inclusive rate of $v/(1 + v)$ must be applied to $(1 - s)(1 - t)y$. A more complex consumption tax schedule involving a number of tax-exempt goods is introduced in Chapter 5.

4.2 A TAX-FREE THRESHOLD

A simple modification of the proportional tax is to suppose that income is not taxable until it exceeds some specified amount, *a*, known as a tax-free threshold. Tax is proportional to income measured in excess of the threshold. The tax schedule becomes:

$$T(y) = 0 \qquad \text{for } y \le a$$
$$= t(y - a) \quad \text{for } y > a \qquad (4.7)$$

The relationship between *z* and *y* for this system follows the kinked line OAB in Figure 4.2. Until the threshold is reached, the 45° line is relevant along OA, after which AB is relevant. The relationship between net income, *z*, and gross income is given, for *y* > *a*, by:

$$z = (1 - t)y + at \qquad (4.8)$$

Hence AB has a slope of $(1 - t)$ and if the line is continued to the vertical axis, the intercept is equal to *at*. For those who must pay tax, this tax function is therefore formally equivalent to a system in which there is a proportional income tax

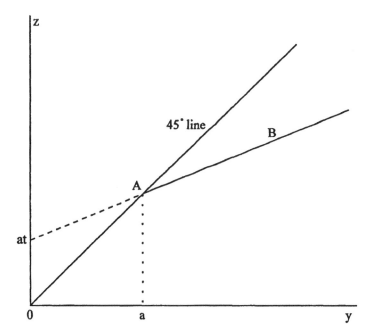

Figure 4.2 A tax-free threshold

combined with a transfer payment such that everyone with $y > a$ receives the transfer payment given by at. What starts as a simple modification of the proportional tax therefore appears, for taxpayers, to be like a tax *and* transfer scheme. Increasing the value of the tax-free threshold raises the value of the effective transfer payment for tax payers. This should be kept in mind when considering tax and transfer schemes combined in Chapter 5.

For those with $y > a$ the marginal tax rate is constant at $dT(y)dy = t$, but the average rate, $T(y)/y$, is $t(1 - a/y)$ and therefore increases from 0, when $y = a$, to t, where y is infinitely large. The schedules are illustrated in Figure 4.3. The property of increasing average tax rates makes the system progressive. The effect on the dispersion of z is discussed below.

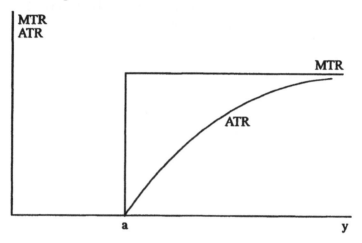

Figure 4.3   Marginal and average tax rates

Total Tax Revenue

The non-linear nature of the schedule means that total tax revenue per person, R, requires more detailed information about the distribution of gross income than with the simple proportional tax. From (4.7), when $y > a$, $T(y) = ty - at$, so that, for those who pay tax, the tax revenue is obtained by multiplying income by t and subtracting the fixed term at. Hence in aggregate it is necessary to determine the average income, for those with $y > a$, and the proportion of people who fall into that category. From the distribution function of income, the latter proportion is given directly by $1 - F(a)$. Denote the average income of those with $y > a$ by $\bar{y}_a$. Then total revenue per person, R, can be expressed as $t\bar{y}_a - at \{1 - F(a)\}$. Hence, if $\bar{y}$ denotes the arithmetic mean income of all individuals:

$$R = t\bar{y}\,[(\bar{y}_a/\bar{y}) - (a/\bar{y})\,\{1 - F(a)\}] \tag{4.9}$$

If $a = 0$ then $\bar{y}_a = \bar{y}$ and (4.9) reduces to $t\bar{y}$ as expected.

It is useful to take a more formal approach to deriving total revenue in this case, because the same type of exercise will be applied in many contexts later in this book. Revenue per person can be written as:

$$R = t\int_a (y - a)\,dF(y) \tag{4.10}$$

where integration is over the range $y > a$. Equation (4.10) can be expanded to give:

$$R = t\int_a y\,dF(y) - at\int_a dF(y)$$

$$= t\left\{\bar{y} - \int_0^a y\,dF(y)\right\} - at\left\{1 - \int_0^a dF(y)\right\} \tag{4.11}$$

The term $\int_0^a dF(y)$ is by definition $F(a)$. The second term inside the first curly brackets in (4.11) is most conveniently expressed using the concept of the incomplete first moment distribution function associated with the distribution function $F(y)$. This was defined in Chapter 2 in terms of the proportion of total income obtained by those with incomes not exceeding a given amount, so that:

$$F_1(y) = (1/\bar{y})\int_0^y u\,dF(u) \tag{4.12}$$

The direct application of this definition therefore gives:

$$\int_0^a y\,dF(y) = \bar{y}F_1(a) \tag{4.13}$$

Substituting into (4.11) and rearranging gives total revenue as:

$$R = t\bar{y}\,[\{1 - F_1(a)\} - (a/\bar{y})\,\{1 - F(a)\}] \tag{4.14}$$

This expression may be compared with (4.9). They are equivalent because $1 - F_1(a)$, the proportion of total income obtained by those with incomes exceeding the threshold, a, is equal to $\bar{y}_a/\bar{y}$, given the definition of $\bar{y}_a$. It is very convenient to write the term in square brackets in (4.14) as $G(a)$, since this type of formula plays such a central role in the analysis of tax and transfer schemes. Hence:

$$R = t\bar{y}G(a) \tag{4.15}$$

Total revenue per person depends on the two parameters, a and t, as well as the form of the distribution of income. The same approach can be used to examine a tax schedule having a larger number of marginal tax rates and thresholds, as shown in Appendix 4. 2. The general forms of the variation in $F(y)$, $F_1(y)$ and $G(y)$ are illustrated in Figure 4.4 for a lognormal distribution having a variance of logarithms of 0.5.

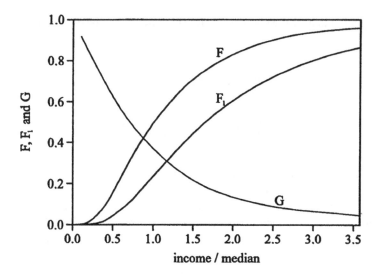

Figure 4.4   The lognormal distribution

Revenue-neutral Changes

Revenue-neutral changes in a and t may be examined by differentiating (4.15) totally with respect to a and t, and then setting $dR = 0$ and rearranging, giving:

$$dR = \bar{y}G(a)dt + t\bar{y}\{\partial G(a)/\partial a\}da$$

$$\left.\frac{da}{dt}\right|_R = \frac{-G(a)}{t\partial G(a)/\partial a} \tag{4.16}$$

The differential of $G(a)$ with respect to the threshold, a, is given by:

$$\frac{\partial G(a)}{\partial a} = -\frac{\partial F_1(a)}{\partial a} - \frac{\{1 - F(a)\}}{\bar{y}} + \frac{a}{\bar{y}}\frac{\partial F(a)}{\partial a}$$

by definition, $\partial F(a) / \partial a = f(a)$ and $\partial F_1(a) / \partial a = af(a) / \bar{y}$, so the first and last terms cancel and:

$$\frac{\partial G(a)}{\partial a} = -\frac{\{1 - F(a)\}}{\bar{y}} \tag{4.17}$$

Associated with any tax function is a set of iso-revenue curves giving the variations in tax parameters that produce the same revenue. In this context, each iso-revenue curve describes, for a given total revenue, a non-linear relationship between a and t. This is shown in Figure 4.5.

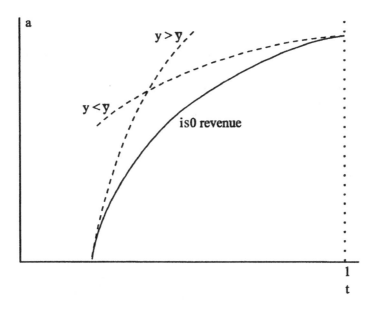

Figure 4.5   Individual tax preferences

Individual Tax Preferences

The above results apply to aggregate tax revenue. Consider the tax paid by a single individual with $y > a$, equal to $t(y - a)$. Total differentiation with respect to t and a gives $dT(y) = (y - a)dt - tda$, so that:

$$\frac{dT(y)}{dt} = (y-a) - t\frac{da}{dt} \tag{4.18}$$

With a fixed pre-tax income, the individual will be indifferent to changes in tax parameters, a and t, such that $dT(y)/dt$ is zero. In order to examine changes which also leave total government revenue unchanged, substitute for da/dt in (4.18), using the iso-revenue curve of (4.16). This gives:

$$\frac{dT(y)}{dt} = y - \bar{y}\frac{\{1-F_1(a)\}}{\{1-F(a)\}} \tag{4.19}$$

For a distribution displaying inequality, the proportion of total income obtained by those with incomes not exceeding a specified amount is less than the corresponding proportion of individuals. This is shown in Figure 4.4, and corresponds to the Lorenz curve being below the diagonal of equal distribution. Hence $F_1(a) < F(a)$, so equation (4.19) shows that all those with $y < \bar{y}$ could reduce their tax burden by moving along the iso-revenue curve to the point where $t = 1$. In this case the threshold, a, is given by the root of $R = \bar{y}G(a)$. Such a situation is illustrated in Figure 4.5, where the highest indifference curve, obtained from equation (4.18) by setting $dT(y) = 0$, reached by an individual with $y < \bar{y}$ and subject to the government's iso-revenue curve, is shown.

Consider a system in which individuals vote for their preferred combination of the tax parameters, a and t, given that a specified total revenue must be collected. It is known from social choice theory that, in the context of a single choice variable, if all individuals have 'single peaked' preferences, then a majority voting equilibrium exists in which the median voter dominates. As shown by the result in (4.19), the present context is one in which all individuals have single peaked preferences regarding the value of the marginal rate, t, remembering that the threshold is determined by the choice of t given the government's revenue constraint. Hence majority voting is dominated by the choice of the median voter, that is, the voter with median income. The above results show that with a skewed distribution for which the median is below the mean, majority voting over the tax structure would result in a unit tax rate. All those with incomes above the tax-free threshold, a, have their incomes reduced to the level of the threshold. All those with $y > \bar{y}$ would prefer a proportional tax system, with $a = 0$ and $t = R/\bar{y}$. This shows the extreme nature of results that can be obtained when pre-tax incomes are assumed to be fixed independent of the tax structure. Majority voting over the tax structure when pre-tax incomes are endogenous, rather than being fixed as here, is considered in Chapter 13.

Dispersion of Post-tax Income

The non-linear nature of the tax function makes it difficult to examine the transformation from the pre-tax to the post-tax income distribution. For those below the tax-free threshold, the distribution is unchanged, whereas for those above the threshold there is a linear transformation, given by (4.8). It is possible to derive the mean and variance of net income for the two sections of the

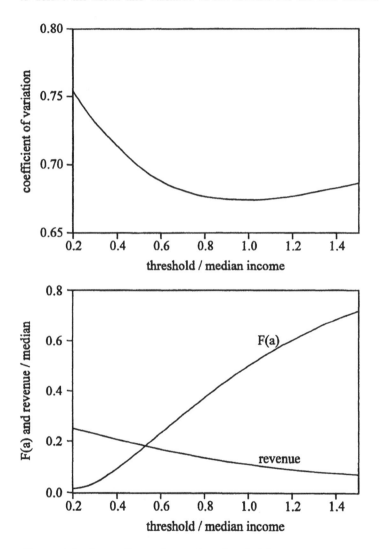

Figure 4.6   Inequality and a tax-free threshold

distribution, and then combine the results appropriately in order to obtain the overall coefficient of variation of net income. The appropriate method is described in Appendix 4.2, which can deal with any number of linear segments in the transformation between z and y.

It is tempting to think that a measure of dispersion of net income, such as the coefficient of variation, falls steadily as the tax-free threshold rises. However, it is necessary to qualify this type of statement. If the threshold is increased while the marginal tax rate is unchanged, then eventually the rising threshold means that very few people pay any tax and the total revenue (as a proportion of total income) becomes negligible. Hence the post-tax distribution ultimately becomes very similar to the pre-tax distribution. This effect is illustrated in Figure 4.6(a) for $t = 0.3$, a lognormal distribution with pre-tax variance of logarithms of 0.5, hence a coefficient of variation of 0.805, using the method given in Appendix 4.2. The corresponding fall in the ratio of tax revenue to mean income, and the rise in the proportion of people below the threshold, is shown in Figure 4.6(b). Depending on the fixed marginal tax rate, the coefficient of variation begins to increase even when less than half the population is paying tax. It is found that as the value of t increases, the value of the threshold, *at* which the coefficient of variation is a minimum, falls.

Alternatively, if the marginal tax rate is adjusted as the threshold is increased, in order to keep total revenue constant, then the coefficient of variation falls steadily. This process must of course come to an end when the tax rate reaches

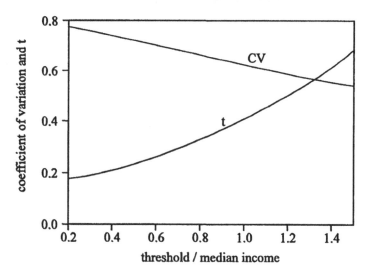

Figure 4.7   Inequality with fixed revenue

unity. The effects of holding revenue constant are shown in Figure 4.7, where the required rise in the tax rate is illustrated, in order to keep $R/\bar{y} = 0.15$.

Alternative Summary Measures

The evaluation of other inequality and progressivity measures, introduced in Chapter 3, requires the use of a simulated population of individuals. This can be constructed for a lognormal distribution using the property that if v is a random variable from a standard normal distribution, $N(0,1)$, then it can also be considered as a random variable from a distribution of the variable $(\log y - \mu)/\sigma$, where y is lognormal, $\Lambda(y \mid \mu, \sigma^2)$. Hence the corresponding value of y is obtained as $\exp(\mu + v\sigma)$. In the calculations reported throughout this book, the random number generator GASDEV was used to generate a set of vs: this is one of the FORTRAN subroutines provided by Press *et al.* (1986).

Table 4.1   A tax-free threshold

| Ratio of threshold/ median | Inequality | | Progressivity | | Welfare Premium | | Aggregate |
	Gini	Atkinson (0.5)	Kakwani	Suits	Gini	Atkinson	Tax rate
0.2	0.354	0.101	0.070	0.071	0.022	0.014	0.253
0.4	0.337	0.091	0.158	0.162	0.042	0.024	0.207
0.6	0.3284	0.0877	0.247	0.264	0.052	0.029	0.168
0.7	0.3272	0.0873	0.288	0.314	0.055	0.030	0.151
0.8	0.3273	0.0875	0.326	0.365	0.056	0.030	0.135
0.9	0.3286	0.0881	0.361	0.413	0.055	0.030	0.121
1.0	0.3306	0.0891	0.392	0.458	0.054	0.029	0.108

Note: The marginal tax rate is constant at 0.3. The Gini and Atkinson (0.5) inequality measures of gross income are 0.3782 and 0.1149 respectively. Results are based on 2000 individuals drawn from $\Lambda(10,0.5)$.

Table 4.1 presents alternative summary measures for a population of 2000 individuals from a lognormal distribution with $\sigma^2 = 0.5$, where the tax-free threshold is varied for a fixed marginal tax rate of 0.3. The fall in tax revenue is shown in the final column of the table, which shows the ratio of the total tax to total income. The first column shows the ratio of the threshold to the median pre-tax income; similarly the welfare premia from progression are shown as ratios of the median. This way of presenting the results means that they are independent of the value of μ used, since the median depends only on μ. This form of presentation will be used in many examples below.

It can be seen from Table 4.1 that the Gini and Atkinson inequality measures eventually start to increase as the threshold rises, just as with the coefficient of variation. Lambert (1985a) has proved the intriguing analytical result that the Gini measure of net income is actually minimized when it is equal to the proportion of people with $y \leq a$; that is, the minimum Gini is simply $F(a)$. Table 4.1 also shows that the welfare premium from progression rises and then falls. However, the progressivity measures continue to rise throughout the range. The increase in the progressivity of the system along with the (eventual) reduction in the redistributive effect results from the reduction in tax revenue.

4.3   A SIMPLE NON-LINEAR FUNCTION

It has been seen that the simplicity of a tax-free threshold combined with a proportional tax applied to income measured in excess of the threshold is in some ways deceptive. The nature of the transformation between pre- and post-tax income can be awkward when introducing the tax schedule into larger economic models and there is no simple result available about the way the parameters affect overall inequality. It is sometimes useful to have a progressive tax function which can be applied easily to the whole range of incomes. A non-linear function that is very tractable is the following, in which $T(y)$ is given by:

$$T(y) = y - \alpha y^\beta \tag{4.20}$$

with $\alpha, \beta > 0$ and $\beta < 2$. It should be noted that this specification is strictly limited to incomes above $\alpha^{1/(1-\beta)}$, otherwise $T(y)$ is negative, but this minimum is negligible in practice, since appropriate values of α are close to unity. The average tax rate is $1 - \alpha y^{\beta-1}$ and the relationship between post and pre-tax income is:

$$z = \alpha y^\beta \tag{4.21}$$

The ability to apply the same function over effectively the whole range of incomes is a useful property. The elasticity of post-tax with respect to pre-tax income, ξ, takes the constant value of β, so this coefficient is also a measure of residual progression. This is useful given the important result of Jacobsson (1976) that, for a fixed pre-tax income distribution, an increase in ξ shifts the Lorenz curve of post-tax income inwards towards the line of complete equality. The function in (4.20) has been used in a number of studies, including Edgeworth (1925), Atkinson (1983), Creedy (1979), Hersoug (1984), Waterson (1985) and Creedy and McDonald (1992). For an interesting derivation of the function, see Dalton (1954, p. 68).

Tax Revenue

A change in β affects the residual progression of the tax function in a simple way, but it also changes the aggregate tax revenue. Total revenue per person, R, is given by integrating $T(y)$ over the whole range of incomes, so that:

$$R = \bar{y} - \alpha \int y^\beta dF(y) \qquad (4.22)$$

This expression can be simplified using the assumption that the distribution of y follows the two-parameter lognormal distribution, $\Lambda(y \,|\, \mu, \sigma^2)$, where μ and σ^2 are respectively the mean and variance of the logarithms of y. The lognormal distribution and its properties have been discussed in Chapter 2, where it was shown that the following convenient transformation exists. If y is $\Lambda\,(y \,|\, \mu, \sigma^2)$ then:

$$z = \alpha y^\beta \text{ is } \Lambda(z \,|\, \log \alpha + \beta\mu, \beta^2\sigma^2) \qquad (4.23)$$

A further property of the lognormal distribution is that the arithmetic mean is given by:

$$\bar{y} = \exp(\mu + \sigma^2/2) \qquad (4.24)$$

Hence R, which is given by $\bar{z} - \bar{y}$, can be written as:

$$R = \bar{y} \left[\alpha \exp\{\mu(\beta - 1) + \sigma^2(\beta^2 - 1)/2\} - 1 \right] \qquad (4.25)$$

which may be compared with (4.22). Total differentiation gives, after setting $dR = 0$:

$$\left.\frac{d\alpha}{d\beta}\right|_R = -\alpha\left(\mu + \beta\sigma^2\right) \qquad (4.26)$$

Hence, revenue-neutral changes in the degree of residual progression can be produced by changing β, with the appropriate adjustment to α taken from (4.26). Changes in revenue which leave the residual progression unchanged can be obtained by changing only the coefficient α.

The present section has considered a non-linear tax schedule over the whole range of pre-tax incomes, while section 4.2 used a tax-free threshold combined with a constant proportional rate. The two aspects can be combined into a single tax schedule combining a tax-free threshold, a constant rate over a range of taxable income, followed by a non-linear range. Such a function is able to capture the complexity involved in some actual functions, as shown in the next section.

4.4 A FIVE-PARAMETER TAX SCHEDULE

Consider the following income tax schedule, which uses a single tax-free allowance applied to every individual:

$$
\begin{aligned}
T(y) &= 0 & y &< a_1 \\
&= t_1 (y - a_1) & a_1 &\leq y \leq a_2 \\
&= t_1 (a_2 - a_1) + (t_2 - hy^{-k})(y - a_2) & y &> a_2
\end{aligned}
\qquad (4.27)
$$

with

$$
h = (t_2 - t_1) \, a_2^k \qquad (4.28)
$$

$$
k < 1 \qquad (4.29)
$$

A 'standard rate', t_1, is therefore applied to incomes between the thresholds a_1 and a_2. Thereafter marginal rates increase non-linearly. The maximum marginal rate is equal to t_2. This schedule can also be applied to tax systems that do not use a standard rate, by setting $a_2 = a_1$. Without a standard rate the function is described by only four parameters, t_1, t_2, and a_1 and k. The condition in (4.28) ensures that the marginal tax rate at the level a_2, beyond which individuals pay higher marginal rates of income tax, is equal to t_2. The condition in (4.29) that $k < 1$ ensures that the marginal tax rate increases as gross income increases, and the marginal rate exceeds the average rate. An increase in k implies that marginal tax rates increase more rapidly from t_1 (at the threshold income a_2) to their maximum.

The tax schedule specified above is extremely flexible and is capable of describing a wide range of profiles of marginal and average tax rates. The tax schedule can be fitted to any actual schedule of marginal tax rates using ordinary least squares regression methods. Over the range $y > a_2$ the marginal rate of tax is given by:

$$
dT(y)/dy = t_2 - (t_2 - t_1)\{(1 - k)(y/a_2)^{-k} + k(y/a_2)^{-1-k}\} \qquad (4.30)
$$

For an assumed value of k and the value of a_2 obtained directly from the actual schedule, a regression of the form $z = \beta + \beta_1 x$, where x is the term in curly brackets in (4.30), may be run. Results using different values of k may be compared to find the one that gives the best fit.

Total Income Tax Revenue

Where the distribution function of before-tax income is denoted by $F(y)$, total tax revenue per person, R, is given as:

$$R = \int T(y) \, dF(y) \tag{4.31}$$

where integration is over the complete range of incomes $0 < y < \infty$. When the tax schedule (4.27) to (4.29) is substituted into this general expression it can be seen that, as in section 4.2, a number of terms appear of the general form $\int_0^a y^r dF(y)$. In section 4.2, terms of the form $\int_0^a y dF(y)$ were found to arise, involving the proportion of total income obtained by those with $y \leq a$. The term $F_1(a)$ was defined such that $\bar{y}F_1(a) = \int_0^a y dF(y)$. The present context therefore requires a generalization of this approach, to allow for powers of y. The term $\bar{y} = \int_0^\infty y dF(y)$ is called the 'first moment' (about the origin) of the distribution. A simple extension is thus to define $\bar{y}_r$ as the rth moment, given by $\bar{y}_r = \int_0^\infty y^r dF(y)$. Hence the functions $F_r(y)$ can be defined as $F_r(y) = (1/\bar{y}_r) \int_0^y u^r dF(u)$, where as before the term u is just an artificial variable. Thus any term of the form $\int_0^a y^r dF(y)$ can be written more succinctly as $\bar{y}_r F_r(a)$. The function $F_r(y)$ is known as the rth moment distribution function.

The use of the first moment distribution has been examined in section 4.2, where it was found useful to introduce a general term $G(y)$, defined in equation (4.14). The present problem is more cumbersome, and it is useful to generalize G somewhat by defining the function as having two arguments; thus define $G(r, y)$ as:

$$G(r,y) = \bar{y}_r \left[\{1 - F_r(y)\} - y \left(\bar{y}_{r-1} / \bar{y}_r\right) \{1 - F_{r-1}(y)\} \right] \tag{4.32}$$

The term $\bar{y}_1$ is the arithmetic mean, also denoted $\bar{y}$, and $\bar{y}_0 = 1$. This approach can be seen to involve the use of non-integer moment distribution functions. Although such functions are unusual, there are no new problems arising from their use. After some manipulation it can be found that

$$R = t_1 \{G(1,a_1) - G(1,a_2)\} + t_2 G(1,a_2) - hG(1 - k,a_2) \tag{4.33}$$

Total revenue per person is therefore a function of just five parameters, a_1, a_2, t_1, t_2 and k, in addition to those required to describe the characteristics of the distribution of income.

The main purpose of this chapter has been to introduce a number of tools of analysis and to illustrate how they can be used to examine tax functions. The same methods will be found useful even when incomes are endogenous. The analyses proceeded by gradually introducing more complex income tax functions. Hence, starting from a proportional function, a tax-free threshold was added. Non-linear functions were then introduced where the evaluation of total tax revenue was seen to require the general concept of the rth moment distribution function, which is a simple but valuable extension of the first moment distribution introduced at the start of Chapter 2. The first, $F_1(y)$, can be described as a straightforward proportion of total income obtained by those with incomes not exceeding y. Such convenient descriptions are not available for $F_r(y)$, $r > 1$, since they involve powers of income, but the same basic principles are involved.

Chapters 2 to 4 have largely concentrated on introducing important concepts, measures and techniques of analysis that are required for analysing tax structures. The next chapter moves a little further towards using the concepts and techniques in order to carry out wider-ranging economic analyses of tax structures.

APPENDIX 4.1   A MULTI-STEP TAX FUNCTION

This appendix sets out the basic analytics of a multi-step tax function, and shows how revenue-neutral changes in tax rates and thresholds can be specified. Suppose there are N steps or thresholds; then, in general, the tax paid on income between the Rth and (R + 1)th thresholds is:

$$T(y) = \sum_{i=1}^{R-1} t_i\left(a_{i+1} - a_i\right)t_R\left(y - a_R\right) + t_R\left(y - a_R\right) \quad a_R < y \le a_{R+1} \quad (4.34)$$

Hence (4.34) holds for R = 2, ..., N. Setting $t_0 = 0$ and $a_{N+1} = \infty$, total revenue per person, T, is given by:

$$T = \sum_{i=1}^{N}\left\{t_i\int_{a_i}^{a_{i+1}}\left(y - a_i\right)dF(y)\right\} + \sum_{i=1}^{N-1}\left\{t_i\left(a_{i+1} - a_i\right)\int_{a_{i+1}}^{\infty}dF(y)\right\}$$

$$= \sum_{i=1}^{N}\left\{t_i\int_{a_i}^{a_{i+1}}y\,dF(y)\right\} - \sum_{i=1}^{N}\left\{a_i\left(t_i - t_{i-1}\right)\int_{a_i}^{\infty}dF(y)\right\} \quad (4.35)$$

This expression can be simplified by noting that:

$$\int_{a_i}^{\infty}dF(y) = 1 - F(a_i) \quad (4.36)$$

$$\int_{a_i}^{a_{i+1}}y\,dF(y) = \bar{y}\left\{F_1\left(a_{i+1}\right) - F_1\left(a_i\right)\right\} \quad (4.37)$$

where $\bar{y}$ is the arithmetic mean value of income and F_1 is the first moment distribution function. Appropriate substitution gives total revenue as:

$$T = \bar{y}\sum_{i=1}^{N} t_i \{F_1(a_{i+1}) - F_1(a_i)\} - \sum_{i=1}^{N} a_i (t_i - t_{i-1})\{1 - F(a_i)\} \qquad (4.38)$$

The change in revenue resulting from a change in any threshold can be found using:

$$\frac{\partial T}{\partial a_i} = -\bar{y}t_i \frac{\partial F_1(a_i)}{\partial a_i} - (t_i - t_{i-1})\{1 - F(a_i)\} + a_i(t_i - t_{i-1})\frac{\partial F(a_i)}{\partial a_i}$$

$$= -(t_i - t_{i-1})\{1 - F(a_i)\} - a_i t_{i-1} f(a_i) \qquad (4.39)$$

The change in revenue resulting from a change in any marginal income tax rate can be found using:

$$\frac{\partial T}{\partial t_i} = \bar{y}\left[\{F_1(a_{i+1}) - F_1(a_i)\} - (a_i / \bar{y})\{1 - F(a_i)\}\right] \qquad (4.40)$$

APPENDIX 4.2   THE DISPERSION OF POST-TRANSFER INCOME

This appendix shows how to calculate the coefficient of variation of after-tax income when it is necessary to decompose the population into a number of separate groups. Analytical results can only be obtained where the measure of dispersion used can also be decomposed in a convenient way. In general there are 'within' and 'between' group effects on overall dispersion. This section presents a general method of calculating the coefficient of variation of net income, z, for any number of groups. Suppose that in the ith group, which covers pre-transfer incomes between y_i and y_j $(y_j > y_i)$, the transformation between z and y is given by:

$$z = \alpha_i + \beta_i y \qquad (4.41)$$

Define the mean and variance of pre-transfer income within the ith group as $\bar{y}_i$ and s^2_{yi} respectively; then from (4.41) the mean and variance of post-transfer income within the ith group, $\bar{z}_i$ and s^2_{zi} respectively, are:

$$\bar{z}_i = \alpha_i + \beta_i \bar{y}_i \qquad (4.42)$$

$$s^2_{zi} = \beta^2_i s^2_{yi} \qquad (4.43)$$

If w_i is the proportion of individuals in the ith group, then the overall mean and variance of z, $\bar{z}$ and s^2_z are:

$$\bar{z} = \sum w_i \bar{z}_i \qquad (4.44)$$

$$s^2_z = \sum w_i (s^2_{zi} + \bar{z}^2_i) - \bar{z}^2 \qquad (4.45)$$

whence:

$$\eta_z = s_z / \bar{z} \qquad (4.46)$$

It is then only necessary to obtain expressions for the w_is and $\bar{y}_i$s and s^2_{yi}s for substitution into (4.44) to (4.46). If $\bar{y}$ and s^2_y are the mean and variance of y, then it can be seen that:

$$w_i = F(y_j) - F(y_i) \qquad (4.47)$$

$$\bar{y}_i = \bar{y}\{F_1(y_j) - F_1(y_i)\}/w_i \qquad (4.48)$$

$$s^2_{yi} = (\bar{y}^2 + s^2_y)\{F_2(y_j) - F_2(y_i)\}/w_i - \bar{y}^2_i \qquad (4.49)$$

Here $F_2(y)$ is the incomplete second moment distribution of y. For the highest income group $F(y_i) = F_1(y) = F_2(y_j) = 1$, while for the lowest group $F(y_i) = F_1(y_i) = F_2(y_i) = 0$. The analysis of the redistributive effects of alternative schemes, in terms of the dispersion of the distributions, is much more cumbersome than the analysis of total revenue, but the above method can be used in a wide variety of situations.

5.   Taxes and transfers combined

The previous chapter considered the modelling of various income tax schemes without regard to the way in which the total revenue is spent by the government. When examining the redistributive effects of taxes, it is not always appropriate to consider a single tax or transfer in isolation, but the methods used in Chapter 4 can be extended to a wide variety of models. The present chapter combines simple income tax schedules with several transfer systems. A scheme in which all the tax revenue is redistributed as transfer payments is referred to as a 'pure' transfer scheme, and this type of system forms the focal point of many analyses.

In practice there are many different types of transfer in operation. Individuals may be eligible to receive certain transfer payments for specified contingencies, for example if they are sick, disabled or unemployed. Furthermore, the level of payments may be fixed, or may depend on several characteristics of individuals in addition to taxes (or special contributions such as National Insurance contributions) paid before being, say, unemployed. The treatment in this book concentrates, as explained in the Introduction, on individuals who are assumed to be homogeneous from the point of view of their treatment by the tax authorities; the only *relevant* differences between individuals are income differences. The exception to this rule is the case of pensions, the receipt of which requires an age qualification; discussion of pensions is deferred until Chapter 8.

The existence of various types of tax and transfer scheme operating simultaneously can lead to unplanned anomalies if the different schemes are not fully integrated. The investigation of such undesired features of tax systems has been an important activity, which is likely to continue, given the fragmentation of policy-making. The schemes examined below therefore involve the further simplification that they treat taxes and transfers as a fully integrated system; that is, the tax authorities are assumed to bring about a desired relationship between the pre-tax and post-tax incomes of individuals. Administrative issues are without doubt extremely important, but they are not the focus of the present study. Different transfers are often based on different time periods; that is, eligibility is based on a variety of lengths of time over which previous experience is considered, and some benefits are awarded for a long period while others are reviewed on a weekly basis. This clearly creates problems from the point of view of integration, again ignored here.

Section 5.1 presents an extreme form of tax and transfer system which has been the subject of an extensive literature. This apparently simple system, which combines universal unconditional benefits with a proportional tax, will be seen to raise many complexities. Section 5.2 examines several modifications, involving the introduction of additional rates of tax. Finally, section 5.3 introduces consumption taxes.

5.1   THE LINEAR INCOME TAX

Considerable emphasis in the literature on taxes and transfers has been placed on what may be called the linear income tax, which combines the simplest possible income tax with the simplest possible transfer system. It is useful to refer back to Figure 4.2, which described the income tax with a tax-free threshold, a. It was noted that, for those who pay tax, the system is equivalent to one in which individuals receive a lump sum, and pay a proportional tax on gross income at the rate t. This non-linear tax system (following the kinked line OAB in Figure 4.2) can be converted into a linear system simply by giving the lump sum to everyone, irrespective of their income level, and imposing a proportional tax on all income. This is shown in Figure 5.1. Those with incomes below the threshold, a, receive a transfer that exceeds their tax payment; the tax schedule is the straight line ABC and those to the left of B are net recipients while those to the right of B are net payers.

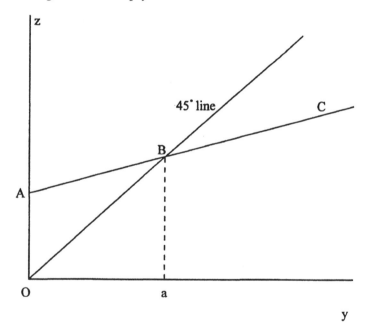

Figure 5.1   The linear income tax

The linear tax can be produced using two different administrative systems which are, however, equivalent if the administrative costs are ignored. The distinction is between what are often called social dividend (SD) and negative income tax (NIT) schemes. Under the social dividend scheme an unconditional payment equal to OA is paid to each person, and all other income is taxed at a constant proportional rate, t, resulting in the line AC. Under the negative income tax, the tax function is written as $T(y) = t(y - a)$ for all incomes, and negative values of $T(y)$ result in transfers which are paid to the individual, depending on the value of y. The two schemes can be expressed as follows. For the negative income tax:

$$z = y - T(y) = y - t(y - a) = y (1 - t) + at \qquad (5.1)$$

while for the social dividend scheme:

$$z = b + y - T(y) = b + y - ty = y (1 - t) + b \qquad (5.2)$$

These two administrative schemes are equivalent when $b = at$. The slope of the line AC is therefore $(1 - t)$. Each scheme requires two policy variables to be set, but there is only one degree of freedom since in a pure transfer system the gross tax revenue must be sufficient to finance the payment of the social dividend. The available choices are given by the government's budget constraint.

The Government's Budget Constraint

Under the linear income tax each person receives the unconditional amount, b, which, for a pure transfer system, must be financed from the proportional income tax. It has been seen in Chapter 4 that revenue per person for a proportional tax is $t\bar{y}$, and depends only on the arithmetic mean income. Hence the government's constraint can be written as:

$$b = t\bar{y} \qquad (5.3)$$

Since b is equivalent to at, it can be seen that $a = \bar{y}$ whatever the tax rate, t. Thus there is net redistribution from those above to those below the arithmetic mean; the extent of the redistribution is determined by the tax rate. It is sometimes useful to express t in terms of the basic minimum or social dividend, b:

$$t = b/\bar{y} \qquad (5.4)$$

Alternatively, a more formal way of writing the constraint is to start from the proposition that net revenue must be zero for a pure transfer scheme. This gives the following:

Fixed labour supplies

$$\int t(y-a)\, dF(y) = 0 \qquad\qquad (5.5)$$

from which it is seen that $at = t\bar{y}$. This approach will be found useful when examining more complex schemes.

If it is required to raise net revenue of Q per person, for purposes other than transfer payments, the general form of the budget constraint is:

$$b = t\bar{y} - Q \qquad\qquad (5.6)$$

Thus b is just replaced by $b + Q$, and the social dividend for a given tax rate is correspondingly lower. This modification can be made to the other pure transfer systems examined below, so it does not need to be included in the formal statement of the schemes.

Individual Tax Preferences

Equation (5.6) defines a straight line, shown in Figure 5.2, inclined at a slope of $\bar{y}$. The government's choice problem may therefore be seen as one of selecting

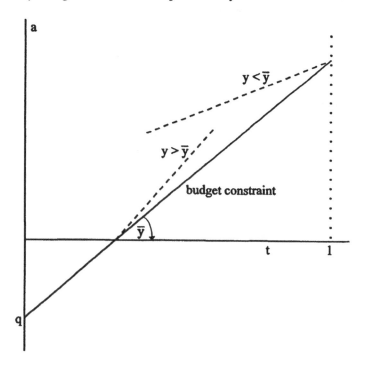

Figure 5.2   Individual tax preferences for the linear tax

an appropriate point on the line, over the range where $b \geq 0$ and $t \leq 1$. It is, however, useful to consider the choice that would be made by any selfish individual with a given income. A similar analysis was carried out in Chapter 4 for the income tax with a tax-free threshold. For an individual with income of y, the relationship between b and t for which a constant net amount of tax, T, is paid is:

$$b = ty - T \qquad (5.7)$$

Remember that in this part of the book individual incomes are assumed to be fixed independently of the tax structure. Hence, each individual prefers to see the personal net tax burden, T, minimized. The preferred value of the tax rate will depend on the individual's value of y in relation to the mean. Equation (5.7) can be regarded as defining a set of iso-tax curves, each of which is linear. Hence, as illustrated in Figure 5.2, all individuals with $y < \bar{y}$ prefer the corner solution with t set at its maximum value of unity. This result can be used to obtain the choice of tax rate based on majority voting, since individuals have single-peaked preferences and the median voter theorem can be applied. With a positively skewed distribution, with the median less than the mean, majority voting would result in $t = 1$. Everyone would receive the after-tax income of $\bar{y} - Q$. The minority with $y > \bar{y}$ would however prefer the corner solution with $b = 0$ and $t = Q/\bar{y}$. This extreme result is modified significantly when pre-tax incomes depend on the tax and transfer system in operation, as discussed in Chapter 13.

Dispersion of Net Income

The linear income tax seems to involve a large amount of redistribution. Any *relative* measure of inequality is unaffected by the proportional income tax, but is reduced by an equal addition to all incomes. The unconditional transfer implies a relatively larger addition to net income for those with relatively lower incomes. For simplicity, consider the use of the coefficient of variation as the inequality measure. Because of the linearity of the schedule over the whole range of income, the redistribution can be expressed in terms of the coefficients of variation of pre- and post-transfer income, η_y and η_z respectively. It can be shown that:

$$\eta_z = \eta_y \{1 + b/(1 - t)\bar{y}\}^{-1} \qquad (5.8)$$

When $t = 1$ the dispersion of z is zero. This is of course an extreme situation, and it is very significantly modified when the distribution of income is affected by the tax system through incentive effects.

Numerical results for other measures can be obtained using a simulated population of individuals. Table 5.1 gives examples of summary measures for the linear income tax, based on a simulated population of 2000 persons drawn from a lognormal distribution with a variance of logarithms of 0.5. Net revenue is held constant at 10 per cent of total income, and the table shows results for variations in the ratio of the social dividend, b, to the median income. These values are independent of the mean of logarithms of the distribution. The Gini and Atkinson inequality measures of net income, the latter based on an inequality aversion coefficient of 0.5, fall rapidly as the threshold rises. The Kakwani and Suits measures of progressivity correspondingly rise rapidly, and are very similar to each other. It will be seen in Part II that such high values cannot be achieved when incomes are endogenous.

Table 5.1   The linear income tax

Ratio of social dividend to median income	Required tax rate, t	Gini	Atkinson (0.5)	Kakwani	Suits
0.2	0.256	0.312	0.078	0.612	0.613
0.4	0.412	0.246	0.049	1.253	1.255
0.6	0.567	0.180	0.028	1.927	1.928
0.8	0.723	0.115	0.012	2.634	2.637
1.0	0.879	0.050	0.003	3.378	3.381

Notes: Net revenue/total income = 0.10; Gini measure of pre-tax income = 0.378; Atkinson (0.5) measure of pre-tax income = 0.115; variance of logarithms of pre-tax income = 0.5.

5.2   A MINIMUM INCOME GUARANTEE

The simplicity of the linear income tax, particularly the use of a single marginal rate, has been attractive not only to analysts but to many policy commentators. However, critics have argued that the linear tax requires a very high marginal rate for a reasonable level of the social dividend, or minimum net income, although average rates are lower and are negative over a range of incomes. It has been argued that a more 'efficient' transfer scheme would concentrate benefits on those who have the greatest need, namely those with very low gross incomes. Such a scheme is a minimum income guarantee, and is discussed in the present section. The choice between transfer systems will be examined further in Chapter 6.

The most basic form of minimum income guarantee involves raising to a guaranteed minimum the incomes of all those with gross incomes below a specified level. However, the use of a minimum income guarantee presents several possibilities. Consider Figure 5.3, where the relationship between z and y for a simple tax structure, involving a single tax rate, t, and a tax-free threshold, a, is shown as OCT. As in section 4.2, individuals pay no tax on earnings below a, and pay a constant proportion of earnings measured above, so that $T(y) = t(y - a)$ for $y > a$. The simplest form of minimum income guarantee would involve the payment of $(a - y)$ to all those with $y < a$. This would produce a relationship between z and y of BCT, and for the same tax rate this would involve the payment of higher transfers to a smaller number of people than under the linear income tax scheme.

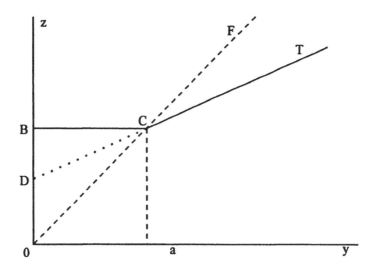

Figure 5.3   A minimum income guarantee

The government's budget constraint is obtained, as before, by imposing the condition that there is zero net revenue. It is therefore required that payments are equal to receipts and:

$$\int^a(a - y)\,dF(y) = t\int_a(y - a)\,dF(y) \qquad (5.9)$$

This can be simplified using the approach described in Chapter 4. The term $G(a)$ was defined there as:

$$G(a) = \{1 - F_1(a)\} - (a/\bar{y})\{1 - F(a)\} \qquad (5.10)$$

and represents the total income, measured in excess of the threshold, a, as a proportion of total gross income. This can be used to simplify equation (5.9) to give the tax rate required to support any specified value of a. After some tedious manipulation it can be shown that:

$$t = 1 - (1 - a/\bar{y})/G(a) \qquad (5.11)$$

This result expresses the tax rate in terms of the value of the minimum income guarantee, which in this model is also equal to the level of the tax-free threshold. This system can however be administered in several different ways. It may use a conventional tax system for those with $y > a$, and means-testing may be used to bring those with $y < a$ up to the level of the minimum income guarantee. Alternatively, it may use some form of the linear income tax to produce the schedule 0DT, along with income dependent transfers to raise the segment DC to BC.

It is not necessary to have the kink in the schedule relating z and y at the point C. It would be possible to extend the range of income, over which the effective marginal rate of tax is 100 per cent, to the right of a. Alternatively a minimum income guarantee scheme may be devised in which fewer individuals receive more generous support. In either case two policy instruments, the earnings level below which individuals receive the minimum income guarantee, y_0, and the level of the minimum net income itself, b, must be set. But it is important to stress that only one of these can be set independently for given values of a and t. This is not because of the government's budget constraint, but arises because of the need to ensure continuity in the relationship between pre- and post-tax and transfer income. The two alternatives are shown in Figure 5.4. In part (a), individuals between a and y_0 pay tax and receive benefits, with the combined effect giving a 100 per cent effective marginal tax rate. In part (b), those between y_0 and a pay no tax and, although they receive smaller absolute transfers than those below y_0, they are not subject to the 100 per cent effective rate.

In each case in Figure 5.4 the necessity to ensure continuity at point C provides a further relationship between y_0, b, a and t. From the equation of the linear segment DT it is required to have:

$$b = at + (1 - t) y_0 \qquad (5.12)$$

However, it is usually more convenient to allow t, b and y_0 to determine the tax-free threshold, a, since b and y_0 are the policy variables of more direct interest. In this case:

$$a = y_0 + (b - y_0)/t \qquad (5.13)$$

With this condition, it is possible to consider the condition required for the net tax revenue to be zero, that is for net revenue to be just sufficient to finance net

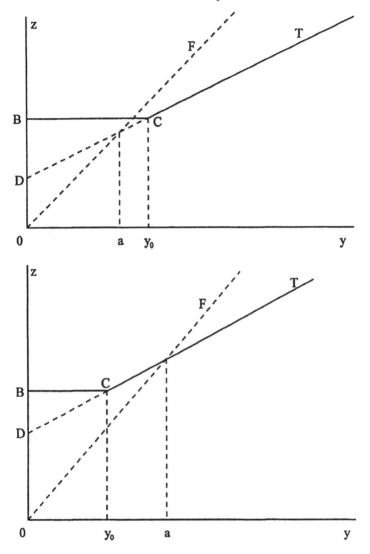

Figure 5.4   Alternative forms of minimum income guarantee

transfers. In either of the above cases the net tax paid by those with y below y_0 is $y - b$, and the net tax paid by those above y_0 is $ty + y_0 (1 - t) - b$. The government's budget constraint is therefore:

$$0 = \int^{y_0}(y - b) \, dF(y) + \int_{y_0} \{ty + y_0 (1 - t) - b\} \, dF(y) \qquad (5.14)$$

After some manipulation, using the term in (3.10), this can be simplified to give

$$t = 1 - (1 - b/\bar{y})/G(y_0) \qquad (5.15)$$

which may be compared with equation (5.11). After obtaining the value of the marginal tax rate, t, for any given minimum income, b, and threshold, y_0, from (5.15), substitution into (5.13) gives the appropriate value of the tax-free threshold. It is important to stress that only combinations that give positive values of the tax-free threshold, a, are sensible, otherwise the income tax system involves lump-sum tax payments rather than 'allowances', thereby making the system regressive.

The introduction of a higher marginal rate, t_2, applied to incomes above, say, a_2 $(> a)$ can also be examined using this framework. The analysis proceeds by writing the net tax paid for individuals in each of the three sections; for $y \leq y_0$; for $y_0 < y \leq a_2$; and for $y > a_2$. The condition that total net tax paid is zero can then be used to express t in terms of a_2, t_2, y_0 and b. After some tedious manipulation, this can be shown to give the result that:

$$t = \{G(y_0) + t_2 G(a_2) - (1 - b/\bar{y})\}/\{G(y_0) + G(a_2)\} \qquad (5.16)$$

It can be seen that the substitution of $t_2 = t$ into (5.16) produces equation (5.15). For further discussion of these types of tax and transfer system, see Creedy (1978, 1982 a, b).

The Modified Minimum Income Guarantee

Each of the minimum income guarantee schemes considered above involves effective marginal rates of 100 per cent below a given income. An alternative scheme may be devised in which the section BC of the relationship between z and y has a slope of $1 - s$, so that the effective tax rate is equal to s. For those below y_0 the net tax paid, $(y - z)$, is $sy - b$; while for those above y_0, net income, z, is $b + y_0(1 - s) + (1 - t)(y - y_0)$. Thus net tax is $ty + y_0(s - t) - b$. If the procedure used above is again applied to ensure that the total net tax is zero, the following relationship is obtained:

$$t = s - (s - b/\bar{y})/G(y_0) \qquad (5.17)$$

and not surprisingly the substitution of $s = 1$ into equation (5.17) gives (5.15).

This modified form of minimum income guarantee does not constrain the kink, in the relationship between pre- and post-tax and transfer income, to occur at some point on the 45° line, just as there is no such constraint in Figure 5.4. A slight simplification therefore involves a modification instead to Figure

5.3, so that those above the tax-free threshold pay income tax and receive no gross transfer, while those below the threshold receive a net transfer. This transfer is progressively reduced as pre-tax income moves towards the threshold.

With this further modification, those below the tax-free threshold, a, receive a transfer of $s(a - y)$ and therefore have a net income of $as + y(1 - s)$. Those above the threshold, as in the simple income tax structure of Chapter 4, pay tax of $t(y - a)$. For a pure transfer system, the government's budget constraint requires:

$$t\int_a^\infty (y - a)\, dF(y) = s\int_0^a (a - y)\, dF(y)$$

This can be simplified to express t in terms of the other variables, whence:

$$t = \frac{(as/\bar{y}) - s\{1 - G(a)\}}{G(a)} \tag{5.18}$$

If additional revenue of Q per person is required for non-transfer purposes, then $Q/\bar{y}$ must be added to the numerator on the right hand side of (5.18). Further use of this type of modified scheme will be made in Part II of this book.

Table 5.2   The modified minimum income guarantee

| Ratio of threshold to median | Fixed net revenue (10%) | | | | Fixed tax rates | |
| | $s = 0.7$ | | $s = 0.9$ | | $s = 0.7\, t = 0.35$ | $s = 0.9\, t = 0.25$ |
	CV	t	CV	t	CV	CV
0.2	0.788	0.119	0.788	0.119	0.743	0.765
0.3	0.775	0.132	0.774	0.133	0.714	0.744
0.4	0.755	0.152	0.751	0.154	0.684	0.720
0.5	0.725	0.179	0.717	0.185	0.653	0.691
0.6	0.685	0.218	0.669	0.230	0.622	0.660
0.7	0.631	0.271	0.604	0.293	0.591	0.625
0.8	0.564	0.342	0.522	0.378	0.559	0.589
0.9	0.481	0.435	0.420	0.489	0.529	0.553
1.0	0.383	0.552	0.298	0.633	0.499	0.517

Note: Coefficient of variation of gross income = 0.805.

Since there is a piecewise linear transformation between gross and net income with the modified minimum income guarantee, it is possible to use the analytical results of Appendix 4.2 to derive the coefficient of variation for any combination of tax parameters, s and t, and the threshold level, a. Some examples are shown in Table 5.2 for a lognormal distribution of gross income having a variance of logarithms of 0.5, that is a coefficient of variation of 0.805. In the case of an income tax system only, it was found in Chapter 4 that increases in the tax-free threshold eventually cause the dispersion of net income to increase unless the marginal tax rate is increased in order to maintain a fixed revenue. In the present case, however, the increase in the threshold involves more people benefiting from the transfer payments. Hence, whether the net revenue is held constant or not, the coefficient of variation falls continuously. There is obviously a limit to which the threshold can be raised in each case: where s and t are fixed, net revenue must be non-negative, and where s and net revenue are constant, t must be less than s. When net revenue is allowed to vary for fixed s and t, it can be seen from Table 5.2 that the coefficient of variation falls relatively slowly as the threshold is raised.

5.3   CONSUMPTION TAXES

A Non-linear Tax Function

In Chapter 4, a general consumption tax, applied at a fixed proportional rate of v to the pre-tax value of all goods, was introduced along with a proportional income tax. It was found that the overall effective tax is also proportional to income, but with a rate that is not equal to the sum of the separate rates. In most practical situations, such as the Value Added Tax systems of European Union member countries, some commodity groups are exempt from tax. For administrative purposes there is an important difference between zero rating and the exemption of goods, but this can be ignored here. Such exemptions are introduced in order to make the consumption tax system progressive, by exempting goods which form a higher proportion of total expenditure for the lower income groups. The most important group in this category is food.

In order to model a consumption tax system with such exemptions, it is necessary to specify the relationship between total expenditure, q, and the proportion of expenditure on exempt goods, $r(q)$. Remembering that the tax-inclusive rate, corresponding to a tax-exclusive rate of v, is equal to $v/(1 + v)$, the consumption tax schedule, $V(q)$, is:

$$V(q) = \left(\frac{v}{1+v}\right)\{1 - r(q)\}q \qquad (5.19)$$

A specification which has been found to provide a very good approximation to household expenditure data is the following:

$$r(q) = \alpha/(q + \theta)^\beta \qquad (5.20)$$

This non-linear form must be estimated using iterative methods; for an application to Australia, see Creedy (1992c). The variation in marginal and average consumption tax rates is illustrated in Figure 5.5, for the case where $v = 0.15$ and the parameters α, β and θ are set at 200, 0.65 and 10,000 respectively. These orders of magnitude are approximately those obtained when food is exempt from taxation, using Australian household expenditure data. The marginal rate is above the average rate and increases more rapidly, but the profiles in Figure 5.5 suggest that the scope for increasing the degree of progression of the tax structure and for introducing progressivity by exempting goods is unlikely to be large.

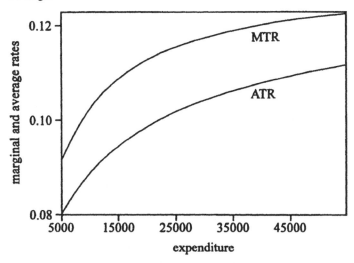

Figure 5.5   Consumption taxation and rate schedules

The overall effect of combining income and consumption taxes depends to some extent on the assumption made about savings. Some commentators have argued that consumption taxes must be regressive, on the grounds that those with higher incomes save relatively more and thereby 'escape' consumption taxes. However, this argument is not appropriate as it is restricted to a single period, whereas savings are ultimately consumed at some future date. This issue will be discussed again in Chapter 7, but for the moment it is most appropriate to ignore savings in the cross-sectional context and write $q = y - T(y)$. The sum of income and consumption taxes, $R(y)$, is thus given by:

$$R(y) = T(y) + q \{1 - r(q)\} \{v/(1 + v)\} \qquad (5.21)$$

If, in addition, there is a minimum income guarantee in operation, a change in the consumption tax rate, v, will affect the real value of the minimum income. The question therefore arises of how the minimum must be adjusted when v is changed. Define b^* as the nominal minimum required to keep the real (that is the after-tax) value constant at b. It is required that the consumption tax paid on b^*, plus the basic minimum, b, must equal b^* itself. The simple 'reimbursement' of the tax paid on b would not be sufficient compensation because the extra expenditure would attract further taxation. Hence:

$$b^* = b + b^* \{1 - r(b)\} \{v/ (1 + v)\} \qquad (5.22)$$

with $r(b)$ given by substituting into (5.20). The non-linear nature of (5.22) means that the nominal value can only be solved iteratively.

A Change in the Tax Mix

Some idea of the role of exemptions in a partial shift, from an income tax structure towards a combination of income and consumption taxes, can be obtained by using the above specification combined with a simulated population of individuals. Suppose the fixed pre-tax distribution of income is lognormal with mean and variance of logarithms of 10 and 0.5 respectively (so that the arithmetic mean is $28,368). Consider the four-parameter form of the non-linear income tax structure described in section 4.4, with a, t_1, t_2 and k given respectively by 5000, 0.25, 0.9 and 0.5. There is also a minimum income guarantee such that all those with disposable incomes less than $6,500 are brought up to that level. With a population of 5000 individuals drawn at random from the lognormal distribution, 6.2 per cent of individuals receive some transfer payment. Concentrating on the effects on Atkinson's inequality measure, with an aversion coefficient of 0.5, the income tax system reduces inequality from 0.1158 for gross income to 0.0386 for after-income-tax income, and the effect of transfers is to reduce this further to 0.0353.

If the value of t_2 is reduced to 0.8, with the other parameters unchanged, and a proportional consumption tax is introduced in order to maintain a fixed net tax revenue, then the tax-exclusive rate must be 0.115, involving a nominal minimum income guarantee of $7,245 which is received by 9.2 per cent of individuals. The Atkinson inequality measure of after-income-tax income is increased to 0.0511 and the inequality of net income is increased to 0.046. Hence the shift increases the inequality of net income. If, however, consumption tax exemptions are introduced such that the schedule of $r(q)$ is the same as that used to produce Figure 5.5 (that is α, β, and θ of 200, 0.65 and 10,000 respectively), then revenue neutrality requires a higher tax-exclusive consumption tax rate of 0.165. However, the nominal minimum income guarantee is reduced to $7,151, received by 8.6 per cent of people. The inequality of net income is 0.0447. The exemptions reduce inequality slightly from 0.046, but the tax shift increases inequality overall.

One strategy that could be used in order to make the tax shift inequality-neutral as well as revenue-neutral is to raise the parameter k at the same time as the maximum marginal tax rate is reduced. This has the effect of increasing the rate at which marginal tax rates increase. With the consumption tax structure assumed above, however, inequality-neutrality can be achieved only with a very small shift in the tax revenue away from income taxation. Although exemptions can introduce progression into the structure of consumption taxation, their effect is very restricted. (For further analysis of a tax shift in Australia, see Creedy, 1992c.) A double-log specification for $r(q)$ was used by Creedy and Gemmell (1984, 1985a) to examine the United Kingdom tax structure; see also Gemmell (1985a).

The consideration of such tax shifts is considerably simplified if transfer payments are ignored and if attention is given only to linear tax functions. For example, if the income tax has a single marginal rate, t, above the threshold, a, then for $y > a$ the tax paid is $T(y) = -at + ty$. If the function $r(q)$ is assumed to be ξ/q, then $V(q) = (q - \xi) v/ (1 + v) = \omega q - \delta$, say. The overall tax structure, the sum of income and consumption taxes, is thus linear and is given, remembering that $q = y - T(y)$, by:

$$R(y) = - \{at (1 - \omega) + \delta\} + y \{t + \omega (1 - t)\} \qquad (5.23)$$

For those who pay income tax, the overall structure is equivalent to a linear income tax with a social dividend equal to $at(1 - \omega) + \delta$ and a constant marginal tax rate of $t + \omega(1 - t)$. With this structure it is much easier to devise tax shifts which are revenue and inequality neutral; for an application of this linear model, see Kay and Morris (1979). However, the restrictive nature of this special case should be kept in mind.

This chapter has examined several simplified tax and transfer systems that have been extensively used in the literature and will also be used in later chapters of this book. These include the linear income tax and various forms of minimum income guarantee. Special attention was given to the form of the government's budget constraint and the implications for inequality measures of variations in tax parameters. It was then shown how consumption taxes, allowing for exempt categories of goods, can be modelled. The implications of such non-linear tax functions can only be investigated using simulation methods; some basic examples, involving a partial shift in the tax mix away from income taxations, were given.

6.   Taxes and transfers over the life-cycle

Previous chapters have concentrated on taxes and transfers in the context of a single period, usually a year. This chapter turns to some issues that arise when attempting to examine taxes in a life-cycle framework. The first problem is that since complete life-cycle data are not available, it is necessary to construct a simulation model. Section 6.1 presents a very simple model which can be used to simulate the lifetime incomes for a group of individuals; the many complexities of household formation and associated changes in household size are ignored, along with events such as unemployment and sickness. Section 6.2 uses the model to compare the effects of taxes in cross-sectional and life-cycle contexts. The effects of changes in the tax mix, involving a partial shift towards consumption taxes, are examined in section 6.3. An issue that arises in the life-cycle framework concerns the precise income concept used. Alternative concepts are presented in section 6.4, and their implications for comparisons between tax structures are examined in section 6.5.

6.1   A SIMULATION MODEL

In the absence of longitudinal data it is necessary to simulate individual earnings profiles. This section describes a simple model that is capable of generating the simulated earnings of a cohort of individuals for each year in the working life. The model requires very few parameters. This approach contrasts with the dynamic microsimulation models which involve using the full details of household expenditure surveys and which are designed to examine different types of question. The present approach concerns the broader evaluation of alternative tax structures.

Earnings Profiles

Individuals' earnings can be modelled as consisting of a systematic component which follows the growth pattern of the geometric mean of earnings in each age group and a random component which introduces a measure of relative earnings mobility. Relative earnings are defined as the ratio of person i's earnings y_{it} to geometric mean earnings m_t in the age group t, that is, y_{it}/m_t. Let

u_{it} be a random variable which is distributed independently of current income and previous proportional changes in income, then if $z_{it} = \log(y_{it}/m_t)$ the generating process can be written:

$$z_{it} - z_{i,t-1} = u_{it} \tag{6.1}$$

If u_{it} has a constant variance of σ_u^2 and if σ_t^2 denotes the variance of z_{it} then the first-order process in (6.1) implies that:

$$\sigma_t^2 = \sigma_1^2 + t\sigma_u^2 \tag{6.2}$$

and the variance of the logarithms of income in each year grows linearly over time. Cross-sectional information on the variance of the logarithms of earnings in different age groups can be used to provide estimates of the parameters in (6.2). More complex processes of earnings movements are discussed in Creedy (1985).

The geometric mean of earnings in each age group is assumed to follow the parabolic pattern typically observed in cross-sectional data. Let μ_t denote the logarithm of the geometric mean income in age group t, then:

$$\mu_t = \mu_1 + \gamma t - \delta t^2 \tag{6.3}$$

Estimates of the parameters in (6.2) and (6.3) can easily be obtained using standard regression analysis, given cross-sectional observations on μ_t and σ_t^2. However, if a set of income distributions is available, it is more efficient to estimate the parameters jointly using an iterative method based on maximum likelihood. An example is given in Creedy (1992b), using data for males from the Australian Bureau of Statistics *Income Distribution Survey* 1985/8; they are reported in Table 6.1. The value of μ_1 can be adjusted to align it with 1984 data used in later sections, giving 9.57436.

Table 6.1   Parameter values for age earnings profiles

σ_1^2	σ_u^2	μ_1	γ	δ
0.1817	0.00575	9.612	0.0385	0.00086

Source: Creedy (1992b, pp. 51–3)

The cross-sectional age profile of earnings on which the estimates are based are representative of a cohort only when factors other than age that affect earnings are absent. While it is difficult, if not impossible, to account for many of these factors, it is possible to account for productivity growth by assuming that every worker in the cohort benefits equally; the rate of growth can then be added to the parameter γ. This adjustment raises lifetime earnings but does not significantly affect the inequality measures.

To generate lifetime earnings profiles for a set of individuals, rewrite (6.1) as:

$$y_{it} = y_{i,t-1} \exp\{(\mu_t - \mu_{t-1}) + u_{it}\} \tag{6.4}$$

This can be used to generate the y_{it}s given a set of random variates from an $N(0, \sigma_u^2)$ distribution. To generate y_{i1}, earnings in the first year of working life (set at age twenty), suppose that the variable v_i is randomly selected from the standard normal distribution, $N(0, 1)$, and use $y_{i1} = \exp(\mu_1 + v_i \sigma_u)$. For simulations reported later in the chapter, it is assumed that the annual growth rate is 0.025 per cent, the inflation rate is 0.07, the nominal interest rate is 0.10, so the nominal growth of earnings is 0.095.

Differential Mortality

Due to the lack of data on differential mortality, it is necessary to make assumptions about the age at death. This is assumed to vary systematically with annual average real earnings relative to the (geometric) mean earnings, so that those with relatively high lifetime earnings tend to live longer. Only those who survive to retirement are considered, so there are no deaths before the age of 65. The relationship between earnings and the number of years of retirement can be specified as:

$$d_i = \bar{d} + d_1 \log(x_i/x_g) + e_i \tag{6.5}$$

where d_i is the number of years person i survives after retirement, $\bar{d}$ is the average of d_is, x_i is person i's annual average earnings, x_g is the geometric mean value of the x_is, and e_i is a random variable distributed as $N(0, \sigma_e^2)$. The values of x_i and x_g can be obtained from the lifetime earnings simulations. In the following simulations the value of $\bar{d}$ was set at 14 years to give an expectation of life of 79 years. After a little experimentation, a value of 8 for d_1 and 50 for σ_e^2 were found to give a very good fit to the Australian survival curve for males. The specification of differential mortality has been used in Creedy (1982b) and was supported by empirical evidence from the UK in Creedy *et al.* (1993).

Savings and Retirement Consumption

In order to calculate the amount of consumption tax paid both before and after retirement it is necessary to model individuals' saving patterns. It would be possible to model formal superannuation systems, but the present discussion ignores these complexities; what is not saved is assumed to be spent, and the expenditure on non-exempt goods incurs consumption tax. Savings are accumulated and then spent in retirement. It might be argued that inheritances and bequests should be modelled explicitly, on the grounds that the relatively wealthy leave larger bequests and thereby avoid consumption taxation. However, any bequests will ultimately be spent and will therefore attract consumption taxation. Some people may perhaps wish to make the value judgement that only consumption during an individual's own life is relevant in considering inequality, but there is clearly no 'correct' approach to this issue.

A simple approach is to assume that during retirement each person takes a constant real amount of accumulated savings each year to spend. This does not constitute a constant yearly level of consumption in the presence of interest income tax since in later years, as the level of wealth is run down, less interest income tax is paid and this allows a higher level of consumption. If W is the accumulated value of savings at retirement, L is the period of retirement, A is the constant annual amount in real terms, and r_r is the real rate of interest, then A is calculated as:

$$A = Wr_r/[1 - v^L] \qquad (6.6)$$

where $v = 1/(1 + r_r)$. The following examples assume that individuals know how long they will live, but this assumption could also be relaxed. The use of this framework is illustrated in the following section.

6.2   CROSS-SECTIONAL VERSUS LIFE-CYCLE COMPARISONS

Earlier studies of taxation in a life-cycle framework include Davies *et al.* (1984), Poterba (1989), Casperson and Metcalf (1993) and Fullerton and Rogers (1993), though only Casperson and Metcalf examine the role of exemptions in a broad-based consumption tax (using current consumption as a proxy for lifetime income, as does Poterba). These authors follow Davies *et al.* in suggesting that income taxes are less progressive and consumption taxes without exemptions are less regressive in a life-cycle than on an annual basis. However, the conclusions are not based on the progressivity measures defined in Chapter 3 above, but on changes in inequality between pre- and post-tax distributions. Furthermore, in their comparisons neither the pre-tax distribution nor the tax revenue are kept constant across the cases being compared. It is quite easy to produce examples showing the opposite results.

Data from 1984 are used in establishing expenditure patterns, so the 1984/85 Australian income tax structure is chosen as the basic structure with which others will be compared and it is shown in Table 6.2 as structure 1. The table also illustrates an alternative and simpler tax structure which is used below. This alternative system raises less income tax revenue and involves higher inequality measures of income after income tax.

Table 6.2   Alternative income tax structures

Structure 1		Structure 2	
Thresholds	Marginal rates	Thresholds	Marginal rates
4,595	0.2667	5,000	0.18
12,500	0.30	10,000	0.28
19,500	0.46	20,000	0.40
28,000	0.4733	30,000	0.50
35,000	0.5533	40,000	0.55
35,788	0.60		

The after-income-tax distributions differ depending on assumptions as to saving behaviour and whether interest income is taxed. In addition, a rate must be set at which the tax brackets are indexed. Since 1983 the Australian income tax structure has not been indexed and as a result there has been a significant amount of 'bracket creep'. However, as the simulations cover a long period, it is more reasonable to model some positive indexation rate, and the following results assume that the rate is set equal to the inflation rate of 0.07.

Table 6.3   Income tax: annual and lifetime effects

	Annual		Lifetime	
	Atkinson (1.2)	Gini	Atkinson (1.2)	Gini
Percentage reduction from income tax	3.73	2.32	4.32	2.60
Kakwani	0.174		0.124	
Suits	0.197		0.131	
Horizontal inequity	—		0.00025	
Aggregate tax ratio	0.336		0.378	

In order to examine the conventional argument that income taxes are less progressive in the life-cycle than in the cross-sectional framework, Table 6.3

presents results for two examples. Income tax structure 1 in Table 6.2 was applied to a population of 2000 individuals selected at random from a lognormal distribution of incomes with mean and variance of logarithms of 10 and 0.5 respectively; these values are reasonable approximations to the cross-sectional distribution. The resulting percentage reductions, from pre- to post-tax distributions, in Gini and Atkinson ($\varepsilon = 1.2$) inequality measures are shown, along with the Kakwani and Suits progressivity measures and the overall tax ratio. The various measures are defined in Chapters 2 and 3. Table 6.3 also shows the effect of applying the same tax structure, suitably indexed, to incomes in each year of life for a cohort of 2000 individuals, using the income generation process described above. The calculations assumed that there was no interest income tax and that individuals saved 10 per cent of disposable income each year of working life. The present values, at age 20, of gross and net incomes were compared. In the lifetime context the variability in incomes, combined with rising marginal tax rates, introduces some re-ranking or horizontal inequity, as shown by the Atkinson–Plotnick measure. These results show that the progressivity of the income tax structure is indeed lower in the life-cycle context, yet because of the difference in aggregate tax ratios, the reduction in the inequality of incomes is greater in the lifetime framework. These results may be compared with the conventional argument in terms of inequality reduction.

Such comparisons between cross-sectional and lifetime frameworks are therefore best avoided. It is, however, much more appropriate to consider specified tax structure *changes* in the two contexts. Examples of such comparisons are shown in the following section.

6.3 CHANGES IN THE TAX MIX

This section examines the implications, in cross-sectional and life-cycle frameworks, of a partial change in the tax mix. Structure 1 of Table 6.2 is replaced by structure 2, where the top rate of income tax is eliminated and other adjustments involve a lower revenue from income taxation. The reduction in income tax revenue is compensated by the introduction of a general consumption tax; this is the type of policy that has been contemplated in Australia in recent years. The consumption tax may have exemptions, following the type of specification introduced in section 5.3. The question raised is: do exemptions have more or less influence in the life-cycle compared with the cross-sectional context?

The Consumption Tax Structure

Exempting various commodity groups from consumption tax is one method of introducing progressivity. It is well established that the proportion of income

spent on food declines as income increases, so that food is typically exempt.
When modelling the consumption tax, two possible structures are considered,
depending on the goods exempt from tax. The alternative structures are described
in Table 6.4.

Table 6.4   Tax-exempt categories

Structure	Categories
0	No exemptions
1	Food
2	Food + fuel and power + medical care and health

The consumption tax paid is affected by the proportion of income spent on exempt
goods. If v denotes the consumption tax rate, q denotes total expenditure and
$r(q)$ the proportion of expenditure on exempt goods, then V(q), the consumption tax paid, can be written:

$$V(q) = [v/(1 + v)][1 - r(q)] \, q \qquad (6.7)$$

As discussed in Chapter 5, the following function, as in (5.20), has been found
to provide a reasonable approximation to consumption patterns:

$$r(q) = \alpha/(q + \theta)^\beta \qquad (6.8)$$

It is therefore necessary to estimate the parameters of $r(q)$ for each of the
structures in Table 6.3. Table 6.5 gives parameter values taken from Creedy
(1992b), where they were estimated using an iterative maximum likelihood
approach with cross-sectional data; no attempt has been made to allow for
variations with age.

Table 6.5   Consumption tax structures

Structure	α	β	θ
0	0.00	—	—
1	177.51	0.653	12,131.60
2	102.41	0.580	8,158.80

Source: Creedy (1992b)

The growth in nominal earnings over time at the rate, g, makes it necessary to adjust the consumption tax parameters every year using the following equations:

$$\alpha_{+1} = \exp\{\log \alpha + \beta \log (1 + g)\} \qquad (6.9)$$

$$\theta_{+1} = \theta(1 + g) \qquad (6.10)$$

The simulation model makes it possible to change the income tax structure and calculate, using an iterative search procedure, the consumption tax rate that gives aggregate revenue-neutrality in terms of the present value of tax payments by the cohort. The simulation results reported in this section were obtained under the same assumptions as mentioned earlier.

Table 6.6   Changes in the tax mix: percentage changes in inequality measures and welfare premia

Type of revenue-Inequality neutral change	Annual Inequality Welfare Atkinson (1.2)	premium	v	Lifetime Welfare rate Atkinson (1.2)	premium	rate v
Income tax structure 1 to 2 with consumption tax 0	4.15	−7.65	0.07	5.72	−7.53	0.069
Consumption tax 0 to 1	−1.09	2.72	0.08	−1.30	1.94	0.091
Consumption tax 0 to 2	−1.63	3.71	0.088	−1.95	2.96	0.101

Results are shown in Table 6.6 for the two frameworks. The effect of introducing exemptions in the consumption tax can be seen by the increase in v. The first row of the table shows that if a revenue-neutral change is made by switching from income tax structure 1 to tax structure 2 combined with consumption tax structure 0, the inequality of net income increases and the welfare premium from progression falls. The increase in inequality is higher in the life-cycle framework, but the fall in the welfare premium is less than in the cross-sectional context. Moving from row 1 to row 2 shows the effect of introducing the exemption of food in the consumption tax; inequality of net income falls and the welfare premium rises. Horizontal inequity is not reported in the table, as it is very small, though the tax shift reduces the Atkinson–Plotnick measure slightly. Exemptions have a larger effect on inequality, but a smaller effect on the welfare premium, in the life-cycle context.

It can be seen that in all cases reported in Table 6.6 the percentage change in the welfare premium exceeds that of inequality, although this need not necessarily hold. For revenue-neutral changes, these two percentage changes can be examined as follows. With a tax shift producing a change in inequality of net income from I_y to I'_y and a change in the welfare premium from Π to Π', then:

$$\Pi = (1 - g)\, \bar{x}\, (I_x - I_y) \qquad\qquad (6.11)$$

$$\Pi' = (1 - g)\, \bar{x}\, (I_x - I'_y) \qquad\qquad (6.12)$$

Combining these expressions gives:

$$\frac{\Pi' - \Pi}{\Pi} = \frac{\left(I_y - I'_y\right)/I_y}{I_x/I_y - 1} \qquad\qquad (6.13)$$

Hence if $0 < I_x/I_y - 1 < 1$, the percentage change in Π will exceed that of I_y.

The results of Table 6.6 are modified if there is a minimum income guarantee in existence and this is adjusted in the way described in Chapter 5 when the consumption tax is introduced. It can be found that the existence of such transfer payments substantially reduces the impact of all the tax structure changes examined. For example, if there is a guarantee of $8,000, indexed to the growth of earnings each year, then (in the lifetime context) the change in the tax mix with no exemptions produces an increase in the inequality of net (present value of) income of 4.5 per cent and a reduction in the welfare premium of 3.85 per cent. Exempting food changes each of the measures by less than 1 per cent. The use of exemptions does appear to provide a rather 'blunt instrument' in terms of introducing progressivity or reducing inequality. An alternative approach might involve the use of a two-rate indirect structure whereby goods that on average form a higher proportion of the budgets of higher income individuals are taxed at a higher rate; such a policy is examined in Creedy (1993a). Experiments with the above model show that increases in the level of the minimum income guarantee are more effective than introducing exemptions in reducing inequality.

6.4   ALTERNATIVE INCOME CONCEPTS

The above comparisons have used the distribution of present values of gross and net income. A different approach has been used by some of those constructing large-scale micro-simulation models; for example, Harding (1994) based comparisons of taxes and transfers on the annual average income of individuals in alternative schemes. Other measures are available, such as the annuity that can be financed over life with the individual's wealth, or the constant value of consumption that gives the same lifetime utility as the actual stream of consumption. The latter approach requires assumptions about the preference patterns of individuals. In computing present values, no special adjustment is made for differential mortality, which means that the income and consumption streams of individuals differ in length, but the other measures allow for such differences in quite different ways. Given the variety of alternative approaches, the important question arises of whether the conclusions reached by empirical or simulation studies are likely to be affected by the income concept used. The issue may thus be stated as follows. Given an earnings stream of x_{it} (for $t = 1, ..., L$) for the ith member of a cohort (with $i = 1, ..., N$), the combined effect of savings and taxes produces a stream of consumption of c_{it} (for $t = 1, ..., T_i$ and $T_i \geq L$). In producing summary measures of the streams, do comparisons depend on the income concept used?

The Alternative Concepts

Consider a single cohort of individuals, all members of which work for L years, obtaining nominal gross earnings in each year of x_{it}, for $t = 1, ...,L$ and $i = 1, ...,N$. The assumptions that the working life is the same for all individuals and that no deaths take place until retirement begins could be relaxed with a simple modification of the following formulae. Suppose also that the nominal interest rate, r_n, and the inflation rate, p, remain constant, so that the real rate of interest, r_r is also constant and is given by:

$$r_r = (1 + r_n)/(1 + p) - 1 \tag{6.14}$$

Nominal earnings x_t are subject to taxation in each year. If the ith individual lives for d_i years after retirement, the length of 'life', measured from entry into the labour force, is given by $L + d_i = T_i$. The tax scheme, combined with savings, transforms the nominal earnings stream into a stream of net consumption. It is convenient to refer to this stream of net consumption as one of 'net income'.

The simplest measures of the stream of gross earnings are as follows. The *present value of gross real earnings*, X_i, is given for each individual by:

$$X = \sum_{t=1}^{L} x_t / (1 + r_n)^{t-1} \tag{6.15}$$

where individual subscripts have been omitted for convenience. Precisely the same form is obtained if earnings in each year are first converted into real terms using the price index, and then the real rate of interest is used. It is, however, necessary to work explicitly in terms of nominal earnings if there is an interest-income tax, since nominal rather than real interest-income is subject to taxation.

The *annual average gross real earnings*, x, of each individual are given by:

$$x = \frac{1}{L}\sum_{t=1}^{L} x_t / (1+p)^{t-1} \tag{6.16}$$

If deaths occur before retirement it is simply necessary to substitute L_i for L.

A common approach is to compare the dispersion of X, the present value of gross real earnings, with that of the *present value of net real income* (or consumption), Y, making no special allowance for the fact that individuals live for different periods. The latter measure is given for each individual by:

$$Y = \sum_{t=1}^{T} c_t (1+r_n)^{t-1} \tag{6.17}$$

where, as before, individual subscripts are omitted from Y, T and c_t.

Some studies compare the inequality of the undiscounted average real gross earnings, x, based on x_t as in equation (6.16), with the equivalent measure of the flow of net income or consumption c_t ($t = 1$, T). The *annual average net real income*, Q, is given by:

$$Q = \frac{1}{T}\sum_{t=1}^{T} c_t / (1+p)^{t-1} \tag{6.18}$$

Comparisons would be made between x and Q. In this type of comparison, neither the net nor the gross income stream is discounted, so that the shapes of the time profiles are ignored. However, the shape of the profile of x_t (for $t = 1, ..., L$) will have a role in the transformation from x_t to c_t because it will influence the time stream of savings and their accumulation, as well as affecting the tax payments. Those individuals whose incomes are more variable over the working life will pay more tax as they will move into higher tax brackets in some years, compared with someone with the same annual average, but constant, income stream. Some studies, such as Harding (1994), which use annual average concepts do not however allow for savings and interest income taxation in examining lifetime redistribution.

Annuity Measures

A different approach involves the transformation of each time-stream into a single measure based on an annuity. Thus, a *constant* value is produced which has the same present value as the actual time profile. This is achieved using the following standard result. If r is the relevant rate of interest, the discount factor is $v = 1/(1 + r)$, and a_n denotes the present value of an annuity in which n payments of \$1 are made, the first received at the end of the first year, then:

$$a_n = (1 - v^n)/r \tag{6.19}$$

The conversion of a present value to an annuity is carried out by dividing the present value by a_n.

The flow of gross income x_t $(t = 1, L)$ would need to be converted, if there were no taxes, into an annuity which is capable of lasting the whole of the lifetime, that is, T periods. Hence the two relevant annuities, A_x and A_c for the gross and net profiles respectively, are defined as:

$$A_x = X r_r \left\{ 1 - \left(\frac{1}{1 + r_r} \right)^T \right\}^{-1} \tag{6.20}$$

$$A_c = Y r_r \left\{ 1 - \left(\frac{1}{1 + r_r} \right)^T \right\}^{-1} \tag{6.21}$$

It might be argued, however, that an annuity as calculated above may not give the individual the same lifetime utility as the actual stream of net income, depending on the inter-temporal elasticity of substitution and the rate of time preference. Such a constant amount, used by Nordhaus (1973), is called the *utility equivalent annuity*. This concept is similar to an equally distributed 'equivalent' measure used in the measurement of inequality. With a concave utility function, income fluctuations are to a certain extent 'wasteful' and a constant annual amount which is less than the arithmetic mean income would provide the same total utility for the individual. The calculation of utility equivalent annuities requires strong assumptions about each individual's preferences. Nordhaus (1973) assumed that all individuals have the same tastes, but a specification for the joint distribution of taste parameters is introduced below.

The utility equivalent annuity can be derived as follows. Define $\beta = -(1 - 1/\eta)$, where η is the inter-temporal elasticity of substitution, and let ξ denote one plus the individual's time preference rate. Write an individual's lifetime utility, U, as:

$$U = \sum_{t=1}^{T} \xi^{-(t-1)} c_t^{-\beta} \tag{6.22}$$

If δ is one plus the real rate of interest and Y is, as above, the present value of net real income, then utility is maximized subject to the lifetime budget constraint:

$$\sum_{t=1}^{T} \delta^{-(t-1)} c_t = Y \tag{6.23}$$

This formulation assumes that there is no interest-income tax and that capital markets are 'perfect', so that corner solutions can be ignored. The solution to this problem is given by:

$$c_t = \left(\frac{\delta}{\xi}\right)^{\eta(t-1)} (kY) \tag{6.24}$$

$$k = \left\{ \sum_{t=1}^{T} \left(\xi \delta^{\beta}\right)^{-\eta(t-1)} \right\}^{-1} \tag{6.25}$$

It can be shown that the utility equivalent annuity, A_c^u is given by:

$$A_c^u = kY \left\{ \left(\frac{1-\xi^{-1}}{1-\alpha}\right) \left(\frac{1-\alpha^T}{1-\xi^{-T}}\right) \right\}^{-1/\beta} \tag{6.26}$$

$$\alpha = (\delta/\xi)^{\eta/\delta} \tag{6.27}$$

The annuity in the absence of taxes and transfers, A_y^u, is given by replacing Y in (6.26) by X.

The various measures can be shown diagrammatically in the case of just two periods. In Figure 6.1 income in periods 1 and 2 is measured respectively on horizontal and vertical axes, so that if an individual has the income stream (y_1, y_2) this gives point Y. The annual average, $\bar{y}$, is obtained from the point of intersection of an upward sloping 45° line through the origin and a downward sloping 45° line through point Y. The present value is the point of intersection of the line through Y, with a gradient of $1 + r$, with the horizontal axis. The annuity measure is the intersection of such a line with the 45° line through the origin. The utility equivalent annuity is given by the intersection of the indifference curve, U, with the 45° line through the origin.

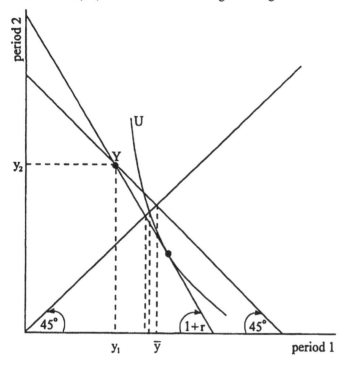

Figure 6.1   Income over two periods

Heterogeneous Preferences

The utility equivalent annuity requires assumptions to be made about each individual's values of ξ and η. Where this concept has previously been used, the assumption has been made that all individuals have the same preferences. However, it is of interest to allow for some heterogeneity by assuming that ξ and η are jointly distributed. Suppose that ξ and η are jointly lognormally distributed as $\Lambda (\xi, \eta \mid \mu_{\xi}, \sigma_{\xi}^2, \mu_{\eta}, \sigma_{\eta}^2, \rho)$, where μ and σ^2 are the mean of logarithms and variance of logarithms of the relevant variables and ρ is the correlation between the logarithms of ξ and η. The following procedure can then be used to generate a set of values. Given a random observation u_i from a $N(0, 1)$ distribution, person i's value of ξ can be obtained from the marginal distribution using $\xi_i = \exp(\mu_\xi + u_i \sigma_\xi)$. The value of η is obtained from the corresponding conditional distribution using

$$\eta_i = \exp[\mu_\eta + \rho(\sigma_\eta/\sigma_\xi)\{\log \xi_i - \mu_\xi\} + v_i \sigma_\eta (1 - \rho^2)^{0.5}] \quad (6.28)$$

where v_i is another random observation from an N (0, 1) distribution. This completes the description of the simulation model.

6.5 COMPARISONS USING ALTERNATIVE CONCEPTS

This section compares simulation results for alternative summary measures and income concepts. The procedure adopted is to examine the measures for alternative tax structures. A wide range of comparisons are made to see if the alternative measures and income concepts give different results. The first stage of the analysis is to generate the earnings profiles. Using the earnings parameters from Table 6.1, with additional productivity growth of 0.015, the earnings of 1,000 individuals were generated. The nominal rate of interest used was 0.10 and inflation was 0.07. The distribution of taste parameters was specified as follows. The arithmetic mean values of ξ and η were set at 0.05 and 1.8 respectively, while their variances (of logarithms) were 0.002 and 0.01. The correlation coefficient between the logarithms of ξ and η was assumed to be –0.75. The tax thresholds were indexed at the rate of 0.07 per year. The assumption was made that each individual saves a fixed proportion, 0.15, of net income in each year of the working life.

In view of the fact that analytical results cannot be obtained, it is important to consider a wide variety of tax structures. This can be done using the flexible functional form introduced in Chapter 4. Values of the Gini and Atkinson measures of inequality of net income, the Kakwani and Suits progressivity measures, and the (Gini- and Atkinson-based) welfare premia from progression, were calculated for a simulated cohort of individuals for each tax structure. The tax function contains five parameters, and 'high' and 'low' values of each parameter were specified. These were as follows: the low values of a_1, a_2, t_1, t_2 and k were 5,000, 10,000, 0.25, 0.6 and 0.5 respectively, while the high values were 10,000, 20,000, 0.3, 0.8 and 0.8 respectively. Taking all combinations of these values gives a total of 32 tax structures, covering a wide range of types of structure. With N tax structures there are $N(N-1)/2$ pairwise comparisons, so that 496 comparisons were made for each measure.

Consider first the inequality measures. For each pair of tax structures, the Gini measure of inequality of the present value of net income was taken as the 'base case'. When comparing one tax structure with another, the extent to which the same ranking was given by the other income concepts was examined.

Similarly, the extent to which the same ranking was given by the Atkinson inequality measure was also examined. The degree of inequality aversion used for the Atkinson measure was 0.5. The results are shown in the first row of Table 6.7, which refers to the case where there is differential mortality and no transfer payments. It can be seen that the case of the annual average measure gave most differences in the ranking of tax structures in pairwise comparisons. The change in the Gini measure of annual average lifetime net income moved in the opposite direction from the Gini measure of the present value of lifetime income in 10 out of 496 comparisons. The case where a transfer payment was in operation is shown in the second row of Table 6.7. Here a minimum income guarantee of $9,000 (indexed in line with inflation) applied in each year. The number of exceptions produced by the annual average measures is similar to the case where there are no transfer payments. The third row shows the results for the assumption of common mortality (each individual lives 14 years after retirement) with no transfer payments. Here only the annual average measure displays any exception.

Table 6.7 Tax structure comparisons: summary of exceptions

Base measure	Present values		Annual average		Annuity		Utility equivalent annuity	
	Gini	Atkinson	Gini	Atkinson	Gini	Atkinson	Gini	Atkinson
Gini								
DM(i)	—	0	10	10	1	1	0	0
(ii)	—	0	11	9	0	0	0	0
CM	—	0	12	12	0	0	0	0
	Kakawani	Suits	Kakawani	Suits	Kakawani	Suits	Kakawani	Suits
Kakawani								
DM (i)	—	6	14	23	1	6	0	6
(ii)	—	7	9	20	0	6	0	7
CM	—	7	26	28	0	7	2	7
	Premium		Premium		Premium		Premium	
	G	A	G	A	G	A	G	A
premium								
Gini DM (i)	—	1	6	14	0	1	0	1
(ii)	—	1	4	13	0	1	0	1
CM	—	1	7	4	0	1	0	1

Notes: DM = Differential mortality. Case (i) – No transfer; case (ii) MIG of $9,000.
CM = Common mortality with no transfer payment. Inequality aversion coefficient: 0.5.
Each entry shows the number of exceptions, compared with the base measure, out of 496 comparisons. Hence each *row* involves 3,472 comparisons.

The middle section of Table 6.7 reports the number of exceptions when the Kakwani progressivity measure, using present value income concepts, is used as the base measure. The number of exceptions between income concepts, and between the Kakwani and Suits measures, is somewhat higher than for the inequality measures. However, the majority of these exceptions are obtained for the annual average income concept. The final set of results shows exceptions for rankings of tax structures according to the welfare premium, taking the Gini-based premium using present value concepts as the base measure.

Each row of Table 6.7 involves 3,472 comparisons between tax structures and income concepts, so that in producing the table, a total of 31, 248 comparisons were made. In aggregate, fewer than 1 per cent gave exceptions, and the large majority of these were for the annual average income concept. The use of homogenous preferences made no difference to the number of exceptions when using the utility equivalent annuity concept. While such simulations cannot be conclusive, they suggest that there is a substantial degree of agreement between the income concepts. The calculation of annuities, and in particular of utility equivalent annuities which involve fairly arbitrary assumptions, is perhaps not necessary in practice, given the agreement with the results using present values.

This chapter has shown how the treatment of taxes and transfers can be extended to the lifetime context using a simulation model of the changing distribution of income with age. Care must be taken in comparing taxes and transfers in cross-sectional and lifetime contexts because neither tax revenue nor the pre-tax distribution of income are the same in each framework. However, comparisons between alternative structures, in the context of the role of exemptions in a partial tax shift towards consumption taxes, were made using simulation analyses. The use of more than one time period also raises the question of the appropriate income concept to use. Several concepts were defined and their implications for tax comparisons were examined, again using simulation methods.

7. Financing state pensions

This chapter examines the special problems that arise in the financing of state pension schemes. Such pensions are typically financed on a pay-as-you-go basis, so that current pensions are financed from current taxes. The observation that many industrialized countries are expected to experience population ageing over the next 50 years has often been used to suggest that there will be a 'pension crisis'. However, the argument that future pensions will impose an excessive burden on future generations of workers is often based on a very simple specification of the government's budget constraint. This suggests that the pension must be equal to the tax rate multiplied by the product of the average income of workers and the reciprocal of the dependency ratio, defined as the ratio of pensioners to workers. Hence a doubling of the dependency ratio doubles the tax rate. However, government pension and tax systems are not usually so simple. For example, countries differ in the extent to which pensions are taxable and means-tested, and some countries rely on revenue from a single source, such as income taxation, while others obtain additional revenue from payroll taxes and consumption taxes. The precise relationship between pension levels and tax rates will depend on the details of the schemes, as well as on the income distributions of workers and pensions, along with dependency rates.

This chapter examines the precise relationship between tax rates and benefits in alternative schemes. It illustrates the use of the same type of approach as in Chapter 4 to a wider range of situations. Section 7.1 begins by presenting a general approach to modelling pension finance. This approach, based on the specification of the government's budget constraint, may be used to examine a large variety of schemes. Section 7.2 adds more structural detail to the general model by considering specific tax schedules and means-testing arrangements. The section shows how more complex tax structures can be accommodated by the general approach. The chapter then selects two systems for further analysis, as special cases of the general model. In the first system, a means-tested flat-rate pension is financed from general income-tax revenue; this system is chosen to represent the pension scheme in Australia. In the second system, a flat-rate pension, with no means-testing, is financed from several taxes, including income, payroll and consumption taxation. The second scheme corresponds in many ways to the flat-rate component of the United Kingdom pension scheme, although of course both schemes involve simplifications. Section 7.3 provides some examples of these two types of scheme. Finally, section 7.4 moves away from pay-as-you-go schemes and examines the basic analytics of pension finance within a single cohort of individuals.

7.1   A GENERAL APPROACH

Government pension schemes are usually very complex. In order to concentrate on the major issues involved, it is necessary to consider simplified systems which nevertheless capture the main elements of those schemes used in practice. The following analysis concentrates on the problem of financing a basic flat-rate pension. Pensioners are assumed to be homogeneous, so that problems associated with dependants' benefits are ignored and the models deal with individuals rather than households or families as the unit of analysis. In addition, eligibility conditions, which are often quite complex, are ignored. Hence just two groups are considered: those over retirement age, all of whom are pensioners, and workers. The aged dependency ratio is defined as the number of pensioners divided by the number of workers; it would be possible to add considerations such as labour force participation and unemployment to the model.

Suppose the income tax paid by each individual is a constant proportion, t, of *taxable* income, however defined. In addition there is a consumption tax in which all tax-exclusive expenditure is taxed at the rate, v; hence the equivalent rate expressed as a tax-inclusive rate is $v/(1 + v)$. There is also a payroll tax based on the gross earnings of workers. The existence of means-testing of the pension may be modelled in terms of a 'pension tax', discussed in more detail below, and applied only to pensioners. Define the following terms:

b = flat-rate pension received by all pensioners
N_w = number of workers
N_p = number of pensioners
Y = total gross income of workers and pensioners combined
Y_T = total taxable income of workers and pensioners combined
C = payroll tax raised from earnings of workers
T_p = 'pension tax' paid per pensioner
E = non-pension government expenditure per person

The central element of the analysis is the budget constraint facing the government. Ignoring government borrowing (by treating E as expenditure net of any borrowing), the budget constraint may be written as:

$$E(N_w + N_p) + N_p b = tY_T + N_p T_p + C + \frac{v}{1+v}(Y - tY_T - N_p T_p - C) \quad (7.1)$$

This formulation abstracts from individuals' savings in evaluating the total tax revenue from the consumption tax, but it would be possible to modify (7.1) to allow for differing saving propensities of workers and pensioners. This constraint can be used to express the proportional tax rate, t, in terms of the other variables as follows:

$$t = \frac{(1+v)\left\{E(N_w + N_p) + N_p b\right\} - vY - N_p T_p - C}{Y_T} \qquad (7.2)$$

This result can be rearranged further by using the following relationships. If $\overline{w}$ and $\overline{y}$ denote the arithmetic mean income of workers and pensioners respectively, then:

$$Y = N_w \overline{w} + N_p \overline{y} \qquad (7.3)$$

Denote by γ the proportion of total workers' gross income which is taxable. Suppose that, in order to avoid double taxation, the 'pension tax' paid by pensioners is deducted from their taxable income. In the system considered below, the total taxable income of pensioners is equal to the difference between their non-pension income and the 'pension tax' paid. Hence:

$$Y_T = \gamma N_w \overline{w} + N_p (\overline{y} - T_p) \qquad (7.4)$$

On the simplifying assumption that all workers' incomes are from employment, and that because of a tax-free threshold the payroll tax involves a proportional tax imposed at the rate c on a proportion, say α, of gross earnings, then:

$$C = \alpha c N_w \overline{w} \qquad (7.5)$$

Similarly, the pension tax per pensioner may be expressed as a proportion, β, of average pensioners' income, so that:

$$T_p = \beta \overline{y} \qquad (7.6)$$

If the replacement ratio, R, is defined as $b/\overline{y}$ and the dependency ratio, D, is N_p/N_w, equation (7.2) may be written as:

$$t = \frac{(1+v)\left\{DR + (1+D)(E/\overline{w})\right\} - v\left\{1 + D(\overline{y}/\overline{w})\right\} - \beta D(\overline{y}/\overline{w}) - \alpha c}{\gamma + D(\overline{y}/\overline{w})(1-\beta)} \qquad (7.7)$$

This general result can be used to examine the implications of a wide variety of schemes. However, care must be taken in modifying (7.7) when there is no means-testing but pensioners' incomes are otherwise taken into account. Without means testing, $\beta = 0$, but it is necessary to assume that there is some tax-free threshold applied to pensioners' incomes. This makes the taxable income of pensioners some proportion, δ, of pensioners' gross income. Hence (7.4) must be replaced by:

$$Y_T = \gamma N_w \bar{w} + \delta N_p \bar{y} \tag{7.8}$$

and the denominator of (7.7) becomes $\gamma + \delta D(\bar{y}/\bar{w})$. The following section presents in further detail the various components of the tax structure included in (7.7).

7.2   SPECIFICATION OF TAX STRUCTURES

Income Tax

If a worker's income is denoted by w, and there is a tax-free threshold applied to workers of a, then the tax paid, $T(w)$, is zero for $w \le a$ and $t(w - a)$ for $w > a$. Let $\bar{w}$ and $F(w)$ respectively denote the arithmetic mean wage and the associated distribution function. Using this income tax system, it has been shown in Chapter 4 that the proportion of total workers' income which is taxed is given by the term $G(a)$. Hence:

$$\gamma = G(a) = \{1 - F_1(a)\} - (a/\bar{w})\{1 - F(a)\} \tag{7.9}$$

where $F_1(a)$ denotes the proportion of total income of those workers with $w \le a$.

If there is no means-testing of the pension, and if the tax threshold for pensioners is the same as that for workers, the tax function facing pensioners, $T_r(y)$, is given by:

$$
\begin{aligned}
T_r(y) &= 0 && \text{for } y + b \le a \\
&= t\{(y + b) - a\} && \text{for } y + b > a
\end{aligned}
\tag{7.10}
$$

When $b > a$, all pensioners pay income taxation, so that δ, the ratio of taxable income to gross income, is $1 + (b - a)/\bar{y}$. But if $b < a$, all those with incomes below $a - b$ will not pay tax and the value of δ is given, where $H(y)$ denotes the distribution function of y, by:

$$\delta = \{1 - H_1 (a - b)\} - \{(a - b)/\bar{y}\} \{1 - H(a - b)\} \qquad (7.11)$$

where $H_1 (a - b)$ denotes the proportion of total income of those pensioners with $y < a - b$, and H_1 is the incomplete first moment distribution function of H.

A Means-tested Pension

Suppose pensioners receive a basic pension which is subject to income taxation and is means-tested according to the pensioner's gross income. If income is below a lower limit, y_e, then the full pension is received. When y exceeds y_e, the pension is reduced by a proportion, s, of income in excess of the lower limit. Thus the pension is reduced by an amount $s(y - y_e)$. This implies that no pension is received once y reaches an upper limit, y_u, which is equal to $y_e + b/s$. This income test is very similar to that used in Australia.

An equivalent way of viewing this type of income test is to regard each individual as receiving an unconditional pension of b, but then paying a special 'pension tax' on non-pension income. The pension tax, $P(y)$, is given by:

$$
\begin{aligned}
P(y) &= 0 & &\text{for } y \le y_e \\
&= s(y - y_e) & &\text{for } y_e < y < y_u \\
&= b & &\text{for } y \ge y_u
\end{aligned}
\qquad (7.12)
$$

In assessing each pensioner for income taxation, it is necessary to avoid the double taxation of the pension tax, by making it tax-deductible. Suppose the income tax threshold for pensioners is a_r. Then the income tax paid, $T_r(y)$, is given by:

$$T_r(y) = t[(y + b) - \{a_r + P(y)\}] \qquad (7.13)$$

Here $y + b$ is total income and $a_r + P(y)$ measures the total 'allowance' against that income for tax purposes. The following analysis uses the assumption, following the Australian system, that $b = a_r$, so that $T_r(y)$ can be rewritten as:

$$T_r(y) = t\{y - P(y)\} \qquad (7.14)$$

Hence taxable income is equal to non-pension income less the amount of pension tax paid. It can be shown, using the methods introduced in Chapter 4, that the ratio, β, of pension tax per pensioner to average income, $\bar{y}$, is:

$$\beta = (b/\bar{y}) \{1 - H(y_u)\} + s\{H_1(y_u) - H_1(y_e)\} - s(y_e/\bar{y})\{H(y_u) - H(y_e)\} \quad (7.15)$$

where $H_1(y)$ represents, as before, the proportion of total income obtained by those pensioners with incomes less than or equal to y. The first term in curly brackets in (7.15) represents the proportion of pensioners who pay the maximum pension tax of b; the second term in curly brackets represents the total income of those who pay pension tax at the rate, s; the third term in curly brackets denotes the proportion of pensioners who pay the pension tax. There is a direct relationship between the structure of the expressions for γ and β, because both are taxes imposed on income measured in excess of a threshold; the pension tax has the added complication of the upper limit, y_u, above which no additional pension tax is paid.

The Payroll Tax

The payroll tax, $C(w)$, paid by employees is assumed to be a constant proportion, c, of the gross income of workers, applied between two limits w_e and w_u. The British system of national insurance contributions took this form for some years. The present analysis ignores employees' contributions. More formally it is given by:

$$
\begin{aligned}
C(w) &= 0 && \text{for } w < w_e \\
&= cw && \text{for } w_e \leq w < w_u \\
&= cw_u && \text{for } w \geq w_u
\end{aligned}
\tag{7.16}
$$

It can be shown, following the usual procedure, that the proportion, α, of total income that is taxable is given by:

$$
\alpha = \{F_1(w_u) - F_1(w_e)\} + (w_u/\overline{w}) \{1 - F(w_u)\}
\tag{7.17}
$$

The first term reflects the proportion of total income of those with income between the limits w_e and w_u, while the second term reflects the fact that all those above the upper limit w_u pay a fixed contribution.

Two Alternative Structures

The general framework set out in section 7.1 can be used to consider a wide range of pension and tax structures. Consider just two structures for comparison purposes. In the first scheme a means-tested pension is combined with only an income tax, as in Australia. Appropriate substitution into (7.7) gives the budget constraint as:

$$t = \frac{DR + (1+D)(E/\overline{w}) - \beta D(\overline{y}/\overline{w})}{\gamma + D(\overline{y}/\overline{w})(1-\beta)} \quad (7.18)$$

In the second scheme, a basic pension is combined with the payroll tax, income tax and the consumption tax, but there is no means-testing. This is similar to the British scheme. The budget constraint, from section 7.1, is thus:

$$t = \frac{(1+v)\{DR + (1+D)(E/\overline{w})\} - v\{1 + D(\overline{y}/\overline{w})\} - \alpha c}{\gamma + \delta D(\overline{y}/\overline{w})} \quad (7.19)$$

These results are much richer than the simplistic constraint mentioned at the beginning of this chapter. They may be used to obtain the precise implications of ageing populations and to consider the way in which the various policy variables can be changed. Care must however be exercised in using these results, in view of the fact that incentive effects have been ignored.

7.3   SOME EXAMPLES

In the following examples, w and y are assumed to be distributed as $\Lambda(\mu_w, \sigma_w^2)$ and $\Lambda(\mu_y, \sigma_y^2)$ respectively, where μ and σ^2 denote the mean and the variance of logarithms. In view of the fact that average pensioner incomes have increased in recent years, calculations are reported for alternative values of $\overline{y}$. However, the results all apply to the following parameter values: $\sigma_y^2 = 0.5$; $\sigma_w^2 = 0.3$; and $\mu_w = 10.446637$. These values imply that $\overline{w} = \$40,000$. Comparisons are made for $\overline{y}$ equal to $\$8,000$ and $\$16,000$, for which μ_y takes the values 8.7372 and 9.43035 respectively. The income tax threshold, a, is set at $\$5,000$ and the additional (non-pension) expenditure per person is $\$7,000$ throughout.

The effect of increasing dependency is illustrated in Figure 7.1 for the means-tested pension scheme combined with income taxation, where $y_e = \$2,000$, $s = 0.5$ and $\overline{y} = \$8,000$. The threshold income level above which means testing applies and the pension tax (taper) rate are similar to those in Australia. Results are shown for four levels of the basic pension, ranging from $\$4,000$ to $\$10,000$. As indicated above, the schedules are approximately linear, with the slope increasing as the basic pension increases. A higher value of $\overline{y}$ reduces the slopes. The values shown in Figure 7.1 may be contrasted with a simplistic framework that is often used in pension debates; this framework has a basic pension financed using a proportional income tax applied only to workers, so that $t = RD + (1+D)(E/\overline{w})$. For $R = 0.25$ (corresponding to $b = 10,000$ and $\overline{w} = 40,000$) and $E = 7,000$, it can be seen that a doubling of D from 0.2 to 0.4 would imply an increase in t

by a factor of 1.33. The corresponding case in Figure 7.1 implies an increase
in the marginal income tax rate by a factor of approximately 1.25; furthermore
the average tax rate increase is correspondingly lower.

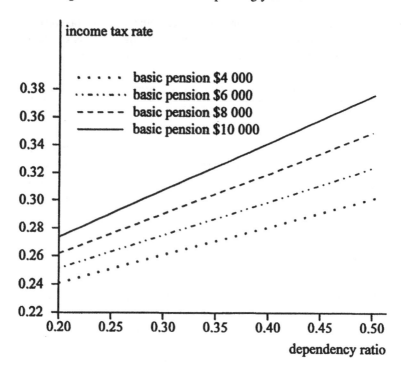

Figure 7.1   The means-tested pension

Figure 7.2 illustrates the second structure where a basic pension is combined
with a payroll and consumption tax in addition to an income tax, and there is
no means-testing of the pension. Results are shown for the same range of basic
pension, b, and dependency ratio, D, and where there is a consumption tax at
the rate $v = 0.15$ with national insurance contributions applied to income
between $8,500 and $75,000 at the rate of 0.075. These values are similar to
those in the UK. As in Figure 7.1, $\bar{y} = 8,000$. Comparison with means-testing
alone may be made by setting $c = v = 0$ in the non-means-tested scheme, shown
in Figure 7.3. Figures 7.1 and 7.3 show, as expected, that the marginal income
tax rates are generally lower where means-testing is used, but other features
are the same. An exception to this general rule is where the basic pension is
relatively high and the value of $\bar{y}$ is relatively low; for values of D above about
0.45 and a pension of $10,000 with $\bar{y} = \$8,000$ the means-tested scheme actually
requires a higher value of t. The explanation for this is the different tax structure

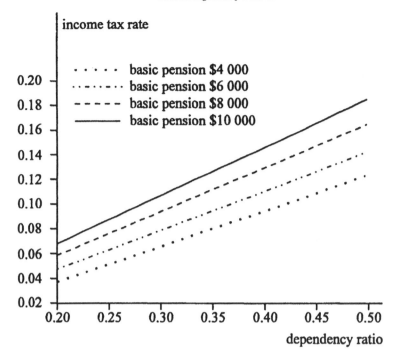

Figure 7.2   Pension with consumption and payroll taxes

applying to pensioners in the two schemes; in the means-tested scheme the threshold is equal to the basic pension, so as the latter rises the taxable income of pensioners falls. For a higher value of $\bar{y}$ than that used in Figures 7.1 and 7.3, there is a much larger difference between required tax rates, with that required in the means-tested structure being much lower.

In comparing the different structures it is more appropriate to measure overall effective marginal tax rates which should be compared at given income levels. Figure 7.4 shows marginal and average rates (calculated at $\bar{w}$) for the means-tested scheme, with two values of the basic pension, and other values corresponding to those used in Figure 7.1. These may be compared with the lower overall effective marginal and average rates shown in Figure 7.5, which in other respects corresponds to Figure 7.2. The interesting result which arises when comparing Figures 7.4 and 7.5 is that the marginal and effective overall rates are much closer together in the structure which uses the combination of income and consumption taxes with the NIC. This means that, for each value of *b* and most values of D, the effective marginal rate is *lower* with the multi-tax system than when means-testing is used with only an income tax, but the average tax rate is *higher*.

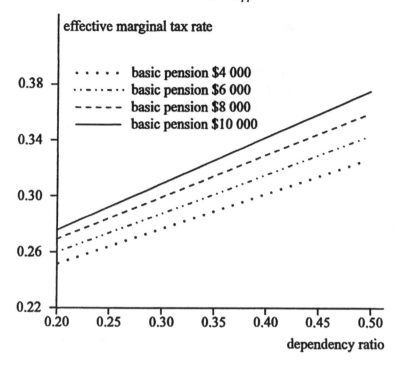

Figure 7.3   Effective tax rates without means-testing

It has been suggested that recent policy debates have typically ignored the extent to which pensioners, on average, receive higher incomes from sources other than state pensions. This means that the 'burden' of financing transfer payments to low-income pensioners is shared between relatively richer workers *and* pensioners. The effect of increasing dependency, with a higher value of $\bar{y}$, can easily be examined using the above results.

The analytical results can also be used to examine the orders of magnitude involved when changing other parameters of the systems. Of particular interest in the means-tested scheme are the effects of changing the pension tax rate, s, and the threshold, y_e, above which the tax is paid (or means-testing begins to operate). For example, it is found that if the value of s is increased from 0.5 to 0.75, while y_e is simultaneously increased from \$2,000 to \$4,000, the required income tax rate is virtually unchanged at all levels of the dependency ratio. This type of change nevertheless has implications for redistribution, since it involves greater transfers to those at the lower end of the distribution of pensioner incomes, at the expense of the relatively better-off pensioners, while those for whom the pension tax is b in each case are not affected.

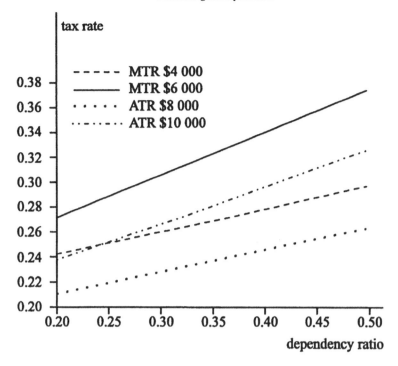

Figure 7.4   Effective tax rates with means-testing

The approach has the advantage of generating the detailed implications of alternative policy proposals. For example, Gruen (1985, p. 621) suggested that the taper rate, or pension tax rate, in the Australian pension scheme should be reduced 'to 25 per cent or at most 33 per cent. One way in which the cost of this reform could be reduced is if the income-free area associated with the pension were abolished.' Many proposals, unlike Gruen's, do not even consider the fact that a policy to increase expenditure must be accompanied by suggestions relating to its finance and an analysis of the combined package. Gruen's proposal may be examined by setting y_e equal to zero, while reducing the value of s in the means-tested scheme, and then finding the new rate of income tax required to ensure that these changes are deficit-neutral. In a wide range of situations (depending on the level of the basic pension and the average non-pension income of pensioners, along with the dependency rate) it was found that a slight increase in the income tax rate would be required to finance the change. However, this increase was less than one percentage point in all cases. Where b and $\bar{y}$ are relatively low (at 4,000 and 8,000 respectively), the use of $s = 0.33$ and $y_e = 0$ involved approximately the same tax rate as when $s = 0.5$ and $y_e = 2,000$.

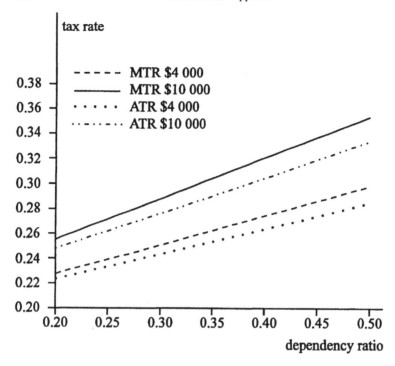

Figure 7.5   Marginal and average tax rates

7.4   A SINGLE COHORT

An alternative approach to the analysis of government pensions is to consider financing pensions within a single cohort. Instead of pensions being financed from the current working population and, as in the previous examples, relatively rich pensioners, the government's budget constraint requires that the present value of pension payments must be equal to the present value of taxes (or special pension contributions). This constraint rules out any redistribution between cohorts. A very simple approach in this context involves using a two-period model such that individuals work in the first period and retire in the second period. Taxes are placed in a fund which accumulates at a rate of interest of r. This simple approach also assumes that all individuals survive over the whole of the two periods.

A variety of tax and pension arrangements may be examined, but for purposes of illustration, consider a flat-rate pension whereby each individual receives a benefit in retirement of b. If the tax system is proportional, then the accumulated contributions per person of $t(1 + r)\bar{y}$ must finance the pension per person, b, so that the replacement ratio, $b/\bar{y}$, is simply $t(1 + r)$. Any individual with income y_i will obtain an implied rate of return from the scheme of r_i, given by:

$$1 + r_i = (1 + r)(\bar{y}/y_i) \tag{7.20}$$

Hence, as with the linear income tax of Chapter 4, there is redistribution from those above the mean to those below the mean.

Alternatively, there may be a two-tier pension scheme whereby the pension $P(y_i)$ is given by:

$$
\begin{aligned}
P(y_i) &= b & \text{for } y_i \leq b \\
&= b + p(y_i - b) & \text{for } y_i > b
\end{aligned} \tag{7.21}
$$

Total pension payments per person are thus:

$$b + p \int_b (y - b) \, dF(y) \tag{7.22}$$

This can immediately be simplified using the function $G(y)$. Thus the budget constraint becomes:

$$(1 + r) \, t\bar{y} = b + p\bar{y} \, G(b) \tag{7.23}$$

and the flat-rate component, expressed as a proportion of average income, is given by:

$$b/\bar{y} = (1 + r)t - p \, G(b) \tag{7.24}$$

The analysis of this type of two-period model does not therefore involve any new basic principles in comparison with the single-period model. It will, however, be necessary to allow for incomes to be endogenous: this extension will be examined in Chapter 12.

This chapter has considered the special problems raised by the financing of government pensions, a form of transfer payment obtained by those above a specified age. The analysis can be regarded as involving the application of the methods discussed in Chapters 4 and 5 to a particular context. Although the specification of the tax and transfer system requires special care, its analysis does not really involve any new techniques or principles. It illustrates the power of the general approach. One of the pension systems examined in this chapter involves the use of means-testing, which implies a lower gross expenditure on pensions and correspondingly lower tax rates. The general question of the relative performance of means-tested versus universal benefits has given rise to a large and important debate. This issue is discussed in the next chapter.

8. Means-tested versus universal transfers

This chapter turns to the issue of whether transfer payments should be universal, as in the basic linear income tax, or means-tested, as in a minimum income guarantee or its variants. Tax and transfer schemes are often evaluated quite narrowly in terms of their role in poverty alleviation. From this point of view, the concept of 'target efficiency' has been developed, particularly by Beckerman (1979a, 1979b). This approach evaluates schemes according to the extent to which transfer payments hit the target group, namely those whose pre-tax and transfer income is below a specified poverty line. Transfers are classified as being inefficient when they are paid to people who would anyway be above the poverty line and when they raise individuals 'unnecessarily' above the line. The approach has been used by Mitchell (1991) and Harding and Mitchell (1992) to compare transfers in a variety of countries. The adoption of this criterion implies that the most efficient transfer system corresponds to a minimum income guarantee whereby all those whose pre-transfer incomes are below the poverty line are brought up to the line, and no net transfers are received by those not initially in poverty. This type of selective scheme is administered using means-testing, and there is effectively a 100 per cent marginal tax rate applying to those below the poverty line. This contrasts with a linear income tax in which every individual receives an unconditional lump-sum transfer and all other income is subject to a proportional tax. For a given amount of expenditure on transfers, the selective scheme is obviously more efficient in this special sense than the universal scheme.

The argument that means-testing is automatically preferred when the focus is on poverty relief has been qualified by Besley (1990), who assumes that individuals incur a non-recoverable transaction cost in order to obtain the means-tested benefit. This means that those who receive benefits nevertheless remain below the poverty line because assessment does not allow for the costs. Furthermore, some individuals who are close to the poverty line will not find it worthwhile to apply for benefits. Using several poverty indices, Besley examines the critical level of costs such that, for the same total government expenditure, measured poverty is the same under both means-testing and universal provision. The critical levels are found to be relatively high, leading Besley (1990, p. 125) to conclude that there is 'a strong presumption in favour of means-testing, at least in the narrowly defined terms of the current exercise'.

The purpose of the present chapter is to compare the use of a minimum income guarantee with a linear income tax involving an unconditional transfer received by everyone. Instead of holding gross government expenditure constant (a rather artificial constraint in a tax and transfer system), the approach involves the comparison of social welfare measures for a given extent of poverty, using several poverty measures. The Beckerman target efficiency measures are presented in section 8.1, and the efficiency characteristics of the linear income tax are examined. Section 8.2 then compares schemes using more general criteria than only the alleviation of poverty. Finally, Appendix 8.1 discusses some alternative schemes, using simple numerical examples in order to reinforce some of the major points of comparison.

8.1   TARGET EFFICIENCY MEASURES

Target efficiency measures are usually defined, following Beckerman (1979a), using a diagram in which income is measured on the vertical axis and the corresponding number of individuals is shown on the horizontal axis, as in Figure 8.1. This approach is based on the assumption that incomes are independent of the tax structure. If the poverty line is agreed to be at the level y_p, then the area enclosed by the poverty line and the pre-tax and transfer distribution measures the 'poverty gap', the total amount of money that would be required to raise all those below y_p up to the line.

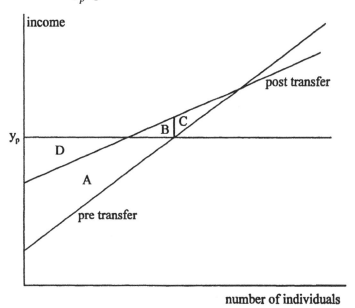

Figure 8.1   Transfer efficiency measures

In Figure 8.1 the area C represents the transfers which are given to those whose pre-transfer income is above y_p, while the area B represents the total transfers which, although received by the pre-transfer 'poor', are considered to be excessive since the individuals are raised above the poverty line. The area A + B represents total transfers received by those with $y < y_p$. In Figure 8.1, there are still some individuals in poverty after transfers; the post-transfer poverty gap is the area D.

Two measures of target efficiency are used. The first, 'vertical expenditure efficiency', measures the proportion of total transfers going to the pre-transfer poor. The second measure, 'poverty reduction efficiency', measures the proportion of total transfers which go to the pre-transfer poor and raises them only to the poverty level y_p. A further measure of 'spillover' is defined as the proportion of transfers received by the poor which are considered excessive. Hence:

Vertical expenditure efficiency $= (A + B)/(A + B + C)$
Poverty reduction efficiency $= A/(A + B + C)$
Spillover $= B/(A + B)$

Notice that none of these measures allows for the post-transfer poverty gap. The various measures are usually calculated using detailed information from household expenditure surveys.

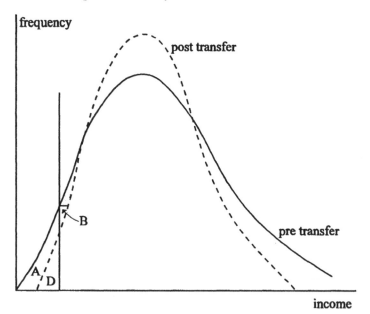

Figure 8.2   Pre- and post-tax income distributions

The form of Figure 8.1 is an unusual way of representing a frequency distribution of incomes, and reflects the concentration of attention on the bottom tail of the distribution in poverty studies. A more familiar representation is shown in Figure 8.2, which shows frequency distributions of pre- and post-tax and transfer incomes. The effect of the tax and transfer scheme is to compress the income distribution by reducing the numbers in both tails. The corresponding areas are also shown in Figure 8.2.

The Linear Income Tax

The standard linear income tax involves a proportional tax of t and an unconditional lump sum benefit, a, which is paid to all individuals, as examined in detail in Chapter 5. It is also helpful to use the more standard tax and transfer diagram with pre-tax and transfer income, y, on the horizontal, and net income, z, on the vertical axis, as in Figure 8.3. The relevant measure of transfers must be net transfers. Suppose the poverty line is deemed to be at y_p. The relationship between y and z is the simple linear function $z = a + y(1 - t)$, and this intercepts

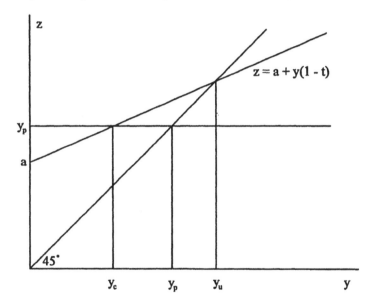

Figure 8.3   Transfer efficiency and the linear income tax

the 45° line at the level y_u. If the scheme is a 'pure' transfer scheme, then $y_u = \bar{y}$, but if additional non-transfer revenue is raised, then $y_u < \bar{y}$. The income level

y_c represents the pre-transfer income which results in a post-transfer income equal to the poverty level. Hence y_c is given by:

$$y_c = (y_p - a)/(1 - t) \tag{8.1}$$

The amounts of money transferred are not represented by areas in Figure 8.3, as they are in Figure 8.1. It is necessary to specify the income distribution explicitly. Let $F(y)$ represent the distribution function of gross income. For those below y_u the net transfer is $z - y = a - ty$, so that total net transfers, corresponding to the area A + B + C of Figures 8.1 and 8.2, are given by:

$$A + B + C = \int_0^{y_u} (a - ty) dF(y) \tag{8.2}$$

Let $F_1(y)$ denote the incomplete first moment distribution function of y, so that $F_1(y)$ is the proportion of total income obtained by those with incomes less than or equal to y. Net transfers in (8.2) can be expressed as:

$$A + B + C = \bar{y}\{(a/\bar{y}) F(y_u) - t F_1(y_u)\} \tag{8.3}$$

For those with $y_c < y < y_p$, the excess of net income over y_p is $a + y(1 - t) - y_p$ so that the net transfer which is needed to get individuals only up to y_p is $(a - ty) - \{a + y(1 - t) - y_p\} = y_p - y$. Hence, the net transfers paid to those below y_p, excluding those transfers which are 'excessive', are given by the area A of Figure 8.1, where:

$$A = \int_0^{y_c} (a - ty) dF(y) + \int_{y_c}^{y_p} (y_p - y) dF(y) \tag{8.4}$$

This expression for A can be expanded and simplified to give:

$$A = \bar{y}\left\{(1 - t)F_1(y_c) - \left(\frac{y_p - a}{\bar{y}}\right)F(y_c) - F_1(y_p) + \left(\frac{y_p}{\bar{y}}\right)F(y_p)\right\} \tag{8.5}$$

Poverty reduction efficiency is (8.5) divided by (8.3). In order to obtain vertical expenditure efficiency, it is required to obtain net transfers going to those with $y < y_p$. This is given by:

$$A + B = \int_0^{y_p} (a - ty)dF(y)$$

$$= \bar{y}\left\{(a/\bar{y})F\left(y_p\right) - tF_1\left(y_p\right)\right\} \tag{8.6}$$

Vertical expenditure efficiency is (8.6) divided by (8.3).

The measure of 'spillover' requires the area B. For those with pre-transfer income between y_c and y_p the excess of their post-transfer income above the poverty line is given by $z - y_p = y(1 - t) - (y_p - a)$. Hence:

$$B = \int_{y_c}^{y_p} \left\{y(1 - t) - \left(y_p - a\right)\right\}dF(y) \tag{8.7}$$

$$= (1 - t)\bar{y}\{F_1(y_p) - F_1(y_c)\} - (y_p - a)\{F(y_p) - F(y_c)\} \tag{8.8}$$

Spillover is therefore given by (8.8) divided by (8.6). Remembering that $y_c = (y_p - a)/(1 - t)$, then if $y_p = a$, (8.8) reduces to $(1 - t)\bar{y}F_1(y_p)$.

These measures do not consider the extent to which poverty is actually reduced; they measure only the extent to which transfers are directed towards those in poverty. For example, if the poverty line were such that $y_p \geq y_u$ in Figure 8.3, the vertical and poverty reduction efficiency measures would be 1 and spillover would be zero, but all the pre-transfer poor would remain in poverty. Hence the value of international comparisons of such efficiency measures is unclear if schemes also differ in the degree to which poverty is actually alleviated. Using a poverty gap measure, a measure of 'poverty gap efficiency' can be defined, based on the proportion of the poverty gap which is actually closed. This is, in terms of the areas in Figure 8.1, defined by:

Poverty gap efficiency = $A/(A + D)$

The area A has already been derived in equation (8.5) for the linear income tax, and the poverty gap, $A + D$, is equal to:

$$A + D = \int_0^{y_p} \left(y_p - y\right)dF(y)$$

$$= \bar{y}\{(y_p/\bar{y}) F(y_p) - F_1(y_p)\} \tag{8.9}$$

Poverty gap efficiency is (8.5) divided by (8.9). Comparisons among schemes which involve different values of poverty gap efficiency would appear to be spurious.

If comparisons are restricted to schemes which have poverty gap efficiency measures of unity, then the most efficient tax and transfer scheme must be the minimum income guarantee. For example, in Figure 8.4 the minimum income guarantee which gives $y_p = a$ is shown as the line EFI. This brings all those with

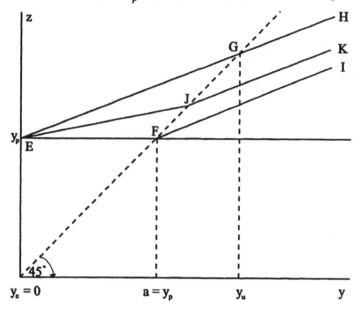

Figure 8.4   Transfer efficiency with alternative transfer schemes

$y < y_p$ up to the level y_p and involves no net transfers to any others; vertical expenditure and poverty reduction efficiency are therefore unity. The most efficient scheme involves 100 per cent marginal tax rates for those with $y < y_p$. Figure 8.4 also shows the linear income tax, in which $a - y_p$, as the line EGH. For this linear tax, the efficiency measures can be obtained by substituting in (8.5), (8.6), (8.8) and (8.9), as:

$$\text{Poverty reduction efficiency} = \frac{(y_p / \bar{y})F(y_p) - F_1(y_p)}{(y_p / \bar{y})F(y_u) - tF_1(y_u)} \qquad (8.10)$$

$$\text{Vertical expenditure efficiency} = \frac{(y_p / \bar{y})F(y_p) - tF_1(y_p)}{(y_p / \bar{y})F(y_u) - tF_1(y_u)} \qquad (8.11)$$

$$\text{Spillover} = \frac{(1-t)F_1(y_p)}{(y_p / \bar{y})F(y_p) - tF_1(y_p)}$$ (8.12)

An increase in the basic minimum level, a, used in the linear income tax is associated with an increase in the poverty gap efficiency measure but a decrease in other efficiency measures. This is illustrated in Table 8.1, which shows the variation in the various measures as the value, a, is increased. These examples are obtained for an assumed lognormal distribution of pre-tax and transfer income with a mean and variance of logarithms respectively of 10 and 0.55, implying an arithmetic mean of approximately \$29,000 and a median income of \$22,000. The calculations also assume a poverty level of \$10,000, and just over 14 per cent of the population are initially in poverty.

Table 8.1 Target efficiency measures for the linear income tax

	Unconditional transfer					
	3,000	4,000	5,000	6,000	7,000	8,000
Marginal tax rate	0.276	0.310	0.345	0.345	0.414	0.448
Poverty reduction efficiency	0.970	0.804	0.654	0.535	0.438	0.360
Vertical expenditure efficiency	0.978	0.863	0.767	0.699	0.649	0.612
Spillover	0.008	0.068	0.147	0.235	0.325	0.441
Poverty gap efficiency	0.358	0.583	0.760	0.885	0.960	0.993

In calculating the values in Table 8.1 it is assumed that, in addition to the tax revenue necessary for the transfer system, the government needs to raise an amount, $R = 5{,}000$, of net revenue per person. For each value of the unconditional transfer it is thus necessary first to solve for the marginal tax rate required to satisfy the government's budget constraint, using:

$$a + R = t\bar{y}$$ (8.13)

so that t is given by:

$$t = (a + R)/\bar{y}$$ (8.14)

As the linear tax reduces the extent of poverty by raising the value of the unconditional transfer, a, the poverty reduction and vertical expenditure efficiencies fall dramatically while the spillovers increase. The minimum income guarantee always has efficiency measures of 1.0 and spillover of 0 so that, for the same poverty gap, it must always dominate the linear income tax. Notice that these comparisons are quite different from those produced by Besley (1990), who imposed revenue neutrality and searched numerically for the individual cost of claiming means-tested benefits that gives the same poverty measure for the two schemes. The following section uses a different set of criteria for evaluating the alternative schemes.

8.2   REDISTRIBUTION AND SOCIAL WELFARE

Consider first a comparison between the means-tested and universal schemes where poverty is eliminated in each case. On the basis of the target efficiency measures alone, it has been seen that the means-tested scheme must dominate. However, the schemes involve different degrees of redistribution over the whole range of the income distribution. It is not obvious that the minimum income guarantee dominates when such broader criteria are used. For example, the 'spillovers' and transfers to those not in poverty may contribute to social welfare generally, rather than being viewed simply as 'bad'. The comparisons reported below are not therefore 'revenue-neutral' (except in so far as they both raise the same net non-transfer revenue), but are 'poverty-neutral' in that they both eliminate poverty.

It is first necessary to obtain the tax rate needed to finance the minimum income guarantee scheme. Suppose that the minimum income is equal to a, so that the revenue needed to finance the transfer payments is equal to:

$$\int_0^a (a - y)\mathrm{dF}(y) \tag{8.15}$$

The revenue obtained from the taxpayers, that is, individuals with $y > a$, is given by:

$$\int_a^\infty t(y - a)\mathrm{dF}(y) \tag{8.16}$$

Adding R, the government net revenue per person, to (8.15) and equating the result with (8.16) gives, after further simplification, the condition that:

$$t = [(R/\bar{y}) - \{F_1(a) - (a/\bar{y})\,F(a)\}]/G(a) \tag{8.17}$$

where the term $G(a)$ is defined as:

$$G(a) = \{1 - F_1(a)\} - (a/\bar{y})\,\{1 - F(a)\} \tag{8.18}$$

Equations (8.17) and (8.14) are used to calculate the appropriate tax rate required to finance transfers in each scheme. Having calculated the tax rates required to eliminate poverty in each scheme, the approach then involves calculating a range of measures of tax progressivity and welfare. These include the Gini and Atkinson inequality measures of post-tax-and-transfer income, and the Kakwani, Reynolds–Smolensky and Suits measures of tax progressivity. These last three measures were calculated using the approach described in Chapter 3. In addition, a measure of the welfare premium from taxation was obtained using abbreviated social welfare functions based on the Gini and Atkinson measures described in Chapter 3. The abbreviated welfare function corresponding to the distribution of x using the inequality measure I_x (either Gini or Atkinson) can be written as $W = \bar{x}(1 - I_x)$, where $\bar{x}$ is the arithmetic mean. If g is the aggregate tax rate (given by total net revenue expressed as a ratio of total income), then the welfare resulting from a proportional tax which raises the same revenue as the actual tax system is given by:

$$W_p = (1 - g)\bar{y}(1 - I_y) \qquad (8.19)$$

The post-tax welfare from the actual tax system, W_z, is given by:

$$W_z = (1 - g)\bar{y}(1 - I_z) \qquad (8.20)$$

The welfare premium from progression, Π, is the difference $W_z - W_p$, and is:

$$\Pi = (1 - g)\bar{y}(I_y - I_z) \qquad (8.21)$$

The various measures of progressivity and inequality cannot be obtained analytically, so it is necessary to use a simulated population. This is achieved by selecting individuals at random from a specified lognormal distribution. Using the same parameters for the distribution of pre-tax-and-transfer income as those used earlier, and a population of 2,000 individuals, the results in Table 8.2 were obtained. In each case the minimum income was set equal to the poverty level, assumed to be $10,000.

For the simulated population, the pre-tax-and-transfer incomes have Atkinson and Gini inequality measures respectively of 0.3317 and 0.3952, where the Atkinson measure is obtained for an inequality aversion coefficient of 1.5. It can be seen that the linear income tax is substantially more progressive than the means-tested minimum income guarantee, for all measures used. The welfare premium from progression, the difference between the social welfare obtained from the progressive system and that obtained from a proportional scheme with the same revenue, is given in the last two rows, using Gini and Atkinson inequality measures. The social welfare functions underlying the use of the different inequality measures are of course very different. Given that the net tax revenue is the same in each scheme, the welfare premium from progression in each case is in fact just proportional to the difference between the inequality of pre- and post-tax income. The comparisons are unchanged for much lower inequality aversion coefficients.

Table 8.2 Minimum income guarantee versus linear income tax

	Minimum income guarantee	Linear income tax
Marginal tax rate	0.279	0.517
Gini inequality of post-tax income	0.3328	0.2290
Atkinson inequality of post-tax income (1.5)	0.2187	0.1116
Kakwani measure of progressivity	0.3020	0.8290
Reynolds–Smolensky measure	0.0623	0.1662
Suits measure	0.2836	0.8301
Welfare premium from progression		
Gini-based measure	0.737	1.976
Atkinson-based measure	1.338	2.618

The comparison in Table 8.2 shows that for zero-poverty structures the linear income tax dominates the minimum income guarantee from the point of view of social welfare. The question arises of whether the ranking still holds when some poverty remains. In order to make 'equal poverty' comparisons, several alternative measures of poverty may be used. The approach followed below is to use the family of poverty measures proposed by Foster *et al.* (1984) and used by Besley (1990), given by:

$$P_\alpha = \int_0^{y_p} \left(\frac{y_p - y}{y_p} \right)^\alpha dF(y) \qquad (8.22)$$

Three different measures are used, where α takes the values 0, 1 and 2. The measure P_0 is the 'headcount' ratio, the proportion of the population below the poverty line. The measure P_1 is the product of P_0 and 1 minus the ratio of the arithmetic mean income of those in poverty, μ_p, to the poverty line, that is $P_0 (1 - \mu_p/y_p) = P_0 \bar{G}$. Thus P_1 reflects the average poverty gap as well as the number in poverty. The third measure P_2 reflects also the coefficient of variation of those in poverty, η_p^2 say, whereby:

$$P_2 = P_0 \{ \bar{G}^2 + (1 - \bar{G})^2 \eta_p^2 \} \qquad (8.23)$$

It is therefore possible to find combinations of the threshold, a, for which measured poverty is the same for both the minimum income guarantee and the linear income tax.

The value of P_0 for the minimum income guarantee remains very high so long as the minimum income remains below the poverty line, so there is very little 'overlap' between the two schemes regarding this measure. The variation in P_1 and P_2 with the minimum income in the two transfer systems is shown in Figure 8.5. These values apply to the same lognormal distribution of pre-tax income as used earlier, with the same poverty line of $10,000 and net tax revenue per person of $5,000. In each case the tax rate, t, is first obtained using the results in equations (8.14) and (8.17) and then the transfer schemes are applied to 'populations' consisting of 2,000 individuals.

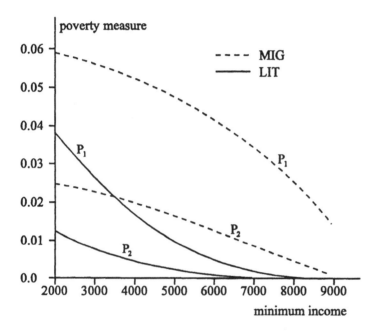

Figure 8.5   Alternative poverty measures

Selected values of poverty measures are shown in Table 8.3 for the two schemes. This table contains one set of values of the minimum income for which the poverty measure P_0 is the same in each scheme, and two sets for each of the other poverty measures. The relevant values of poverty are indicated by being underlined; for example a minimum income of $2,000 in the linear income tax gives the same value of P_0 as a value of $8,400 in the minimum income guarantee scheme. This table gives five pairs of equal poverty comparisons.

Table 8.3   Alternative poverty measures

Minimum	Linear income tax			Minimum income guarantee		
income, a	P_0	P_1	P_2	P_0	P_1	P_2
2,000	*0.1595*	*0.0364*	0.0124	0.1970	0.0576	0.0241
3,400	0.1220	0.0214	*0.0059*	0.1905	0.0532	0.0211
3,800	0.1050	*0.0179*	0.0047	0.1895	0.0517	0.0200
4,200	0.0940	0.0148	*0.0036*	0.1880	0.0501	0.0189
6,600	0.0340	0.0028	0.0004	0.1785	*0.0363*	0.0098
7,600	0.0135	0.0008	0.0001	0.1660	0.0281	*0.0058*
8,200	0.0055	0.0003	—	0.1605	0.0223	*0.0036*
8,400	0.0035	0.0002	—	*0.1595*	0.0202	0.0029
8,600	0.0025	0.0001	—	0.1575	*0.0180*	0.0023

Notes: Poverty line = $10,000; net revenue per person = $5,000.

Table 8.4   Equal poverty comparisons

Tax	Minimum	Poverty	Tax	Kakwani	Welfare premium	
system	income		rate	progressivity	Gini-based	Atkinson-based
Poverty measure = P_0						
LIT	2,000	0.1595	0.241	0.1616	0.395	0.729
MIG	8,400	0.1595	0.251	0.2128	0.520	1.029
Poverty measure = P_1						
LIT	2,000	0.0364	0.241	0.1616	0.395	0.729
MIG	6,600	0.0363	0.226	0.1388	0.340	0.725
LIT	3,800	0.0179	0.303	0.3088	0.751	1.259
MIG	8,600	0.0180	0.254	0.2226	0.544	1.066
Poverty measure = P_2						
LIT	3,400	0.0059	0.290	0.2759	0.672	1.148
MIG	7,600	0.0058	0.239	0.1769	0.433	0.888
LIT	4,200	0.0036	0.317	0.3417	0.830	1.366
MIG	8,200	0.0036	0.248	0.2033	0.497	0.993

Notes: Poverty line = $10,000; net revenue per person = $5,000; LIT = Linear income tax;
MIG = Minimum income guarantee.

The progressivity and welfare measures corresponding to the different
threshold income levels in each scheme can also be calculated. Results are shown

in Table 8.4. In view of the fact that the various progressivity measures provide the same ranking, only the Kakwani measure is shown in Table 8.4 for each case. Furthermore, the rankings are not influenced by the degree of inequality aversion used to calculate the Atkinson inequality measures, so results for the single value of 1.5 are shown in the table. For all the comparisons involving the poverty measures P_1 and P_2, the Kakwani progressivity measure and the welfare premia from progression are higher for the linear income tax compared with the minimum income guarantee. Although the minimum income is significantly higher for the minimum income guarantee, the tax rate required to finance the linear income tax is higher. This is not surprising, given the nature of each of the relationships between net and gross income. The equal poverty comparison involving the headcount measure P_0 is the only one which gives a higher welfare premium and higher progressivity for the minimum income guarantee. This arises because the minimum income has to be so much higher in the latter scheme, for the proportion below the poverty line to be the same as in the linear income tax.

In examining the 'target efficiency' involved in allocating a given amount of gross government expenditure, it is obvious that a means-tested tax and transfer scheme such as the minimum income guarantee will dominate a 'universal' scheme such as the linear income tax. However, this chapter has argued that it is inappropriate to hold gross expenditure fixed in comparing transfer schemes and to evaluate schemes without any regard to the extent to which they actually reduce poverty or achieve wider aims involving income redistribution more generally. Equal poverty comparisons between schemes were carried out using alternative criteria such as progressivity measures and, in particular, measures of the welfare premia involved in raising a given amount of net revenue from the tax system (compared with a proportional tax which provides no transfers). It was seen that the linear tax dominated the means-tested scheme, the minimum income guarantee, except when the schemes were required to have the same value of the 'headcount' measure of poverty.

APPENDIX 8.1   ALTERNATIVE SCHEMES

Table 8.5 presents details of five hypothetical individuals under four different tax and transfer schemes. These are 'pure' transfer systems, so that gross revenue from taxation is exactly matched by gross expenditure on transfer payments. In schemes (i), (ii) and (iii) the gross revenue raised by income taxation is 30, and the transfer payment systems are such that only those in poverty, judged by pre-tax income, receive benefits and none is raised above the poverty line. The individuals are ranked in ascending order of their incomes and it is assumed that the poverty level is equal to 40, so that individuals 1 and 2 are in poverty before taxes and transfers. The alternative schemes are as follows:

(i)   The income tax is such that the tax paid $T(y)$ on an income of y is given by:

$$T(y) = 0 \qquad\qquad \text{for } y \leq 20$$
$$= 0.10(y - 20) \qquad \text{for } y > 20 \qquad\qquad (8.24)$$

Hence there is a single marginal tax rate of 0.10 applied to income measured in excess of a tax-free threshold of 20. In addition, there is a minimum income guarantee (MIG) such that those individuals with incomes (after income tax) below 30 have their net incomes brought up to 30. This is referred to as a 'fully integrated' MIG.

(ii) The income tax is the same as in (i) above, but the transfer payments are designed in order to minimize the number of people with net income below the poverty line; that is, the headcount poverty measure is minimized.

(iii) The income tax is the same as in (i) but the transfer system has means-tested 'tapered' benefits. Those with $y < 50$ receive a basic benefit of 25 which is reduced at a rate of 2/3 of pre-tax income. Hence net income, z, is given by:

$$z = 25 + y(1 - 2/3) \qquad\qquad (8.25)$$

This transfer system, given the pre-tax income distribution, just exhausts the 30 raised from income taxation imposed on the three richest individuals.

(iv) This structure has a linear income tax with a universal benefit, or social dividend, of 30 which is received by all individuals. Income taxation is imposed at a fixed proportional rate on all income. With a gross revenue requirement of 150, the tax rate required is 0.3846. Hence net income is given by:

$$z = 30 + y(1 - 0.3846) \qquad\qquad (8.26)$$

For each of the four tax and transfer schemes, the net incomes are shown, along with several measures of poverty and inequality.

In comparing the four structures, the gross revenue raised by income taxation is rather an arbitrary measure to take as a criterion. This is because the numerical examples have assumed that there are no administrative costs of collecting taxation or of administering benefits. In practice the administrative costs of the different structures would be expected to vary, and it may be that they vary in proportion to the total (gross) revenue raised and disbursed. The linear income tax can indeed be administered in two ways; either everyone is taxed at the rate 0.3846 to produce revenue of 150, or revenue is only obtained from those with incomes, y_i above the arithmetic mean, $\bar{y}$, in which case the gross revenue is effectively 55.38 rather than 150.

Table 8.5   Alternative tax and transfer schemes

Person	Pre-tax	Net income under tax structures			
Number	Income	(i)	(ii)	(iii)	(iv)
1	10	30	20	28.33	36.15
2	20	30	40	31.66	42.31
3	60	56	56	56	66.92
4	100	92	92	92	91.54
5	200	182	182	182	153.08
P_0	0.4	0.4	0.2	0.4	0.2
P_1	0.25	0.1	0.1	0.1	0.0192
P_2	0.1625	0.025	0.05	0.0257	0.0018
Gini	0.472	0.375	0.386	0.377	0.290
Atkinson (0.5)	0.199	0.116	0.123	0.116	0.068

The structures (i)–(iii) all have target efficiency measures of 100 per cent, reflecting the fact that only those who have $y < y_p$ are better off after taxes and transfers and none has a net income exceeding the poverty line. However, poverty is not eliminated in any of the schemes, according to any of the poverty measures.

A feature of the income tax system of structures (i)–(iii), involving a tax-free threshold, is also worth emphasizing as it is often ignored by those in favour of means-testing. For those with $y > y_p$, inspection of (i) shows that income after the deduction of income tax is given by $(0.1)(20) + y(1 - 0.1) = 2 + 0.9y$. This is the same basic form as the linear income tax (with universal benefits) of equation (8.26). An increase in the tax-free threshold would increase the effective social dividend received by those who pay tax.

A comparison of the structures shows that if target efficiency is thought to be an important criterion, the choice among structures (i)–(iii) depends on which poverty measure reflects the value judgements of whoever is making the evaluation. The MIG of structure (i) would be chosen if P_2 is used. Although structure (ii) is designed to minimise P_0 it does badly according to P_2. However, all three structures have the same value of P_1. In this latter case, reference may be made to the inequality measures. This is a case where a lexicographic approach may be applied; that is, a primary aim is to minimize poverty (for a given measure) and a secondary aim is then to minimize inequality among schemes which achieve the minimum poverty level. Here the choice depends on value judgements which are involved in the choice of inequality measure. Thus schemes (i) and (iii), the MIG and the modified MIG with tapered benefits, tie when P_1 and Atkinson's measure (with aversion coefficient of 0.5) are used, but the MIG dominates if the Gini measure is used along with P_1.

The linear income tax of structure (iv) performs badly from the point of view of target efficiency since person 2's net income is above the poverty line and person 3 has a higher net income than gross income (all those with $y < \bar{y}$ in this scheme are better off), yet it does not eliminate poverty because the net income of person 1 is below y_p. However, it has lower poverty measures P_1 and P_2 than any of the other schemes. If P_0 is used, then (iv) ties with (ii), but the lexicographic approach results in (iv) dominating because it has lower inequality measures. A concentration on inequality reduction as a sole criterion would, not surprisingly, also give a preference for the linear income tax.

In comparing the four structures of Table 8.5, there is therefore no single scheme that can be regarded as economically superior to any other. The evaluation inevitably involves value judgements, and such values may involve rather complex issues relating to views about poverty and inequality. Although the term 'target efficiency' has been used in the literature, the use of such measures really has nothing to do with economic efficiency but involves the value judgement that transfers to the non-poor are 'bad', as are excessively generous payments to the poor. Efficiency considerations cannot really be applied in this context of a fixed pre-tax income distribution.

PART II

Variable Labour Supplies

9. Taxation and labour supply

Part I of this book examined taxes and transfers on the assumption that the pre-tax income distribution remains unchanged when taxes and transfers change. This assumption is often appropriate when taxes are included in wider economic models and when only a small range of tax rates is being considered. The analytical methods presented in part I are also useful when the assumption of fixed labour supplies is relaxed. However, when taken to extremes it can obviously lead to absurd results; for example, it suggests that complete equality of post-tax-and-transfer income can be achieved. Part II relaxes this assumption by making the pre-tax distribution of income endogenous, depending on the labour supply of individuals.

In introducing labour supply variations it is still necessary to make a number of simplifying assumptions. For example, labour supply involves effort as well as hours worked, but only variations in hours will be modelled. In practice the labour supply decision may not simply be a question of working longer hours or taking more leisure, since time away from paid employment may be used in producing goods and services which are consumed at home rather than being purchased in the market. Such household production is, however, ignored below. Labour supply may also involve a complex joint decision within households, but, as in earlier chapters, the analysis concentrates on single individuals.

The income-earning ability of individuals is assumed to be reflected simply in the wage rate faced, which is treated as being exogenous in a single-period context. Individuals are considered to work in only one job; thus hours worked are supply-determined and there is no need to work at any other than the highest possible wage. General equilibrium aspects are ignored at this stage, but are considered in detail in part III. Despite these simplifications, the analysis is not straightforward.

Early studies of labour supply approached it directly in terms of the associated demand for consumption goods, or real income. The number of hours of labour supplied is obtained by multiplying the demand for consumption (net income) by the ratio of a price index of goods to the wage rate per hour. This is the reciprocal demand property that lies at the heart of the theory of exchange and can be used to show that the labour supply curve will be 'backward bending' when the demand for goods is inelastic; see Creedy (1992a). The modern approach is, however, a direct application of the utility analysis of demand where the individual's utility function has as its arguments an index of the consumption of goods and the consumption of leisure time. The supply of labour is a residual; it is the total number of hours available less the number of hours of leisure consumed. The effects of changes in wages or taxes are examined in terms of the standard income and substitution effects. However, the problem is complicated by the fact that the budget constraint resulting from the existence of tax and transfer schemes is usually non-linear, so careful attention must be paid to the possibility of corner solutions.

Section 9.1 considers some general features of the analysis of labour supply and shows that for further results it is necessary to consider a specific form of the utility function. Comparative statics of the general case are examined in Appendix 9.1. Section 9.2 concentrates on the simplest type of utility function, the Cobb–Douglas form, and obtains basic results in the absence of taxation. The more complicated case of the constant elasticity of substitution (CES) utility function is discussed in Appendix 9.2. Taxes and transfers are introduced in section 9.3, which examines several alternative schemes.

9.1   THE GENERAL CASE

Let c denote an index of consumption of all goods and services, where for convenience the price index is normalized to unity. The proportion of time devoted to leisure is represented by h, so that $0 \le h \le 1$. The individual is considered to maximize utility, $U = U(c,h)$, subject to the budget constraint that consumption is equal to post-tax-and-transfer income, z. The utility function is assumed to be twice continuously differentiable. If w denotes the fixed wage rate faced by the individual, and if earnings from employment are augmented by non-labour income of g, then pre-tax income, y, is $g + w(1 - h)$. Let τ denote a vector of tax and transfer parameters, which may include tax rates, thresholds and unconditional transfers; hence the budget constraint facing the individual is considered to be piecewise linear. Net income may in general be written as a function of y and the vector τ, so that $z = z(y, \tau) = z(g + w(1 - h), \tau)$.

Diagrammatically the individual's utility-maximizing position is represented by the position on the piecewise budget constraint which enables the individual to reach the highest indifference curve attainable. But the diagrammatic analysis does not take the discussion very far, so it is necessary to take a more formal approach. Ideally, the Kuhn–Tucker approach would be used, given the non-linear nature of the problem, but the following treatment will start by examining interior (tangency) solutions and then consider the conditions under which they will hold. The Lagrangean is:

$$L = U(z,h) + \lambda(z - c) \tag{9.1}$$

The first-order conditions for an interior solution to this problem, where subscripts denote partial derivatives, are:

$$L_c = U_c - \lambda = 0 \tag{9.2}$$

$$L_h = U_h + \lambda z_h = 0 \tag{9.3}$$

$$L_\lambda = z - c = 0 \tag{9.4}$$

The partial derivative, z_h, is the negative of the after-tax wage rate. An interior solution to these equations represents a tangency position between an indifference curve and one of the linear sections of the budget constraint, corresponding to a particular tax rate. Comparative statics are therefore awkward because continuity in the solution functions requires the assumption that a change in the relevant tax rate is sufficiently small to avoid a movement either to a corner solution or to another linear segment of the budget constraint. This naturally rules out many of the interesting types of change which may occur in practice. Even if such continuity is assumed, few unambiguous qualitative results are available. The comparative statics of the general case are examined further in Appendix 9.1.

The complexity of the general case makes it desirable to examine specific functional forms which allow explicit solutions to the first-order conditions to be considered. For this reason the following discussion concentrates on the use of the Cobb–Douglas utility function. However, the Cobb–Douglas form has severe limitations, and for this reason the more complicated constant elasticity of substitution (CES) form is examined in Appendix 9.2. As suggested above, it is also important to handle corner solutions, which are particularly likely to arise when dealing with tax and transfer systems that imply budget constraints having a number of kinks. The restriction that $h \leq 1$, along with the non-negativity constraints on c and h, must also be imposed.

9.2 COBB–DOUGLAS UTILITY FUNCTIONS

The simplest case to examine is the situation where there are no taxes or transfers. The Cobb–Douglas form of utility function is given by:

$$U = c^\alpha h^{1-\alpha} \tag{9.5}$$

and is maximized subject to the constraint that:

$$c = w(1 - h) + g \qquad (9.6)$$

There is no loss of generality in using the constant returns to scale form of (9.5), since demand functions are invariant with respect to monotonic transformations of the utility function. It is a straightforward matter to substitute into the first-order conditions given in the previous section for utility maximization, using these functions. Combine (9.2) and (9.3) to eliminate λ and express c in terms of h. Finally, substitute the resulting expression into (9.4) to solve for h in terms of α, g and w. This approach is equivalent to the following method, which is convenient when introducing non-linear tax schedules. From (9.5), the marginal rate of substitution of leisure for consumption is given by:

$$\frac{dc}{dh}\Big|_U = -\left(\frac{1-\alpha}{\alpha}\right)\frac{c}{h} \qquad (9.7)$$

From (9.6), the rate of substitution along the budget line is given by:

$$\frac{dc}{dh} = -w \qquad (9.8)$$

For interior solutions, equate (9.7) and (9.8) to get c in terms of h as:

$$c = \left(\frac{\alpha}{1-\alpha}\right)wh \qquad (9.9)$$

Then substitute (9.9) into (9.6) and solve for h, giving:

$$h = (1 - \alpha)(w + g)/w \qquad (9.10)$$

The maximum potential labour income is w, which is obtained when $h = 0$. The 'price' of leisure is also w, so that (9.10) shows the familiar Cobb–Douglas result that expenditure functions are linear and demand functions are rectangular hyperbolas. It is convenient to write the maximum possible income as $M = w + g$ and to refer to M as *full income*. Notice that if there is no non-wage income, so that g is zero, leisure is constant at $1 - \alpha$ and labour supply is fixed at α. When g is positive, labour supply approaches the value α asymptotically as the wage increases. The Cobb–Douglas specification cannot therefore generate a backward-bending labour supply curve in a diagram where the wage is plotted on the vertical axis and labour supply is measured along the horizontal axis.

Consumption can be obtained from (9.9) by substituting for h using the result in (9.10). It can be seen that c is a proportion, α, of M; in relating this simple result to the standard property of Cobb–Douglas functions, remember that the price of c is unity. It is useful to rearrange (9.10) to solve for gross earnings, $y = w(1 - h)$, so that:

$$y = w(1 - h) = \alpha w - g(1 - \alpha) \tag{9.11}$$

Earnings from employment are thus a linear function of the wage rate, above some critical value, w_L say, for which earnings are non-negative, that is, for which $h \leq 1$. Using either (9.10) or (9.11), the critical value of w below which the individual supplies no labour at all is given by:

$$w_L = g(1 - \alpha)/\alpha \tag{9.12}$$

Having established these results, it will be shown below how they can be extended to allow for a wide range of tax and transfer schemes involving several linear segments.

The above analysis applies to a single individual. Within any population, individuals may be expected to differ according to their preferences (determined by α) and their non-wage income, in addition to the wage rate they face. Heterogeneity would therefore be described by a three-dimensional distribution in α, g and w. In the context of tax and transfer schemes, concentration is usually on employment income only, so that g is influenced only by the transfer system. This non-wage component of income is assumed to be the same for all individuals, given that non-income characteristics are assumed to be irrelevant in assessing taxes and transfers. Dealing with variation in both w and α is still rather awkward, and it is necessary to impose *a priori* restrictions on the nature of variations in preferences. In order to avoid these problems, the literature typically assumes that individuals differ only by the wage rate faced. However, further aspects of heterogeneity are examined in later chapters.

9.3 TAX AND TRANSFER SYSTEMS

A Linear Income Tax

Consider the linear income tax introduced in Chapter 4, where each individual receives a lump sum payment of a, and pays tax at a proportional rate, t, applied to all wage income. This can also be seen as a system in which there is a tax-free exemption of a/t, where all those with income below the exemption receive a payment (or pay a negative amount of tax) which depends on their income.

The two ways of looking at the linear tax imply different administrative arrangements, but for those above the tax-free exemption, they give rise to precisely the same relationship between net and gross income. The budget constraint is thus:

$$c = a + w(1-h)(1-t) \tag{9.13}$$

The effect of taxes and transfers is to alter only the budget constraint facing each individual. Hence the results in section 9.2 can be applied directly to this case by substituting the fixed transfer for g and writing $w(1-t)$ instead of w. Full income, M, therefore becomes $a + w(1-t)$, and (9.10) becomes $h = (1 - \alpha) M/\{w(1-t)\}$. Similarly the earnings function, using (9.11), is:

$$y = w(1-h) = \alpha w - a(1-\alpha)/(1-t) \tag{9.14}$$

Since y must be positive, this expression applies for $w > w_L$, where:

$$w_L = \frac{a(1-\alpha)}{\alpha(1-t)} \tag{9.15}$$

Since the right-hand side of (9.15) exceeds that of (9.12), the proportion of the population not working is higher, the higher the tax rate. The linear income tax and the simple case discussed in section 9.2 are similar because they share the same basic form of budget constraint, shown in Figure 9.1. The length BD is either g or a, since both represent non-wage income, and the slope of the section AB is either w or $w(1-t)$, the post-tax wage rate. If there is a proportional tax system, so that $a = 0$, the supply of labour is always α and a change in the tax rate has no effect on labour supply. If $a > 0$, labour supply increases, for $w > w_L$, until it approaches α asymptotically. Increases in the wage rate (above w_L) and reductions in the proportional tax rate both lead to increases in labour supply.

The question arises of whether labour supply would ever be expected to increase as a result of an increase in the tax rate which is accompanied by a change in the transfer, a, in order to ensure revenue-neutrality. This can be considered using the result in (9.14) above, which implies that $(1-h) = \alpha - a(1-\alpha)/(1-t)w$. Total differentiation with respect to a and t gives:

$$\frac{d(1-h)}{dt} = -\frac{a(1-\alpha)}{w(1-t)}\left[\frac{da}{adt} + \frac{1}{1-t}\right]$$

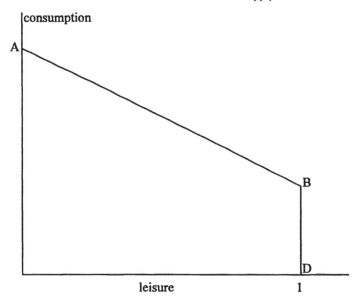

Figure 9.1   The individual's budget constraint

Thus so long as da/dt along the government's budget constraint is non-negative, labour supply will fall whatever the wage rate. With a fixed income distribution it has been seen that da/dt is positive and constant, but it will be seen that with endogenous incomes there is a range over which the fall in the tax base dominates the rise in t, and the value of the lump sum transfer falls as t increases. In the range where da/dt < 0, labour supply falls so long as the absolute value of the elasticity of the transfer, a, with respect to t is less than $1/(1 - t)$. There is therefore a range where an increase in t leads to an increase in labour supply; it will however be shown that this range can be ruled out as being sub-optimal.

It will also be shown that a revenue-neutral increase in t always leads to a reduction in a measure of inequality, hence it is unequivocally progressive in its effect. It can therefore be said that an increase in the progressivity of the linear income tax system reduces labour supply at all wage levels. There is an extensive debate on the effects of progressivity on labour supply, starting from the work of Barlow and Sparks (1964). This includes Chatterji (1979) and Hemming (1980), who consider a single individual paying a constant amount of tax, and Sandmo (1983) who uses aggregate revenue neutrality.

A Tax-free Threshold

Suppose that the tax schedule has a tax-free threshold but there are no transfer payments for those below the threshold. Hence the tax paid is zero for earnings,

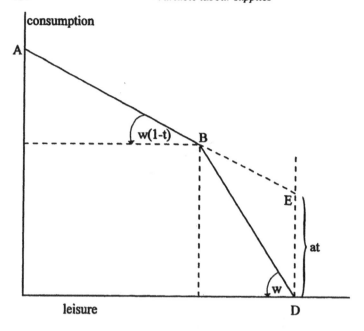

Figure 9.2 Budget constraint with tax-free threshold

$y = w(1 - h)$, below an amount, a, but is equal to $t(y - a)$ for $y \geq a$. The budget constraint takes the form shown in Figure 9.2. For $y > a$ the section AB is relevant and its equation is given by:

$$c = at + w(1 - h)(1 - t) \tag{9.16}$$

When $w(1 - h) < a$, the constraint is the section BD, for which:

$$c = w(1 - h) \tag{9.17}$$

The individual's optimization problem is therefore essentially a programming problem, but the main characteristics can be obtained using the above results. First, notice that (9.16) is precisely like (9.13) except that the term at replaces the transfer a. Hence along the range AB, full income, M, is equal to $at + w(1 - t)$, $h = (1 - \alpha) M / \{w(1 - t)\}$, and earnings are given by substituting directly into (9.14), giving:

$$w(1 - h) = \alpha w - at(1 - \alpha)/(1 - t) \tag{9.19}$$

This holds for $w(1 - t) > a$, so that w must exceed the level, w_T, given by $a(1 - \alpha t)/\{\alpha (1 - t)\}$. Along the section BD, earnings are αw; this is obtained from (9.19) by setting $a = t = 0$. This result applies when earnings are less than the amount, w_0, given by:

$$w_0 = \frac{a}{\alpha} \tag{9.20}$$

There is consequently a range of values of w for which individuals are bunched at the corner solution, B, in Figure 9.2. This range is $w_0 < w < w_T$, so that:

$$\frac{a}{\alpha} < w < \frac{a(1 - \alpha t)}{\alpha(1 - t)} \tag{9.21}$$

The basic results of section 9.2 can therefore be extended to any tax schedule which has a piecewise linear budget constraint involving several thresholds and marginal tax rates. Each threshold will produce a kink like that at B and a range similar to (9.21). No new principles are involved so long as the budget constraint continues to be concave. Convexities are considered in the following subsection.

A Convex Budget Constraint

Consider the modified minimum income guarantee in which those above an earnings threshold, a, pay tax equal to $t(y - a)$. But if $y < a$ the individual receives a transfer payment equal to $s(a - y)$, with $s > t$. Hence the transfer is withdrawn at a rate that exceeds the marginal tax rate t. Individuals below the threshold therefore 'pay' a negative tax of $-s(y - a)$, which in absolute terms is more than under the corresponding linear income tax, for which $t = s$. This type of scheme was examined by Lambert (1985b, 1990, 1993a), although the following treatment extends that of Lambert in several ways.

The convex budget constraint is illustrated in Figure 9.3, and is the kinked line ABDE. For the range AB, the analysis of the previous subsections has shown that equation (9.19) applies, over a range of wage rates to be specified below. For the range BD, it is necessary to substitute s for t in (9.14) and (9.15), and allow for the restriction that earnings must be positive. Hence for this range to be relevant, the wage rate must be greater than w_L, given by:

$$w_L = \frac{as(1 - \alpha)}{\alpha(1 - s)} \tag{9.22}$$

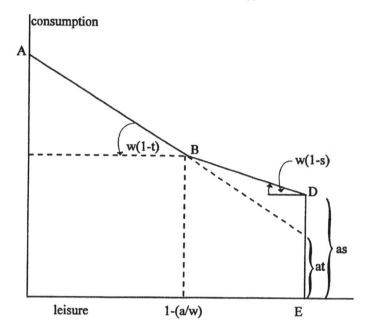

Figure 9.3   The modified minimum income guarantee

The point D is reached for all wage rates below w_L. Similarly, the straight line defined by (9.19) intercepts the wage axis in the relationship between gross earnings and the wage at the wage w_G, given by:

$$w_G = \frac{(1-\alpha)at}{\alpha(1-t)} \tag{9.23}$$

It can be seen that $w_L > w_G$, since $s > t$. The kink at B corresponds to a situation where net and gross income both equal a; the individual neither pays tax nor receives a transfer. But this point would never be chosen because a discrete jump would take place from one linear section to the other before B could be reached. Over the convex part of the budget constraint in Figure 9.3 an indifference curve can be simultaneously tangential to the sections AB and BD for a particular wage rate. Hence as the wage rate rises, individuals move away from the corner at D, but switch from the section BD to AB at some value of w. It is thus necessary to determine the precise wage rate for which the switch occurs. Notice that as w changes, the segment BD pivots about the fixed point D and the segment AB shifts accordingly.

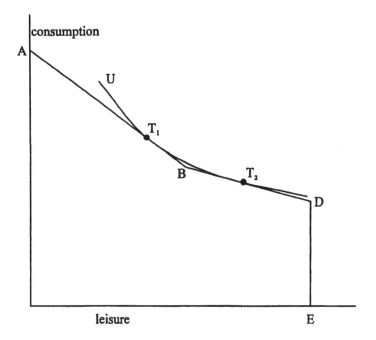

Figure 9.4   Two simultaneous tangency positions

Consider Figure 9.4, which shows the indifference curve U which is tangential to BD at T_2 and at the same time tangential to AB at T_1. Suppose that the combinations of c and h at T_1 are c_1 and h_1 and at T_2 they are c_2 and h_2. These points are on a common indifference curve, so it must be the case that:

$$c_1^\alpha h_1^{1-\alpha} = c_2^\alpha h_2^{1-\alpha} \tag{9.24}$$

This can be rearranged to give the ratio c_1/c_2 as:

$$\frac{c_1}{c_2} = \left(\frac{h_2}{h_1}\right)^{(1-\alpha)/\alpha} \tag{9.25}$$

Furthermore, equating marginal rates of substitution to slopes of the respective sections of the budget line gives:

$$\left(\frac{1-\alpha}{\alpha}\right)\frac{c_1}{h_1} = (1-t)w \quad \text{and} \quad \left(\frac{1-\alpha}{\alpha}\right)\frac{c_2}{h_2} = (1-s)w \qquad (9.26)$$

Eliminating w from these equations gives the relation:

$$\frac{c_1}{c_2} = \left(\frac{1-t}{1-s}\right)\frac{h_1}{h_2} \qquad (9.27)$$

Substituting for c_1/c_2, from (9.25), into (9.27) and rearranging gives:

$$\frac{h_1}{h_2} = \left(\frac{1-s}{1-t}\right)^\alpha \qquad (9.28)$$

Substituting in (9.28) for h_1 and h_2 in terms of w where, for example, $h_1 = (1-\alpha)\{at + w(1-t)\}/\{w(1-t)\}$ finally produces an equation in w. The solution of this equation is the 'switching' value, w_s, which can be shown to be:

$$w_s = \frac{a(\theta s - t)}{(1-t) - \theta(1-s)} \qquad (9.29)$$

where: $\qquad\qquad \theta = \{(1-t)/(1-s)\}^{1-\alpha} \qquad (9.30)$

Inspection of (9.22) and (9.29), which give expressions for w_L and w_s respectively, shows that if s is large (close to unity) and t is small, it is possible to have $w_L > w_s$; otherwise $w_s > w_L$. Hence these two possibilities need to be considered. A similar phenomenon, though in the context of earnings-related pensions, is examined in Chapter 12. The results in terms of earnings are illustrated in Figure 9.5, showing the variation in $w(1-h)$ as w increases. In Figure 9.5(a) earnings follow the line O to A when the wage rate is too low to induce any labour supply and the individual receives the transfer, as. Then from A to B the individual works and receives a reduced transfer, until the 'jump' is made at w_s from B to C, after which the individual pays tax and does not receive any transfer. If individuals differ only according to the wage rate faced, then no individual would be expected to have gross earnings in the range BC of Figure 9.5.

In the case where $w_L > w_s$, the tangency position, corresponding to the point T_2 in Figure 9.4, is beyond the feasible range, so that the constraint that $h \le 1$ is violated. This means that the individual never simultaneously works and receives

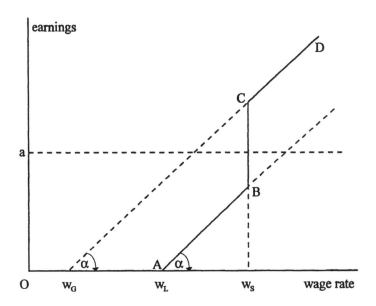

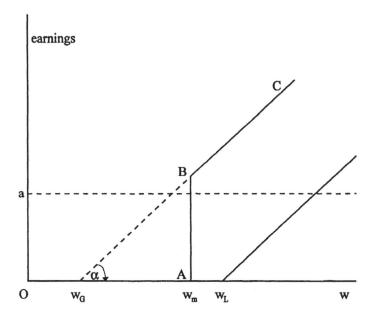

Figure 9.5 Earnings with the modified minimum income guarantee

transfer payments; only the corner solution where $h = 1$ or the section of the budget constraint for which $y > a$ are relevant. An alternative minimum wage must therefore be produced, w_m, such that an indifference curve is tangential to the range AB of Figure 9.4 and at the same time touches the corner at point D. The condition requires that:

$$c_1^\alpha h_1^{1-\alpha} = (as)^\alpha \qquad (9.31)$$

where $c_1 = \alpha\{at + (1-t)\,w_m\}$ and $h_1 = (1-\alpha)\{at + (1-t)w_m\}/\{w_m(1-t)\}$. Substituting for c_1 and h_1 using these expressions gives w_m as the root of the equation:

$$\theta_1\, w_m^{1-\alpha} - \theta_2\, w_m - \theta_3 = 0 \qquad (9.32)$$

where:

$$\theta_1 = (as)^\alpha$$
$$\theta_2 = (1-t)\alpha^\alpha\,\{(1-\alpha)/(1-t)\}^{1-\alpha}$$
$$\theta_3 = at\alpha^\alpha\,\{(1-\alpha)/(1-t)\}^{\,1-\alpha} \qquad (9.33)$$

Figure 9.5(b) illustrates this case, where the individual does not work for $w < w_m$, but jumps from A to B; that is, moves from receiving a transfer, as, to paying tax and receiving no transfer payment. Equation (9.32) cannot be solved explicitly because of the non-linearity, so it is necessary to use a numerical method of solution. The most convenient approach in this situation is to use Newton's Method, as follows. Rewrite (9.32) as $\Phi(w) = 0$, and obtain the differential:

$$\frac{d\Phi(w)}{dw} = \theta_1(1-\alpha)w^{-\alpha} - \theta_2 \qquad (9.34)$$

Given an initial trial value of w_m, say w_1, the new value, w_2, in the iterative sequence is given by:

$$w_2 = w_1 - \Phi(w)/(d\Phi(w)/dw) \qquad (9.35)$$

The process converges when w_1 and w_2 are sufficiently close. A useful initial value is that of w_s obtained from (9.29). The basis of Newton's Method is to approximate the function using the straight line given by the tangent at the relevant point. Some examples of the values produced using equations (9.29) and (9.32) are given in Table 9.1.

Table 9.1   Wage thresholds with the modified minimum income guarantee

s	t	w_L	w_s	w_m
0.9	0.1	1928.57	1160.26	1116.44
0.9	0.3	1928.57	1261.24	1221.26
0.9	0.5	1928.57	1418.31	1387.85
0.9	0.7	1928.57	1712.68	1704.23
0.8	0.1	857.14	986.58	—
0.8	0.3	857.14	1058.03	—
0.8	0.5	857.14	1168.25	—
0.8	0.7	857.14	1372.42	—

Note: In all cases $\alpha = 0.7$ and $a = 500$.

Each example in Table 9.1 was produced using $a = 500$ and $\alpha = 0.7$. In the cases where $w_L > w_s$, it can be seen that the threshold w_m is slightly lower than w_s. This is expected from the basic indifference curve diagram.

This chapter has examined an individual's choice of consumption and leisure, subject to a budget constraint in which the wage rate, rather than the income level, is fixed. The effect of taxes and transfers is to alter the budget constraint, and the chapter has shown how any type of piecewise linear budget constraint, containing convexities and concavities, may be handled. The crucial problem is to deal appropriately with the different types of corner solution. In one case individuals bunch at the corners of concave sections, while in another case no one would be expected to be at the corner of convex sections. The following two chapters use these results to explore the implications of endogenous earnings for the government's budget constraint and social welfare.

APPENDIX 9.1   COMPARATIVE STATICS

Assuming that the set of equations (9.2) to (9.4) can be solved, the optimum values may be denoted λ^*, c^* and h^*, which can be regarded as functions of w, g and the vector τ. After substituting the optimum values into equations (9.2) to (9.4) and differentiating each equation totally, the resulting equations can be rearranged into the following matrix form:

$$\begin{bmatrix} U_{cc} & U_{ch} & -1 \\ U_{hc} & U_{hh} + \lambda^* z_{hh} & z_h \\ -1 & z_h & 0 \end{bmatrix} \begin{bmatrix} dc^* \\ dh^* \\ d\lambda^* \end{bmatrix} = \begin{bmatrix} 0 & 0 & 0 \\ -\lambda^* z_{hw} & -\lambda^* z_{hg} & -\lambda^* z_{h\tau} \\ -z_w & -z_g & -z_\tau \end{bmatrix} \begin{bmatrix} dw \\ dg \\ d\tau \end{bmatrix} \qquad (9.36)$$

All first and second derivatives in the matrices in (9.36) are evaluated at the optimal values of the endogenous variables. Consider the effect of a change in one parameter of the vector τ representing the tax system, that is a change in the tax rate corresponding to the linear section of the budget constraint on which the interior solution lies, with the wage rate and the value of non-employment income constant, so that $dw = dg = 0$. If H denotes the bordered hessian matrix on the left hand side of (9.36), then:

$$\begin{bmatrix} dc^*/d\tau \\ dh^*/d\tau \\ d\lambda^*/d\tau \end{bmatrix} = H^{-1} \begin{bmatrix} 0 \\ -\lambda^* z_{h\tau} \\ -z_\tau \end{bmatrix} \tag{9.37}$$

The inverse, H^{-1}, is obtained by dividing the adjoint of H by its determinant. If attention is restricted to the effect on the consumption of leisure, $dh^*/d\tau$, then only the last two elements of the second row of H^{-1} need to be considered, in view of the zero in the first element of the vector on the right hand side of (9.37). Hence:

$$|H| \frac{dh^*}{d\tau} = -\lambda^* z_{h\tau} \begin{vmatrix} U_{cc} & -1 \\ -1 & 0 \end{vmatrix} + z_\tau \begin{vmatrix} U_{cc} & U_{ch} \\ -1 & z_h \end{vmatrix}$$

$$= -\lambda^* z_{h\tau} + z_\tau (z_h U_{cc} + U_{ch}) \tag{9.38}$$

The second-order condition for a maximum is satisfied by assumption, so that the determinant, $|H|$, is negative. Therefore equation (9.38) shows that the tax change increases leisure, or reduces labour supply, if the right-hand side of (9.37) is negative. In general, no clear result is available without further assumptions about the form of the utility function and the tax-and-transfer system. For example, suppose that $U_{cc} < 0$, $U_{ch} > 0$, and $z_h < 0$, $z_\tau < 0$ and $z_{h\tau} < 0$ (as in the linear income tax). Substitution into (9.33) shows that labour supply is unambiguously reduced by an increase in the relevant tax rate.

APPENDIX 9.2   THE CES UTILITY FUNCTION

A limitation of the Cobb–Douglas utility function $U = c^\alpha h^{1-\alpha}$ is that it has a constant unitary elasticity of substitution between consumption and leisure. In the absence of any non-wage income, this implies a fixed labour supply equal to α, independent of the wage rate. With positive non-wage income, then labour supply increases asymptotically towards α as the wage increases. Consider instead the use of a constant-elasticity-of-substitution, CES, utility function which can be written as:

$$U = (\alpha c^{-\rho} + (1 - \alpha)h^{-\rho})^{-1/\rho} \tag{9.39}$$

where $\rho > -1$, $0 < \alpha < 1$ and $1/(1 + \rho) = \sigma$, the elasticity of substitution. In this case the marginal rate of substitution of leisure for consumption is given by:

$$\left.\frac{dc}{dh}\right|_U = -\left(\frac{1-\alpha}{\alpha}\right)\left(\frac{h}{c}\right)^{-(1+\rho)} \tag{9.40}$$

Hence equating (9.40) and the rate of substitution along the budget line, which is simply $-w$ given in (9.8), gives c in terms of h:

$$c = h\left\{\left(\frac{1-\alpha}{\alpha}\right)\frac{1}{w}\right\}^{-\sigma} \tag{9.41}$$

Suppose that there is no taxation, but a non-wage income of g, so that the budget constraint is $c = w(1 - h) + g$. Substituting for c from (9.41) and rearranging gives:

$$h = \psi M\left(\frac{1-\alpha}{w}\right)^{\sigma} \tag{9.42}$$

where M is, as before, full income, $w + g$, and ψ is given by:

$$\psi = \left[\alpha^{\sigma} + w\left(\frac{1-\alpha}{w}\right)^{\sigma}\right]^{-1} \tag{9.43}$$

Furthermore, substituting (9.42) into (9.41) gives consumption as:

$$c = \psi M\alpha^{\sigma} \tag{9.44}$$

It is necessary to consider the minimum wage, w_L, above which the individual works, that is for which $h < 1$. It can be shown that:

$$w_L = g^{1+\rho}\left(\frac{1-\alpha}{\alpha}\right) \tag{9.45}$$

For those who work, earnings are therefore given by:

$$y = w(1-h) = w\left\{1 - \psi M\left(\frac{1-\alpha}{w}\right)^\sigma\right\} \tag{9.46}$$

This expression for earnings is much more awkward than the corresponding formulae for the Cobb–Douglas case. This has implications for evaluating the government's budget constraint and means that the very convenient Cobb–Douglas approach given in the next chapter cannot be used.

The above results can easily be modified to allow for a tax and transfer system by suitable adjustment of the non-wage component and the wage rate. For example, in the case of the linear income tax with universal transfer, a, and tax rate, t, w is replaced by $w(1-t)$ and g is replaced by a.

The relationship between labour supply, $1-h$, and the wage rate (or the net of tax wage rate) is also more complex than the Cobb–Douglas case, but in some respects this is an advantage because it has greater flexibility. As shown by Stern (1976), two cases need to be distinguished. If $\sigma > 1$, labour supply increases continually as the wage rate increases, so the wage elasticity of labour supply is positive once w exceeds w_L. If $\sigma < 1$, labour supply eventually falls as the wage increases, so that (with w on the vertical axis and $1-h$ on the horizontal axis of a diagram) the labour supply curve can become 'backward bending'. Stern (1976, p. 139) shows that the turning point occurs where $h = 1 - g/\rho w$. The implication is that σ must be less than 1 if it is thought that labour supply is backward bending, and empirical results suggest the use of a value of around 0.5. Furthermore, if the non-wage income is zero, only the backward bending part of the supply curve is relevant when $\sigma < 1$.

Care needs to be taken in the calibration of the model, in addition to the choice of the elasticity of substitution. For example, it is known that as σ approaches unity, (9.39) approaches the Cobb–Douglas form and α indicates the proportion of time spent working, in the absence of non-wage income and taxation. But the appropriate value of α in the CES case depends on the units in which w is measured. In the no-tax case, with $g = 0$, the rearrangement of (9.42) gives:

$$\alpha = (1 + k^{1/\sigma})^{-1} \tag{9.47}$$

where:
$$k = \left(\frac{h}{1-h}\right) w^{\sigma-1} \qquad (9.48)$$

It is therefore possible to specify a particular wage for which it is desired that labour supply should take a certain value, for a given value of the elasticity of substitution. These three variables can be substituted into (9.48) to obtain the value of k, giving in turn the required value of α from (9.47). For example if $\sigma = 0.5$ and it is required that the individual works 70 per cent of the time, so that $h = 0.3$, when $w = 80$, the solution for α is 0.9977. The required value of α is higher for higher wage rates, and α is lower for higher values of σ. Indeed α is very sensitive to the elasticity of substitution: for $h = 0.3$ and $w = 80$, α takes the values 0.987, 0.896, and 0.755 when σ is respectively 0.6, 0.8, and 0.95. Further aspects of the sensitivity of results to σ will be discussed in later chapters. For empirical use of the CES case, see Zabalza (1983), and for an extensive treatment of optimum income taxation using simulations with the CES function see Stern (1976).

Finally, consider the utility function given by:

$$U = (-1/\beta\varepsilon)\,(ch^{\beta})^{-\varepsilon} \qquad (9\,49)$$

where $\varepsilon > -1$, $\varepsilon \neq 0$, and $0 < \beta < 1$. When $\varepsilon = 0$ this takes the form $(1/\beta)\log(ch^{\beta})$. This form of the utility function was used by Jenkins and Millar (1989), following Cowell (1981) and Barzel and McDonald (1973). The marginal rate of substitution of leisure for consumption is found simply to be $-\beta c/h$, so that for interior solutions $c = wh/\beta$ and:

$$h = \left(\frac{g+w}{w}\right)\left(\frac{\beta}{1+\beta}\right) \qquad (9.50)$$

Hence the relationship between y and w is linear, as with the Cobb–Douglas form.

10.   The government's budget constraint

It has been stressed that whatever the government's objective in designing a tax and transfer scheme, its choice of policy variables must satisfy a budget constraint. In a pure transfer scheme, the need for tax revenue to finance transfer payments means that the various tax rates and transfer levels cannot be set independently; one degree of freedom in policy choices is lost. The form of the budget constraint in alternative schemes in the context of fixed pre-tax incomes has been examined in Part I. The various expressions are in terms of the pre-tax income distribution, and these expressions continue to hold even when incomes are endogenous. However, these results for the budget constraint need to be extended when the more fundamental distribution is that of wage rates, rather than of earnings.

The purpose of the present chapter is therefore to examine the government's budget constraint when incomes are endogenous. Section 10.1 considers the linear income tax which has received so much attention in the literature. It is seen that the constraint, even in this simple tax and transfer scheme, cannot be solved analytically, so a numerical procedure for solving the equation is described. The alternative schemes involving a tax-free threshold and the minimum income guarantee are discussed in sections 10.2 and 10.3. Heterogeneous tastes are introduced in section 10.4. Finally, the relationship between revenue and aggregate tax rates is discussed in section 10.5. All the results in this chapter apply to the case where individuals have Cobb–Douglas utility functions.

10.1   THE LINEAR INCOME TAX

In the linear income tax scheme, the unconditional transfer, a, is paid to all individuals. In a pure transfer system in which taxes are used only to finance transfer payments, this transfer must equal the tax revenue per person. The tax revenue is the tax rate, t, multiplied by arithmetic mean earnings, $\bar{y}$, so that there is a simple relationship between a and t given by $a = t\bar{y}$. When earnings are endogenous, the arithmetic mean depends on individuals' labour supplies and the wage rate distribution. The derivation of average earnings depends on the way in which heterogeneity is introduced into the model. In Chapter 9 it was stated that most studies assume only that there is a dispersion in the wage rate faced by individuals, who have identical preferences. This means that a distribution of wages, $F(w)$, is sufficient. The case of variations in tastes will be discussed in section 10.4. For the moment, average earnings are obtained using the fact that each individual's earnings are $w(1 - h)$, by:

$$\bar{y} = \int_{w_L}^{\infty} w(1-h)dF(w) \tag{10.1}$$

The value of w_L is $a(1 - \alpha)/\{\alpha(1 - t)\}$, as shown in equation (9.18). It is the threshold level of the wage rate above which individuals work. The relationship between earnings and the wage rate is given by (9.17). It is convenient to rewrite this expression as:

$$y = \alpha w - \psi$$

where:

$$\psi = a(1 - \alpha)/(1 - t) \tag{10.2}$$

Substituting for $w(1-h)$ into (10.1), using (10.2), gives arithmetic mean earnings of:

$$\bar{y} = \alpha \int_{w_L}^{\infty} wdF(w) - \psi \int_{w_L}^{\infty} dF(w) \tag{10.3}$$

If $F_1(w)$ denotes the incomplete first moment distribution function of w, the arithmetic mean can be rewritten as:

$$\bar{y} = \alpha\bar{w}\{1 - F_1(w_L)\} - \psi\{1 - F(w_L)\} \tag{10.4}$$

This is determined using a direct application of the approach introduced in section 4.2. In the present context $F_1(w)$ represents the proportion of maximum potential earnings (when $h = 0$) obtainable by those facing a wage rate not exceeding w. It has been seen that the general function $G(y)$, introduced in Chapter 4, is very useful. Inspection of (10.4) shows that a similar function, $G_\psi(w)$, in terms of the wage rate, may be defined. Hence write:

$$G_\psi(w_L) = \{1 - F_1(w_L)\} - (\psi/\alpha\bar{w})\{1 - F(w_L)\} \tag{10.5}$$

so that average income is conveniently expressed as $\bar{y} = \alpha\bar{w}G_\psi(w_L)$. The government budget constraint, as with a fixed distribution of earnings, is given by $a = t\bar{y}$, but with $\bar{y}$ as given by (10.4). The complexity arises because $\bar{y}$

depends on w_L and ψ, both of which depend on the values of a and t. The budget constraint is therefore highly non-linear and can only be solved using numerical methods. This requires the use of an explicit functional form for $F(w)$.

An iterative procedure for solving the constraint is as follows. Select a tax rate, t, and an appropriate 'starting value' for the transfer, a, say a_0. Then evaluate the various terms such as w_L and the corresponding integrals, and by substituting into the constraint $a = t\bar{y}$, obtain another value of a, say a_1. If $a_1 > a_0$, increase a_0 slightly and repeat the process, while if $a_1 < a_0$ reduce a_0 slightly. The process is stopped when the two values of the transfer are sufficiently close. Notice that the approach proceeds by finding the value of the threshold corresponding to a specified tax rate, rather than the other way round. This is because there is no unique tax rate corresponding to a given threshold, and the attempt to solve for t would give rise to convergence problems. If the distribution of wage rates follows the lognormal form, then the useful properties of this distribution can allow the various integrals to be evaluated quite easily.

An example of the type of relationship between a and t obtained for the linear income tax is shown in Figure 10.1. With no labour supply responses, there would simply be a straight line through the origin, but in the present case the social dividend is lower and there is a maximum value that can be financed. The precise maximum depends on the distribution of wage rates and the preference parameter α. Each value of the unconditional transfer, a, can be financed with two tax rates, the higher of which involves a larger proportion of individuals who do not work at all. This relationship may intercept the tax rate axis before t reaches unity if $F(w_L)$ reaches unity first. In considering alternative rates it should be remembered that in a pure transfer system such as that examined here, all redistribution is from those above to those below the arithmetic mean value of earnings. Those

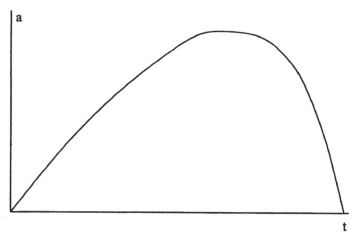

Figure 10.1   Government constraint with the linear income tax

below the arithmetic mean face a negative effective average tax rate, irrespective of the marginal rate.

Some detailed examples are given in Table 10.1, which is based on a lognormal distribution of wage rates with a variance of logarithms of 0.5. The government budget constraint was solved numerically using the above approach, and results are given for values of α, the coefficient on consumption in the Cobb–Douglas utility functions, of 0.5 and 0.9; these represent relatively low and high values. The values of the social dividend, a, and the wage, w_L, below which individuals do not work (and are at a corner solution) are given relative to the median value of the wage rate. This means that the results in Table 10.1 do not depend on the mean of logarithms of the wage rate distributions. Not surprisingly, a higher value of α implies that a larger proportion of people work and the value of the social dividend, a, can be increased much more, compared with the lower value of α.

Table 10.1   The linear income tax

	$\alpha = 0.5$			$\alpha = 0.9$		
t	a	w_L	$F(w_L)$	a	w_L	$F(w_L)$
0.2	0.114	0.142	0.003	0.225	0.031	—
0.3	0.158	0.226	0.018	0.332	0.053	—
0.4	0.193	0.322	0.054	0.433	0.080	—
0.5	0.216	0.432	0.118	0.524	0.117	0.001
0.6	0.226	0.565	0.210	0.602	0.167	0.006
0.7	0.221	0.735	0.332	0.656	0.243	0.023
0.8	0.195	0.977	0.487	0.665	0.369	0.080
0.9	0.141	1.408	0.686	0.569	0.633	0.259

Note: Values of a and w_L are given as ratios of the median wage rate.

10.2   THE TAX-FREE THRESHOLD

The linear income tax is the simplest possible form of tax and transfer system. More complex transfer schemes can be approached in the same manner, with particular attention given to the limits of integration of the various ranges of w which need to be considered, using the results from Chapter 9. However, they do not generate fundamentally different problems, and iterative methods of solution are always required. For example, with a proportional tax system applied to income measured in excess of a threshold, the condition under which a constant amount of revenue per person, R, is raised *ex post* can be established.

As before, earnings can be written as the linear function, $y = w(1 - h) = \alpha w - \psi$ where ψ is now equal to $at(1 - \alpha)/(1 - t)$. The budget constraint of the government is obtained as:

$$R = t \int_{w_L}^{\infty} (\alpha w - \psi - a) dF(w)$$

$$= t \left[\alpha \bar{w} \{1 - F_1(w_L)\} - (\psi + a)\{1 - F(w_L)\} \right] \qquad (10.6)$$

where w_L is in this context given by $w_L = at(1 - \alpha)/\alpha(1 - t)$. This form of the constraint can be expressed more succinctly using the function $G_\psi(w)$ defined in (10.5) above. Comparison shows that $R = \alpha t \bar{w} \, G_{\psi+a}(w_L)$. Again, this can be solved iteratively for the threshold, a, given a specified tax rate, t, and other parameters of the system.

10.3 THE MODIFIED MINIMUM INCOME GUARANTEE

Consider next the non-linear tax and transfer system with a taper, giving rise to the convex budget constraint discussed in Chapters 5 and 9, and described as a modified minimum income guarantee. It was found that two cases need to be distinguished according to the relative values of w_L and w_s. Where $w_s > w_L$, each individual with $w > w_s$ pays tax equal to $t(y - a)$ while all those with $w_L < w < w_s$ receive benefits of $s(a - y)$. Furthermore, those with $w < w_L$ each receive a benefit equal to as. For a pure transfer scheme, the government's constraint can be expressed in the following form:

$$as \int_0^{w_L} dF(w) + s \int_{w_L}^{w_s} \{a - (\alpha w - \psi_s)\} dF(w) = t \int_{w_s}^{\infty} \{(\alpha w - \psi_t) - a\} dF(w) \quad (10.7)$$

This uses the general expression for earnings, introduced in (10.2) of $y = \alpha w - \psi$, where two values of ψ need to be distinguished according to which range of the individual's budget constraint is relevant. These values are given by $\psi_s = as(1 - \alpha)/(1 - s)$ and $\psi_t = at(1 - \alpha)/(1 - t)$.

It has been shown in Chapter 9 that the minimum wage above which individuals work, w_L, is equal to $as(1 - \alpha)/\{\alpha(1 - s)\}$. The wage at which individuals switch from one linear section of the convex budget constraint to the other, w_s, is from Chapter 9 given by:

$$w_s = \frac{a(\theta s - t)}{(1-t) - \theta(1-s)} \tag{10.8}$$

$$\theta = \left\{ \frac{1-t}{1-s} \right\}^{1-\alpha} \tag{10.9}$$

Suppose first that $w_s > w_L$, which is the typical situation. The expression in (10.7) can be rearranged and simplified using the now familiar approach involving the first moment distribution function, as follows. Expanding each side of (10.7) and using the first moment distribution, $F_1(w)$, gives:

$$asF(w_L) + s(a + \psi_s) \{F(w_s) - F(w_L)\} - \alpha s \bar{w} \{F_1(w_s) - F_1(w_L)\}$$
$$= \alpha t \bar{w} \{1 - F_1(w_s)\} - t(a + \psi_t) \{1 - F(w_s)\}$$

In order to simplify this expression, it is useful to define the function $G_x(w_1, w_2)$, based on a modification of (10.5) as follows:

$$G_x(w_1, w_2) = \{F_1(w_1) - F_1(w_2)\} - (x/\alpha \bar{w}) \{F(w_1) - F(w_2)\} \tag{10.10}$$

Hence $G_x(\infty, w) = G_x(w)$. Using this expression, the above result can be written more succinctly as:

$$asF(w_L) - \alpha \bar{w} s\, G_{a+\psi_s}(w_s, w_L) = \alpha \bar{w} t\, G_{a+\psi_t}(w_s)$$

and by collecting terms, the parameter, a, can be expressed as

$$a = \frac{\alpha \bar{w} \{ s G_{\psi_s}(w_s, w_L) + t G_{\psi_t}(w_s) \}}{[sF(w_s) + t\{1 - F(w_s)\}]} \tag{10.11}$$

This is non-linear because various terms on the right-hand side contain the threshold, a, but it can be used to solve iteratively for the threshold, given the other parameters, following the type of procedure described earlier, in section 10.1. If net revenue is required to be positive, then the value of revenue per person is subtracted from the numerator of (10.11).

Where $w_L > w_s$, it was shown in Chapter 9 that an alternative threshold, w_m, needs to be calculated using the non-linear equation (9.32). In this situation individuals either do not work and receive a transfer, as, or they work and pay tax of $t(y - a)$. Hence the revised budget constraint is given by:

$$as \int_0^{w_m} dF(w) = t \int_{w_m}^{\infty} \{(\alpha w - \psi_t) - a\} dF(w) \qquad (10.12)$$

Following the usual procedure, this reduces to the following expression for the threshold in terms of other values:

$$a = \frac{\alpha \bar{w} t G_{\psi_t}(w_m)}{sF(w_m) + t\{1 - F(w_m)\}} \qquad (10.13)$$

This can be solved iteratively for the threshold, given a set of tax parameters and a specified wage rate distribution.

Some examples of the various thresholds and rates are given in Table 10.2. These values were obtained for a lognormal wage rate distribution having a variance of logarithms of 0.5, and a value of α of 0.7. The values of a and w reported in the table are actually the corresponding values expressed as ratios of the median wage rate. A positive net revenue per person of 2,000 was assumed, with a value of the mean log-wage of 10. For the higher value of s of 0.9, it was found that $w_L > w_s$ in all cases except that of the high value of $t = 0.8$. Hence it was necessary to obtain w_m and use the constraint in (10.13), with net revenue per person deducted from the numerator. Otherwise $w_s > w_L$ and the form in (10.11) is appropriate. In each case there is an upper limit to the size of the threshold, a, that can be financed. The incentive effects of the higher taper rate, s, are clearly shown in the table by the lower thresholds for each value of t and the higher values of w_m with $s = 0.9$ compared with w_L when $s = 0.8$. With the higher taper rate, a substantially larger proportion of people do not work, and therefore receive the maximum transfer available.

Table 10.2   The modified minimum income guarantee

		$s = 0.9$				$s = 0.8$	
t	a	w_L	w_s	w_m	a	w_L	w_s
0.2	0.230	—	—	0.535	0.255	0.437	0.519
0.3	0.289	—	—	0.705	0.323	0.554	0.684
0.4	0.322	—	—	0.834	0.364	0.624	0.806
0.5	0.341	—	—	0.946	0.390	0.668	0.910
0.6	0.347	—	—	1.051	0.402	0.689	1.005
0.7	0.338	—	—	1.153	0.399	0.684	1.095
0.8	0.310	1.102	1.244	—	—	—	—

Note: $\sigma_w^2 = 0.5$; $\alpha = 0.7$. All values are reported as ratios of the median wage rate.

10.4 HETEROGENEOUS TASTES

It has been explicitly assumed that individuals differ only in the wage rate that they face, but they have the same tastes and face the same tax structure. Suppose instead that all individuals have the same type of Cobb–Douglas utility function, but have different parameters α with $0 \leq \alpha \leq 1$. In the linear income tax scheme, it is useful in this context to indicate that ψ now differs between individuals. Therefore, write gross earnings as:

$$y = w(1 - h) = \alpha w - \psi_\alpha \qquad (10.14)$$

where $\psi_\alpha = a(1 - \alpha)/(1 - t)$. This interior solution holds for $w > w_{L,\alpha} = a(1 - \alpha)/\alpha(1 - t)$. Let $S(\alpha)$ denote the distribution function of the coefficient on consumption in individuals' utility functions, and $F_\alpha(w \mid \alpha)$ the conditional distribution of w, for given α. Arithmetic mean earnings can be written as follows:

$$\bar{y} = \int_0^1 \left\{ \int_{w_{L,\alpha}}^\infty (\alpha w - \psi_\alpha) dF_\alpha(w \mid \alpha) \right\} dS(\alpha) \qquad (10.15)$$

This expression can be further simplified to give:

$$\bar{y} = \int_0^1 \left[\alpha \bar{w}_\alpha \left\{ 1 - F_{1,\alpha}(w_{L,\alpha}) \right\} - \psi_\alpha \left\{ 1 - F_\alpha(w_{L,\alpha}) \right\} \right] dS(\alpha) \qquad (10.16)$$

where $F_{1,\alpha}$ denotes the first moment distribution function of the marginal distribution of w, for a given value of α, and $\bar{w}_\alpha$ denotes the conditional arithmetic mean wage, for given α. Again, the function G, defined in (10.5), may be used, so that (10.16) may be written as:

$$\bar{y} = \int \alpha \bar{w}_\alpha G_{\psi_\alpha}(w_{L,\alpha}) \, dS(\alpha) \qquad (10.17)$$

The introduction of heterogeneous tastes therefore requires the specification of a set of conditional distributions in addition to the marginal distribution of α, and complicates the government budget constraint, but it does not really introduce any fundamentally new problems. Numerical exercises show that if those with higher wages have, on average, a lower preference for consumption relative to leisure (lower α), then arithmetic mean income is lower than if the high-wage people preferred consumption to leisure. For example, suppose that the coefficient α is lognormally distributed with parameters μ_α and σ_α^2. If the wage rate of the ith individual is w_i, then the corresponding simulated value of

α_i, can be obtained from the appropriate conditional distribution. Hence if v_i is a random variable drawn from $N(0,1)$:

$$\alpha_i = \exp\left[\mu_\alpha + \rho(\sigma_\alpha / \sigma_w)(\log w_i - \mu_w) + v_i \sigma_\alpha \sqrt{1 - \rho^2}\right] \quad (10.18)$$

It is thereby possible to generate a simulated joint distribution of w and α. Using a variance of log-wages of 0.5 and a simulated population of 5,000 individuals, the resulting examples are given in Table 10.3. The assumed arithmetic mean of α is 0.7 while the variance of logarithms is 0.10 (so that the mean of the logarithms of α is -0.41).

Table 10.3   The linear income tax with heterogeneous preferences

	$\rho = -0.75$			$\rho = 0.75$		
t	a	$\bar{z}$	A(0.5)	a	$\bar{z}$	A(0.5)
0.2	0.136	0.682	0.050	0.172	0.859	0.134
0.4	0.241	0.602	0.034	0.309	0.773	0.095
0.6	0.293	0.490	0.022	0.401	0.669	0.057
0.8	0.258	0.322	0.011	0.416	0.520	0.023

Note: $\bar{\alpha} = 0.7$; $\sigma_\alpha^2 = 0.10$; $\sigma_w^2 = 0.5$. The values of the social dividend, a, and the arithmetic mean net income are given as ratios of the meidan wage rate. Results are based on a simulated population of 5,000 individuals.

These results are for two alternative values of the correlation between the logarithms of w and α. In addition to showing the social dividend that can be financed with alternative tax rates, the arithmetic mean, $\bar{z}$, of net income is also shown, in both cases as ratios of the median wage rate. Furthermore, Atkinson's inequality measure of net income is reported. The high positive correlation, so that those who have a relatively lower preference for leisure face a higher wage rate, substantially increases not just the level of incomes, but also its inequality.

10.5   TAX REVENUE AND THE AGGREGATE TAX RATE

Previous sections of this chapter have concentrated on the interdependencies between tax rates, thresholds and net revenue which are implied by the government's budget constraint.

In the simplest case of a tax-free threshold with no transfer payments, section 10.2 shows how the threshold and the marginal tax rate are related, for a given amount of revenue per person. It is, however, also of interest to consider the variation in tax revenue as one of the tax parameters changes with the other held constant. For example, as the marginal rate, t, increases, with the threshold fixed, the tax revenue per person, R, rises initially as the higher rate outweighs the reduction in the tax base resulting from labour supply effects. Eventually dR/dt becomes negative as the incentive effects dominate, and at some stage revenue is zero when no individual works. This relationship can be converted into one between revenue and the aggregate tax rate. Where $\bar{y}$ and $\bar{z}$ denote average gross and net income respectively, the aggregate tax rate, T, is defined as $(\bar{y} - \bar{z})/\bar{y}$ while total revenue per person is $\bar{y} - \bar{z}$. Notice that if pre-tax incomes are independent of the tax structure, $\bar{y}$ is fixed and the relationship between T and R is trivial. In the present context the inverted U-shaped relationship between R and t converts into a loop, starting and ending at the origin, between R and T. There is a limit to values of both T and R that can be achieved.

The case of the modified minimum income guarantee is more complicated because of the existence of an additional tax parameter, the taper rate, s, applied to the transfer payments obtained by those below the threshold, a. The range of variation in the marginal tax rate, t, applied above the threshold is constrained since $0 \leq t \leq s$. Examples of the general type of relationship obtained between R and T are shown in Figure 10.2. In 10.2(a) the taper rate, s, is relatively low, while in 10.2(b) the taper rate is high, allowing the marginal tax rate to increase more. The figure illustrates schedules for three alternative thresholds, such that $a_1 < a_2 < a_3$. When the taper is low, the schedules end before they become backward-bending, whereas if the taper is high the increase in t means that the schedules turn backwards. For a high threshold and a high taper, the relationship becomes a complete loop when the increasing tax rate reduces the tax base to zero and no individual works. It is important to realize that the schedule may loop back all the way to the origin before the marginal rate, t, reaches unity.

This chapter has extended previous expressions for the government's budget constraint, by allowing for endogenous labour supplies. The results were obtained for the linear income tax, the tax-free threshold and the modified minimum income guarantee, where all individuals are assumed to have Cobb–Douglas utility functions. In each case the expression for the budget constraint involved various integrals of lognormal wage distributions.

The limits of integration typically include the parameters of interest, so that the equations are highly non-linear. However, they can be solved numerically using simple iterative methods. The emphasis of this chapter has inevitably been on the technicalities of deriving the expressions for the constraints and their solution. These results provide the foundations for the further analysis of tax and transfer systems, given in the following chapter.

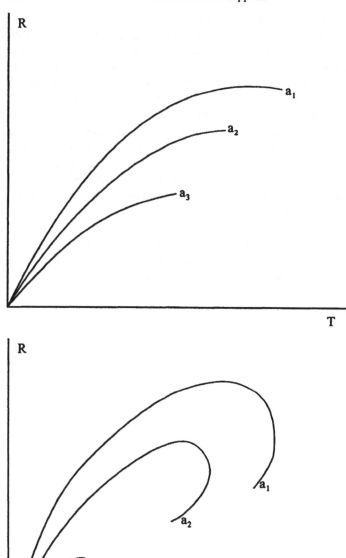

Figure 10.2   Tax revenue and the aggregate tax rate

11. Equity and efficiency

An increase in taxation can be designed to reduce inequality, but there may be a cost in terms of the effect on labour supply incentives. This raises the standard problem of the trade-off between 'equity and efficiency' – more clearly stated in terms of equity versus average (or total) income. This forms the subject of the present chapter.

Individuals are assumed in Chapter 9 to be maximizing their own utility by an appropriate choice of consumption and labour supply, given the parameters of the tax and transfer system imposed by the government. The government must in turn set the parameters in order to ensure that the independent actions of many individuals are mutually consistent. Thus, the transfers must be financed from the endogenous earnings which in turn depend on those transfers. This consistency is achieved when the government's budget constraint, discussed in the previous chapter, is satisfied. However, it is also appropriate to suppose that the government has some objective of its own which it attempts to achieve, subject to its need to ensure the mutual consistency of all individuals' plans. The context is one in which some individuals gain from a change in the tax structure while others lose, so that the concept of Pareto efficiency is of little use, although a range of Pareto-inefficient changes can be identified.

Further analysis therefore requires the use of explicit value judgements involving interpersonal comparisons. A welfare function, specified in terms of individuals' utilities, is discussed in section 11.1. The optimal tax problem is examined in section 11.2, and section 11.3 presents the typical form taken by the relevant relationships. Section 11.4 then turns to the problem of evaluating alternative tax and transfer systems raised in Chapter 8. This section extends the earlier result, relating to equal poverty comparisons, to the case of endogenous earnings. An alternative mechanism for modelling the government's choice of tax systems, that of majority voting, is examined in Chapter 13.

11.1 A SOCIAL WELFARE FUNCTION

It is first necessary to stress that in this chapter a cardinal concept of utility is used, and interpersonal comparisons are involved. The analysis can be described as one of exploring the implications of adopting specified value judgements. The government may be assumed, given a fixed population size, to maximize a simple sum of utility; this is the basic 'classical utilitarian' position, which attaches an equal weight to all individuals. Alternatively, the government may be concerned only to maximize the welfare of the worst-off members of society. Analytically, it is necessary to specify an objective function that is sufficiently flexible to allow for a wide range of value judgements. Alternative welfare functions were discussed in Chapter 2, and associated abbreviated welfare functions were examined. However, the literature on taxes and transfers has concentrated on the form of social welfare function where welfare, W, is defined as a weighted sum of individual utilities U_i, as follows:

$$W = \frac{1}{1-\varepsilon} \sum_i U_i^{1-\varepsilon} \qquad \text{for } \varepsilon \neq 1 \qquad (11.1)$$

$$= \sum_i \log(U_i) \qquad \text{for } \varepsilon = 1 \qquad (11.2)$$

The case where $\varepsilon = 0$ corresponds to a social welfare function which is the unweighted sum of individual utilities; this is the 'classical utilitarian' type. From (11.1), $\partial W/\partial U_i = U_i^{-\varepsilon}$, so that for $\varepsilon > 0$ marginal social welfare is a decreasing function of individual utility. A higher value of ε indicates therefore a greater preference for equality, or a higher degree of inequality aversion. An infinitely large value of ε leads to a social welfare function of the 'maxi-min' type, whereby the objective is to maximize the utility of the least well-off person. Notice that the discussion has been in terms of individual *utilities* rather than incomes; where individuals place value on leisure it is more appropriate to do this than to specify a social welfare function in terms of incomes.

It is important to recognize that the results of adopting this approach depend on both the value of ε and the particular cardinalization of individuals' utility functions. For example, in considering individual utility maximization, the optimal choice of leisure and consumption is identical whether the utility function $c^\alpha h^{1-\alpha}$ is used or the monotonic transformation $\alpha \log c + (1 - \alpha) \log h$. But it can be seen that the former, when combined with $\varepsilon = 1$, leads to exactly the same form of W as when the latter is combined with $\varepsilon = 0$. However, the use of (11.1) is useful, as seen in Chapter 2, partly because it allows for an explicit trade-off between efficiency and equality, when the measure of inequality used is Atkinson's measure, $A(\varepsilon)$, defined (in terms of the distribution of utility) by:

$$A(\varepsilon) = 1 - U_e /\bar{U} \qquad (11.3)$$

where $\bar{U}$ is arithmetic mean utility and U_e is the 'equally distributed equivalent' utility level which, if enjoyed by each individual, would generate the same social welfare as the actual distribution. This measure was introduced in Chapter 2 in terms of incomes. Hence:

$$U_e = \left\{ \frac{1}{N} \sum_i U_i^{1-\varepsilon} \right\}^{1/(1-\varepsilon)} \tag{11.4}$$

and since from (11.3), $U_e = \bar{U}\{1 - A(\varepsilon)\}$, social welfare per person can be written as:

$$\frac{W}{N} = \frac{\left[\bar{U}\{1 - A(\varepsilon)\}\right]^{1-\varepsilon}}{1-\varepsilon} \tag{11.5}$$

Hence indifference curves have the slope $d\bar{U}/dA(\varepsilon) = \bar{U}\{1 - A(\varepsilon)\}^{-1}$. The optimal rate for any given tax and transfer structure is represented by a tangency position of a social indifference curve with the curve of average utility plotted against the inequality measure, where both sets of curves are obtained using the same value of ε.

11.2   OPTIMAL LINEAR TAXATION

The tangency solution described above represents the diagrammatic analog of the first-order conditions for maximization of the social welfare function, subject to the restriction that all individuals achieve their constrained optimum and the government budget constraint is satisfied. Some insight into the nature of these first-order conditions may be obtained by considering the linear income tax. The government must select the values of the transfer, a, and the tax rate, t, which maximize $W = \sum_i G(U_i)$, subject to the constraint that $a = t\bar{y}$.

Simultaneously individuals are maximizing $U(c_i, h_i)$ subject to the constraint that $c_i = a + w_i (1 - h_i)(1 - t)$, giving $U_i = V(w_i, a, t, \alpha)$. Remembering that $\bar{y}$ is a function of α, a, t and $F(w)$, the Lagrangean for the optimal tax problem is thus:

$$L = W + \lambda (t\bar{y} - a) \tag{11.6}$$

The first-order conditions can be written as:

$$\frac{\partial L}{\partial a} = \sum_i \frac{\partial G}{\partial U_i} \frac{\partial U_i}{\partial a} + \lambda \left(t \frac{\partial \bar{y}}{\partial a} - 1 \right) = 0 \qquad (11.7)$$

$$\frac{\partial L}{\partial t} = \sum_i \frac{\partial G}{\partial U_i} \frac{\partial U_i}{\partial t} + \lambda \left(\bar{y} + t \frac{\partial \bar{y}}{\partial t} \right) = 0 \qquad (11.8)$$

These may initially appear to be fairly straightforward, but the general treatment of the first-order conditions is very awkward; see, for example, Mirrlees (1976), Dixit and Sandmo (1977) and Atkinson and Stiglitz (1980, pp. 405–8). Further progress requires more structure to be imposed on the model, along with numerical analysis. Few general comparative static results are available. For a diagrammatic comparative static analysis of the linear income tax in a model with just two individuals, see Ihori (1987).

When making numerical calculations it is necessary to search for the combination of tax parameters, satisfying the government's budget constraint, which maximize social welfare, W. With a two-parameter income tax function, search involves iterating over just one parameter, because the government's budget constraint removes a degree of freedom. Chapter 10 has shown how the government's budget constraint can be written analytically in terms of the underlying distribution of wage rates, even though its solution needs an iterative procedure. The maximization of W is, however, more complicated because the relationship between each individual's utility and the wage rate faced is too awkward to allow W to be expressed in terms of the tax parameters, which in turn depend on the distribution function of w; this is mainly because of the existence of non-wage-related income.

This awkward problem must be overcome by generating a simulated population of individuals. For each individual, a simulated wage rate can be generated as follows: if v represents a random variable drawn from an $N(0,1)$ distribution, then $\exp\{\mu + v\sigma\}$ is a random wage from a $\Lambda(\mu,\sigma^2)$ distribution. The use of iterative methods to solve non-linear government budget constraints, along with large simulated populations of thousands of individuals, can be handled without serious difficulties using modern microcomputers. The analytical results derived in Chapter 10 can be used to solve for the government's budget constraint (using an iterative routine), giving the tax parameters. These parameters can then be used with the simulated population in order to derive each person's choice of labour supply, consumption and hence level of utility.

Some illustrative examples are shown in Table 11.1, which is based on a simulated population of 5,000 individuals and a variance of logarithms of wage rates of 0.5. The optimal tax rate is given for alternative values of α, the coefficient on consumption in each individual's utility function, and ε, the inequality aversion coefficient. The corresponding values of the social dividend, a, and the wage rate above which individuals work, w_L, are shown in relation to the median wage rate, so that the results in Table 11.1 are independent of the mean of logarithms of wage rates. The effect of a higher aversion to inequality is, as expected, to raise the optimal tax rate. Similarly, a higher preference for consumption relative to leisure not only implies a higher optimal tax rate, but also gives rise to a substantially larger social dividend. As expected, the wage above which individuals work is much lower for the higher values of α.

Table 11.1   The optimal linear income tax

	$\varepsilon = 0.5$			$\varepsilon = 1.5$
α	0.5	0.7	0.9	0.7
t	0.35	0.39	0.48	0.46
a	0.177	0.294	0.508	0.330
w_L	0.273	0.207	0.109	0.262

Notes: All values are produced for a lognormal wage rate distribution with $\sigma_w^2 = 0.5$.
The values of a and w_L are expressed as ratios of the median wage rate. Simulated population size is 5,000 individuals.

Redistribution and Progressivity

Chapter 3 presented a number of summary measures of tax progressivity, along with the concept of the welfare premium from progression, in the context of a fixed distribution of pre-tax incomes. The behaviour of these measures is considered briefly here, where incomes are endogenous. Consider a linear income tax which, unlike the pure transfer system discussed above, raises some net revenue from taxation. First, it is necessary to obtain appropriate measures regarding a proportional tax system which raises the same revenue. If individuals maximize $U = c^\alpha h^{1-\alpha}$, face a proportional tax and have no non-wage income, their full income is $w(1 - t)$ and labour supply is constant at α, while net income, c, is given by $\alpha(1 - t)w$. Hence if revenue of R per person is raised, this requires a tax rate, t, given by solving $R = t\bar{y} = t\alpha\bar{w}$. Net income is proportional to the wage rate, so the Atkinson and Gini measures of inequality of net income can be obtained directly from the explicit expressions for lognormal distributions given in the appendix to Chapter 2. These can be used to obtain post-tax social welfare, based on net incomes, from the corresponding abbreviated social welfare functions.

Substituting for c and h into the utility function gives:

$$U = \{\alpha w (1 - t)\}^{\alpha} (1 - \alpha)^{1-\alpha}$$
$$= kw^{\alpha} \qquad (11.9)$$

where $k = \{\alpha(1 - t)\}^{\alpha} (1 - \alpha)^{1-\alpha}$. Thus, from the general relationship regarding transformations, stated in Appendix 2.1, utility is distributed as $\Lambda (\log k + \alpha\mu_{w}, \alpha^{2}\sigma_{w}^{2})$. This result can be used to find average utility and the measures of inequality, from which the abbreviated welfare function, in terms of cardinal utility, can be obtained.

A point to stress when incomes are endogenous is that under the linear income tax an increase in the tax rate, t, will produce an increase in the inequality of pre-tax incomes, although that of post-tax incomes falls. The redistributive effect of taxation appears therefore to increase, as t increases, by more than it would if incomes are fixed. As t increases, some individuals move to the corner of the budget constraint where they do not work, so their pre-tax incomes are zero. Where any incomes are zero the Atkinson inequality measure cannot be calculated as it is only defined for positive incomes. Hence, in the following examples, only Gini measures are reported.

Results are shown in Table 11.2 for a population of 5,000 individuals selected at random from a lognormal wage rate distribution with μ_{w} and σ_{w}^{2} of 8 and 0.5 respectively. All individuals have $\alpha = 0.70$ and the net revenue is set at 200. This net revenue could be obtained from a proportional tax system with a tax rate of 0.0746, and this would give rise to a Gini-based measure of welfare, based on the abbreviated welfare function in terms of net income, of 0.5132 (expressed as a ratio of the median wage rate). Table 11.2 shows, in the second two columns, the extent to which pre-tax inequality increases while post-tax inequality falls. The table also shows how the overall tax rate, that is total tax revenue (held constant at 200) divided by total pre-tax income, rises because of the fall in labour supply as t increases. The Kakwani and Suits progressivity measures are very similar and increase rapidly as t increases; this increase in measured progressivity is much larger than when pre-tax incomes are constant.

The final two columns of the table give alternative measures of the welfare premium, based on the Gini measure in terms of incomes. The last column shows the values that would be obtained using the formula given in Chapter 3 for the case where pre-tax incomes are assumed to be fixed. These increase substantially as t rises, and this result is associated with the increasing spread between pre- and post-tax income distributions. However, the penultimate column shows the 'true' premium; that is, the difference between social welfare under the linear tax and social welfare under the proportional tax raising the same net revenue. This premium can be seen to be negative for the higher tax rates; social welfare based on incomes would be higher with a proportional (non-progressive) tax system rather than the linear income tax.

Table 11.2   Linear taxation with net revenue

	Income inequality		Tax ratio	Kakwani	Suits	Welfare premium from progression	
t	Pre-tax	Post-tax				True	Measured
0.1	0.384	0.374	0.0752	0.1266	0.1268	0.00185	0.00847
0.2	0.398	0.346	0.0778	0.6262	0.6266	0.00426	0.04174
0.3	0.417	0.317	0.0811	1.1250	1.1256	0.00103	0.07476
0.4	0.441	0.289	0.0855	1.6210	1.6218	–0.00934	0.10736
0.5	0.472	0.260	0.0916	2.1063	2.1073	–0.02855	0.13907

Notes: Net revenue = 200: μ_w = 8.0; σ_w^2 = 0.5; α = 0.70. Results are based on a simulated population of 5,000 individuals. Welfare measures are given as ratios of median wage rate. Inequality and welfare are all based on the Gini measure.

All these values are based on incomes rather than utilities, and it has been suggested that a welfare evaluation would include the value of leisure to individuals. The optimal rate, based on a welfare function of the form (11.1), or of course its abbreviated form, is in this case $t = 0.45$ when $\varepsilon = 1.2$. The relative performance of these alternative measures displayed here should be kept in mind when evaluating empirical distributions.

The Optimal Rate Schedule

The above discussion has concentrated on the optimal linear income tax, and this has received most attention in the literature. However, it is important to ask whether the linear tax, with its constant marginal tax rate, is itself optimal. Would a different schedule of marginal rates raise social welfare above the maximum that can be achieved with the linear income tax? It might perhaps be thought that a high aversion to inequality would tend to favour a schedule with increasing marginal rates. However, one of the few theoretical results concerning the rate schedule immediately contradicts this supposition, since it states that the marginal tax rate at the top of the income distribution should be zero; see Heady (1993, p. 26) and Stern (1976) for discussions. This can be seen intuitively by supposing that the richest person (with the highest wage rate) has an income of y^m and that the marginal rate above y^m is positive. A reduction in that marginal rate to zero may increase the labour supply of the richest person, who becomes better off, although there is no effect on total tax revenue. Hence the change is a Pareto improvement. However, this argument is largely of theoretical interest only, since it does not always apply to continuous wage distributions and it is anyway very difficult to identify the highest income in practice.

Early numerical studies showed that the optimal rate schedule is indeed approximately linear. This result shows that a concern for inequality does not necessarily mean a preference for increasing marginal rates. A further implication is that there is no conflict between optimality and administrative convenience. It is an open question as to whether this theoretical result had an influence on policy; most OECD countries have reduced their top marginal rates substantially and moved towards a flatter rate structure (though this is not true of Australia). More recently, Kanbur and Toumala (1994) have examined the optimal rate schedule (using CES utility functions with an elasticity of substitution of 0.5) for a range of values of the dispersion of wage rates and the degree of inequality aversion of the social welfare function. They found that a combination of low wage rate inequality and high inequality aversion leads to a pattern of declining marginal tax rates. But if wage rate inequality is high, marginal rates rise over a substantial range.

Numerical results have therefore shown that a high aversion to inequality does not necessarily lead to high or increasing marginal tax rates. Stern (1976), using an extensive range of simulations, found that (for the linear income tax), the argument for very high tax rates must be based on the argument that the elasticity of substitution is very low. When net revenue is zero, the optimal tax rate is found to fall when the elasticity of substitution rises. However, for positive net revenue, the optimal rate can fall and then rise as the elasticity of substitution rises. This result arises because a minimum rate is required to raise the net revenue, and the minimum increases with the elasticity of substitution.

11.3   THE TYPICAL FORM OF SCHEDULES

The typical shapes of the various relationships involved are illustrated in Figure 11.1 for the linear income tax structure and the Atkinson inequality measure expressed in terms of individual utilities. The top left-hand side of the figure shows arithmetic mean utility plotted against equality, $1 - A(\varepsilon)$, giving a convex set of possibilities. As the tax rate, t, initially increases from $t = 0$, both the measure of equality and arithmetic mean utility increase until the latter reaches a maximum. The tax rate corresponding to this maximum is therefore the optimal tax rate under the so-called classical utilitarian maximand. At high tax rates, increases in equality can only be 'purchased' with large reductions in mean utility; the profile is typically quite flat at lower t and steep for high t. As indicated earlier, realistic choice would not extend beyond the point of maximum transfer, a, even though equality may increase slightly as everyone becomes worse off. Even with extreme aversion to inequality, that is an infinitely large, ε, the best situation for the least well-off person is the combination giving the maximum value of the transfer.

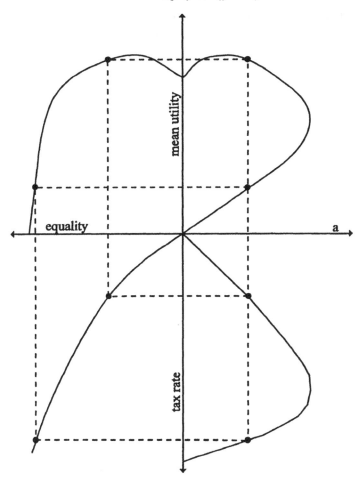

Figure 11.1   Equality, efficiency and tax rates

In Figure 11.1, the top right and bottom left-hand quadrants show how the tax rate and transfer can be read directly from the selected point on the trade-off relationship between equity and efficiency. It should be stressed that an increase in equality, measured in terms of utility, will typically be associated with an increase in the inequality of *pre*-tax-and-transfer income, especially when *t* is increased from relatively low values, although the inequality of *post*-transfer income falls. This suggests that comparisons between pre- and post-tax *income* distributions may be misleading. The discussion has concerned the linear income tax, but the use of a tax-free threshold and constant government revenue produces a set of schedules very similar to those in Figure 11.1.

Inequality has been discussed in terms of the distribution of utility, but within the types of model considered so far, the inequality of *net* income and utility always change in the same direction. The general form of the relationship between the two measures is shown in Figure 11.2. At higher levels of inequality the relationship is virtually linear, though at lower levels the inequality of net income increases much more rapidly than that of utility.

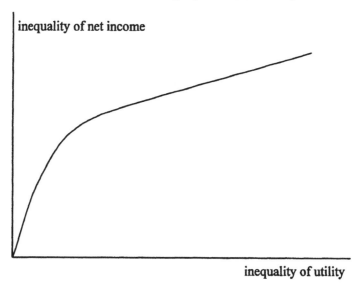

Figure 11.2   Net income and utility

For the modified minimum income guarantee, there is a larger variety of methods of increasing the marginal tax rate while satisfying the government's revenue-neutrality condition. This structure has been examined in detail by Lambert (1985b), who concentrates on the effects of tax changes on the distribution of post-tax-and-transfer income rather than the distribution of utility. Changes which are progressive, in terms of their effect on the inequality of net income, are identified. Constraints on the government's ability to raise the average tax rate within the system are also identified. Lambert (1990) has also used the non-linear tax structure to examine the relationship between the Gini measure of the inequality of consumption (rather than utility) and total income. This provides a rigorous treatment of Breit's (1974) 'output possibility curve', and shows that it may not be concave. The modified minimum income guarantee is used in the following section in order to consider the question of means-testing versus universal benefits.

11.4   EQUAL POVERTY COMPARISONS

A comparison of the minimum income guarantee scheme with a linear income tax involving universal benefits was made in Chapter 8. The comparisons did not use the arbitrary restriction of holding gross expenditure constant but examined a range of social welfare and tax progressivity measures for schemes which involve the same extent of poverty, using measures from the Foster *et al.* (1984) class. It was found that the linear income tax dominated the minimum income guarantee scheme, in the sense that social welfare was higher, except where the 'head count' measure of poverty was used.

A limitation of Chapter 8 is that it did not allow for any potential incentive effects of tax and transfer schemes. In contrast, Kesselman and Garfinkel (1978) compared means-testing and universal provision by explicitly allowing for incentive effects in a two-class model. They examined the conditions under which Pareto improvements can be obtained; that is, by holding the welfare level of the poor group constant across the two schemes, they found the conditions which ensure that the rich class is better off under universal provision. Kesselman and Garfinkel, allowing for administrative aspects and the political control of expenditure, favoured the use of universal benefits. Their analysis has the advantage of allowing for incentives and, by concentrating on two groups, using the weaker value judgement underlying Pareto efficiency rather than using a specific social welfare function. The analysis was extended by Sadka *et al.* (1982) to five groups of workers and an explicit social welfare function, with similar results. Nevertheless the comparisons do not allow for the relief of poverty as an important objective, which is the primary focus of those who use the target efficiency measures and who are in favour of means-testing.

Lambert (1990) evaluated a range of transfer schemes, using the modified minimum income guarantee, in terms of the 'output possibility curve' (OPC) defined in terms of income per head and the Gini measure of income inequality. The tax schedule is sufficiently flexible to range from the minimum income guarantee to the linear income tax, depending on the level of the taper. He referred to this instead as a 'dual-rate negative income tax (NIT)', and when the taper and tax rates are equal the resulting linear income tax was called a 'credit income tax (CIT)'. Allowing for labour supply effects, with identical Cobb–Douglas utility functions for all individuals and a lognormal wage rate distribution, Lambert (1990, p. 97) found that, 'any dual-rate ... NIT can be improved upon by another dual-rate NIT with a higher threshold – and by a flat-rate CTT with a higher threshold'. Furthermore, 'redistribution schemes designed to secure perfect equality below the tax threshold are inferior to all others' (ibid., p. 99). The linear income tax dominates in terms of the output possibility curve because it implies less distortion to labour supply. The evaluation is thus in terms of an abbreviated social welfare function defined in terms of average income and the Gini inequality measure. It is of interest to use alternative social welfare functions and, in view of the fact that utility is attached to leisure, to define social welfare over individuals' utilities rather than incomes.

Neither Kesselman and Garfinkel nor Lambert allow for the extent of poverty in any of their comparisons, although this is the major focus of the target efficiency studies. This section provides comparisons between tax and transfer systems which have more 'common ground' in the way the systems are evaluated. Comparisons are made between schemes in terms of both social welfare and poverty, and labour supply effects are modelled. The relief of poverty is thus to a certain extent regarded as a major objective which places a constraint on a tax and transfer scheme, but the schemes are evaluated using a social welfare function approach, thereby considering redistribution more broadly and allowing for an aversion to inequality. The approach therefore involves a lexicographic ordering, as discussed by Atkinson (1987a).

Simulation Results

The tax and transfer schedule is sufficiently flexible to provide a contrast between the two extremes of means-testing with 100 per cent marginal rates applying to transfer recipients as in the minimum income guarantee, and the case of universal benefits combined with proportional tax applied to everyone as in the linear tax function. The approach used below is to allow the taper rate, s, to vary. For each value of s, the tax rate, t, is varied while the threshold, a, is adjusted to ensure that the government's budget constraint is satisfied with all individuals maximizing utility. For each combination, several poverty measures (based on a specified poverty level) are calculated along with a measure of social welfare based on the abbreviated social welfare function:

$$W = \bar{U}(1 - I_u) \tag{11.9}$$

where $\bar{U}$ is arithmetic mean utility and I_u is a measure of inequality. Two measures of inequality are used, Atkinson's measure and the Gini inequality measure. The rationale for the Gini measure is Sen's (1973) pairwise maxi-min criterion according to which the welfare of any pair of units is the minimum value, and social welfare is the arithmetic mean welfare of all pairs.

The following numerical results are based on the use of a lognormal wage rate distribution with mean and variance of logarithms of 10.0 and 0.5 respectively (implying an arithmetic mean wage of $28,283). The coefficient, α, on consumption in each individual's utility function is set at 0.7. The poverty line below which individuals are judged to be in poverty is $8,000, and it is assumed that the government must raise net (non-transfer) revenue equal to $2,000 per person. Inequality aversion, ε, is set equal to 0.8. The general results discussed

below are not affected by these specific assumptions. The simulated populations consist of 2,000 individuals, drawn at random from the lognormal wage
rate distribution.

The variation in social welfare (both Atkinson- and Gini-based) in three alternative schemes is shown in Figure 11.3 for variations in the marginal tax rate,
t. The schemes shown are the linear income tax, and the modified minimum
income guarantee scheme with the taper, s, equal to 0.8 and 0.5. The profiles
for the various schemes must obviously meet at the point where $s = t$. While t
is varied, the value of the parameter a is calculated to ensure that the government's
budget constraint is met at all times. For the assumed value of ε, the Gini
inequality measure is always greater than the Atkinson measure, so that social
welfare is higher using the Atkinson-based abbreviated welfare function.

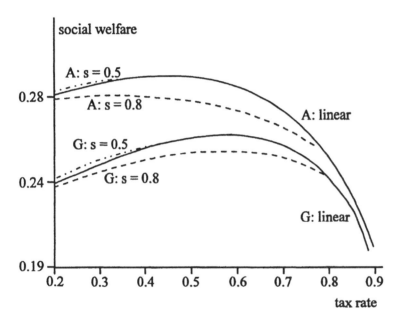

Figure 11.3 Social welfare with alternative transfer systems

It is shown in Figure 11.3 that social welfare is always higher for the linear
income tax than for the means-tested modified minimum income guarantee with
$s = 0.8$ (except of course where $s = t$, when they are equivalent). However, for
the lower value of $s = 0.5$, the social welfare profiles are slightly above those
for the linear income tax. Nevertheless, the maximum value of social welfare
(for both the Atkinson- and Gini-based abbreviated welfare functions) is higher
with the linear tax than with the two-rate schedule.

As suggested earlier, it is important to examine the associated poverty measures, in view of the central role attached to poverty by those using target efficiency measures which support means-testing. The variation in the headcount measure, P_0, with the marginal tax rate, t, is shown for each scheme in Figure 11.4. The values are of course equal when $s = t$. In the case where $s = 0.8$ the intersection occurs where poverty is very high. With the particular poverty line used here of $8,000 (and the other parameters), it is impossible to eliminate poverty whichever scheme is used. This contrasts with the use of a simple assumption of a fixed pre-tax and transfer income distribution where there are, by assumption, no limits to redistribution. For higher tax rates the incentive effects dominate, as both the minimum income falls and the proportion of the population who do not work increases. In the case of the modified minimum income guarantee, with $s = 0.8$, the headcount poverty measure increases for all values of t. However, for lower values of s, this measure initially increases more rapidly and then turns sharply downwards, until it reaches the linear tax schedule (where $t = s$).

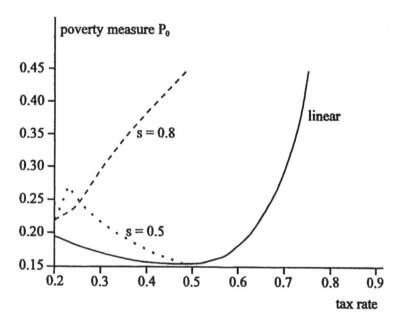

Figure 11.4   Headcount poverty measures

The other poverty measures are shown in Figure 11.5, where it can be seen that these are again lower for the linear income tax than for the modified minimum income guarantee, except for the lower value of the taper rate, s, and the poverty measure P_2. The other poverty measures are, however, always higher than in the linear tax. It is therefore possible to find ranges of the tax rate, t, in the modified minimum income guarantee scheme (with low taper rates) for which social welfare is higher and the poverty measure, P_2, is lower than the linear tax. Despite this result, it should be stressed that even where this result occurs, the *optimum* marginal rate in the linear tax will always produce both a higher value of social welfare, and a lower poverty measure, than any modified minimum income guarantee scheme. The difference is more marked the greater the degree of inequality aversion of the welfare function.

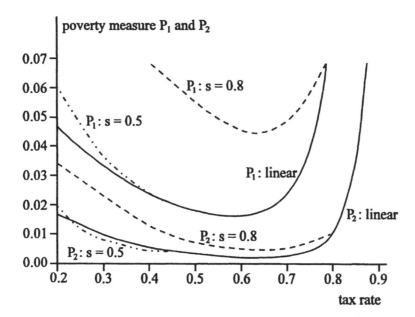

Figure 11.5   Alternative poverty measures and transfer systems

If therefore attention is restricted to optimum tax structures, the adverse incentive effects of the modified minimum income guarantee are such that it is dominated by the optimal linear income tax from the point of view of social welfare *and* a range of poverty measures. Inspection of Figures 11.3 and 11.5 shows that, even for the case where $s = 0.8$ in the two-rate structure, it is possible to find a tax rate, t, (and usually a range of such rates) for which a measure of poverty is the same as in the linear income tax, while social welfare is higher. All that is required is to find a tax rate for which a selected poverty measure is the same in both schemes, but which is sufficiently far from the optimal linear income tax rate. For example, when $s = 0.8$ and $t = 0.31$ in the two-rate structure, the value of P_2 is the same as when $t = 0.83$ in the linear income tax; social welfare (either the Atkinson- or Gini-based measure) is higher in the former than in the latter. But such an equal-poverty comparison does not support the modified minimum income guarantee because both poverty alleviation and social welfare can be improved by lowering the tax rate in the linear income tax.

As mentioned above, Lambert (1990) showed that a linear income tax (with appropriate unconditional transfer) dominates the two-rate scheme in terms of the 'output possibility curve' specified in terms of arithmetic mean net income, $\bar{z}$, and the Gini measure of inequality of net income, G_z. The evaluation is thus in terms of an abbreviated social welfare function of the form $\bar{z}(1 - G_z)$. The present results confirm Lambert's conclusions, but using abbreviated social welfare functions based on individuals' utility rather than net income (which seems more appropriate, given that, with labour supply responses, individuals attach utility to leisure). Furthermore, the welfare functions used included those based on Atkinson as well as Gini measures of inequality; these imply very different social evaluation functions. In addition, the results of this section have shown that the *optimal* linear income tax also dominates the modified minimum guarantee scheme in terms of poverty alleviation, using several poverty measures. This result holds despite the fact that it is possible to find ranges of tax rates over which social welfare in the two-rate scheme and the poverty measure P_2 are superior to the linear income tax at the same tax rates. It is also possible to make equal-poverty comparisons in which social welfare is higher in a two-rate scheme than in a linear income tax scheme. But such non-optimal-rate comparisons are not appropriate, as a better linear income tax rate can be found which improves poverty alleviation and social welfare.

This chapter has shown how the results of the previous two chapters can be applied to the analysis of the trade-off between 'equity and efficiency' in alternative tax systems. The restriction to a single time period of analysis is relaxed in the following chapter.

12.   Two-period models

Chapters 9 to 11 have concentrated on the single-period framework. Relatively less attention has been devoted in the literature to taxation in a multi-period framework, and much of that work has been concerned with the debate over the choice between income and consumption as the appropriate tax base. Even in simple models the relative merits of income and consumption taxes cannot be established unambiguously. Given the extra complexity of the multi-period problem, strong simplifying assumptions have been used. Some studies use an exogenous income stream, while others examine the life-cycle of a representative individual. As with the single-period models, homogeneous preferences are often assumed and the context typically involves a single consumption good. Other studies examine a two-period model in which labour supply is relevant only in the first period. For discussion and further references, see Atkinson and Stiglitz (1980), King (1980), Kay (1990), Auerbach and Kotlikoff (1987).

This chapter provides an exercise in modelling the tax structure in a two-period partial equilibrium framework. Individuals make choices concerning their consumption of two goods and leisure in each period. In producing the model it is necessary to specify the joint distribution of wage rates in the two periods. An approach is used which allows for a variety of types of change in the wage rates of individuals from the first to the second period. However, wage rates are exogenous, so that individual investment in education is not considered. An important component of the model is the specification of heterogeneity.

Individuals have the same basic form of utility function but have different parameter values, including time preference rates. It is necessary to specify the joint distribution of such parameters. The model allows for some correlation between wage rates and preference parameters, in particular the preference for leisure. The analysis uses a Cobb–Douglas form of utility function. The modelling strategy allows the various joint distributions to be specified so that those with relatively higher incomes over the two periods consume relatively more of one of the goods, on average. This allows for systematic redistributive effects of the consumption tax structure. The analysis is of a pure transfer scheme in which all tax revenue is used to provide an unconditional transfer payment to each individual in each period. The emphasis is on the modelling strategy, the process of generating numerical results and the general features of the model.

The framework is described in section 12.1. Great care needs to be taken in dealing with the various corner solutions, and a suitable algorithm is developed. Section 12.2 presents the approach used in specifying population heterogeneity, which is an important component of the model. Section 12.3 considers the government's budget constraint and the nature of the social welfare function used. The section also discusses several examples, including the role of an interest income tax. Finally, section 12.4 considers the case where the second period is a period of retirement for all individuals.

12.1 DEMANDS AND LABOUR SUPPLY: THE BASIC MODEL

Each individual must choose amounts of goods X and Y to consume in each period, denoted x_t and y_t ($t = 1, 2$) respectively, along with leisure, h_t. If the rate of time preference is denoted ξ, with $\theta = 1/(1 + \xi)$, the utility function of each individual is assumed to take the form:

$$U = \alpha \log x_1 + \beta \log y_1 + \gamma \log h_1 + \theta\,(\alpha \log x_2 + \beta \log y_2 + \gamma \log h_2) \quad (12.1)$$

The relative preferences for consumption and leisure, governed by the parameters α, β and γ, remain the same in each period, and there is no loss of generality in writing $\gamma = 1 - \alpha - \beta$. It can be seen that (12.1) is equivalent to a multi-good, single period, Cobb–Douglas utility function. Suppose that in each period there is a linear income tax in operation, with a fixed social dividend of δ paid to each person and a marginal tax rate of t applied to all earned income. In addition, there is an interest income tax applied to all interest income at the same rate, t, as for wage income. Let r denote the nominal rate of interest, so that the proportionality of the tax implies an after-tax interest rate of $r(1 - t)$. In addition, there is a consumption tax scheme such that tax-exclusive rates of t_x and t_y apply to goods X and Y respectively in both periods. With pre-tax prices of p_x and p_y respectively, the tax-inclusive prices are denoted $p'_x = p_x\,(1 + t_x)$ and $p'_y = p_y\,(1 + t_y)$. The general form of the two-period budget constraint can be written:

$$x_1 p'_x + y_1 p'_y + v\,(x_2 p'_x + y_2 p'_y)$$
$$= \delta(1 + v) + (1 - t)\,\{w_1(1 - h_1) + vw_2\,(1 - h_2)p'_x p'_y\} \quad (12.2)$$

where the discount factor, v, is equal to $1/\{1 + r(1 - t)\}$ if the individual lends in the first period, but is simply $1/(1 + r)$ if the individual borrows. The wage rates faced by the individual are w_t ($t = 1, 2$), and these are assumed to be exogenous.

Given the form of the utility function in (12.1), the form of the interior solutions is quite straightforward. For example, the demand for each good is equal to the product of two terms: the first term is the ratio of the coefficient on the (logarithm of the) good in the utility function to the sum of the coefficients on all goods; the second term is the ratio of 'full income', M, to the price of the good. Full income in the present context is the maximum present value of income that can be obtained (that is, if $h_1 = h_2 = 0$). The price of leisure in periods 1 and 2 respectively is $w_1(1 - t)$ and $vw_2(1 - t)$.

Great care must, however, be taken in dealing with the various corner solutions. These concern the labour supply in each period as well as the decision to borrow or lend. The form of the budget constraint in (12.2) is only applicable when there is an interior solution in which the individual works in both periods. A procedure for solving each individual's optimization problem is described in Appendix 12.1. This solution procedure must be carried out for every individual, where individuals differ in their wage profiles and preferences. The specification of population heterogeneity is described in the following section.

12.2   WAGE AND PREFERENCE DISTRIBUTIONS

Wage Profiles

The standard approach in the single-period optimal tax literature is to impose an exogenous distribution of wage rates. A similar approach is adopted in the present context, with the addition of a specification of the process by which the wage rate changes from period 1 to period 2. For the first period, w_1 is assumed to be distributed lognormally as $\Lambda(\mu_1, \sigma_1^2)$ where μ_1 and σ_1^2 are respectively the mean and variance of the logarithms of wage rates. The median wage, m_1, is thus $\exp(\mu_1)$. Individual values of w_{i1} can be generated for simulation purposes using the following expression:

$$w_{i1} = \exp(\mu_1 + \sigma_1 u_i) \tag{12.3}$$

where u_i represents a random variable drawn from an $N(0,1)$ distribution.

If μ_2 denotes the mean of logarithms of w_2, and b denotes the proportionate change given by $(\mu_2 - \mu_1)/\mu_1$ then:

$$\mu_2 = (1 + b)\mu_1 \tag{12.4}$$

But not all individuals receive the same proportional change in the wage rate. In addition to a random component it is useful to allow for alternative degrees of Galtonian regression towards the mean in the process of wage rate changes. This can be achieved by writing:

$$w_{i2} = \left(\frac{w_{i1}}{m_1}\right)^g \exp(\mu_2 + \sigma_\varepsilon u_i) \qquad (12.5)$$

where u_i represents another random observation from $N(0,1)$, σ_ε^2 is the variance of the distribution of proportional relative wage changes, and g is the measure of regression towards the mean. Hence there is a systematic component of relative changes associated with the position of individuals in the wage distribution, and a random component influenced by the term in σ_ε. If $g = 1$, the average proportionate change is the same for all percentiles of the distribution of w_1. This is seen by rearranging (12.5) to get:

$$\log w_{i2} - \log w_{i1} = (\mu_2 - \mu_1) - (1 - g) \log(w_{i1}/m_1) + \sigma_\varepsilon u_i \qquad (12.6)$$

Hence if $g = 1$ the appropriate term on the right hand side of (12.6) vanishes and the average proportionate change (or change in the logarithms) is independent of the wage in the first period. But if $g < 1$, (12.6) shows that percentiles of the wage distribution for which $w_1 < m_1$ have a higher percentage change, on average, than those for which $w_1 > m_1$. Taking variances of (12.6) gives, with σ_2^2 denoting the variance of logarithms of wage rates in the second period:

$$\sigma_2^2 = g^2 \sigma_1^2 + \sigma_\varepsilon^2 \qquad (12.7)$$

If there is no regression towards the mean, so that $g = 1$, it can be seen from (12.7) that the variance of logarithms in the second period is simply the variance in the first period plus the variance of the stochastic component of relative changes. The relative values of σ_2^2 and σ_1^2 depend on the strength of any regression effect, which tends to reduce the dispersion of wage rates, compared with the term σ_ε^2, which tends to increase the dispersion. The variance of log-wage rates will remain unchanged only if $\sigma_2^2 = \sigma_1^2$, and from (12.7) this requires that the following relationship holds:

$$g^2 = 1 - \sigma_\varepsilon^2/\sigma_1^2 \qquad (12.8)$$

The above specification, in particular (12.3)–(12.5), can be used to generate a joint distribution of wage rates in the two periods for any number of individuals.

Heterogeneous Preferences

Each individual's preferences are characterized, given the form of the utility function which is common to all individuals, by the parameters α, β, γ and ξ, although the condition is imposed that $\alpha + \beta + \gamma = 1$. It is required to specify heterogeneity in a way that allows a wide variety of alternative situations to be examined, though there is virtually no direct evidence on which to draw. One obvious constraint is that the parameters must be strictly positive. This adds support to the use of the lognormal distribution in this context as well as for the generation of wage rate distributions.

It is useful to have some control over the extent to which those who have a strong preference for leisure also have a relatively strong preference for any of the goods. Hence suppose that β and γ are jointly distributed as $\Lambda(\beta, \gamma \mid \mu_\beta, \sigma_\beta^2, \mu_\gamma, \sigma_\gamma^2, \rho)$ where μ and σ^2, with appropriate subscripts, are means and variances of logarithms, and ρ is the correlation coefficient between log-values. For a given value of γ for any individual, a corresponding value of β can be obtained by taking a random observation from the appropriate conditional distribution. For the ith individual, then:

$$\beta_i = \exp\left\{\mu_\beta + \rho\frac{\sigma_\beta}{\sigma_\gamma}\left(\gamma_i - \mu_\gamma\right) + u_i\sigma_\beta\left(1 - \rho^2\right)^{0.5}\right\} \qquad (12.9)$$

where u_i is a random drawing from N(0, 1). The term $\rho\sigma_\beta/\sigma_\gamma$ is the appropriate regression coefficient and $\sigma_\beta^2(1 - \rho^2)$ is the variance of logarithms of the conditional distributions of β for given γ, which are of course homoscedastic.

It is also desirable to have some control over the extent to which relatively high-wage individuals have a stronger, or weaker, preference for leisure. The model does not allow for an endogenous wage rate distribution, resulting perhaps from investment in human capital, but it is possible to impose a degree of correlation between wages and preferences. First, denote the ith individual's mean log-wage rate over the two periods as $\bar{w}_i$, where the mean and variance of $\bar{w}_i$ are $\mu_{\bar{w}}$ and $\sigma_{\bar{w}}^2$ respectively. Secondly, suppose that the joint distribution of $\bar{w}$ and γ is also lognormal, given by $\Lambda(\bar{w}, \gamma \mid \mu_{\bar{w}}, \sigma_{\bar{w}}^2, \mu_\gamma, \sigma_\gamma^2, \rho_w)$, where ρ_w is the correlation between the mean log-wage and the coefficient on leisure. The values of $\bar{w}_i$ and the corresponding means and variances can be obtained directly from the simulated wages generated using the procedure described earlier. Simulated values of γ_i can then be obtained from the appropriate conditional distributions. Hence:

$$\gamma_i = \exp\left\{\mu_\gamma + \rho_w\frac{\sigma_\gamma}{\sigma_{\bar{w}}}\left(\bar{w}_i - \mu_{\bar{w}}\right) + u_i\sigma_\gamma\left(1 - \rho_w^2\right)^{0.5}\right\} \qquad (12.10)$$

where u_i is another random drawing from $N(0, 1)$. The process of generating taste parameters therefore begins with equation (12.10), following the generation of wage profiles. Having obtained the γ_i values, equation (12.9) is then used to obtain corresponding β_i values. Finally α_i is simply obtained as $1 - \gamma_i - \beta_i$. Any values resulting in negative α are rejected, and it should be recognized that the distribution of α will not itself be lognormal since it is a sum rather than a product of lognormal variates.

It remains to specify the distribution of the rate of time preference, and this is assumed to be independently lognormally distributed with parameters μ_ξ and σ_ξ. Hence values of ξ_i are obtained using:

$$\xi_i = \exp(\mu_\xi + u_i \, \sigma_\xi) \tag{12.11}$$

with u_i as yet another random observation from $N(0, 1)$.

Using the above procedure it is possible to generate a simulated population such that, for example, those who face relatively high wage rates (on average over the two periods) also work relatively more and therefore typically have higher earnings. Those with relatively higher earnings can also be assumed to spend relatively more, on average, on a specified good. Despite the variability within the population the proportion of income devoted to a specified good can be made, on average, to fall or rise with (endogenous) income. For example, setting ρ_w to be negative and ρ to be positive, there is a tendency for higher-wage individuals to earn higher incomes and to consume relatively less of good Y. This type of variation is observed in budget studies, the most prominent case being that of food, and is important when considering alternative tax systems. If the correlation coefficients are zero, there is no systematic tendency to vary the proportion of income devoted to one good as income changes.

12.3   TAX STRUCTURES

The Government's Budget Constraint

In the present context the government's budget constraint may be specified in terms of the present value of transfers per person, $\delta\{1 + 1/(1 + r)\}$, being equal to the present value of tax payments per person. Consumption taxes paid by any individual are $t_x p_x\{x_1 + x_2/(1 + r)\}$ plus $t_y p_y\{y_1 + y_2/(1 + r)\}$ for goods X and Y respectively. The present value of income tax for any individual is $t\{w_1 (1 - h_1) + w_2(1 - h_2)/(1 + r)\}$ plus the tax paid on interest income, if relevant. Given the complexity of each individual's optimization problem, the government's budget constraint cannot be expressed in any convenient analytical form.

In the present model there are three tax rates, t, t_x and t_y, and one transfer payment, δ, to be determined, but the government's budget constraint means that one degree of freedom is lost in the choice of setting the levels. Hence only three of the four tax 'parameters' can be set independently. For a given set of consumption taxes, t_x and t_y, the budget constraint can be regarded as allowing the transfer payment, δ, to be determined for any specified value of the income tax rate, t. This must be carried out using an iterative search procedure, given the highly complex and non-linear nature of the budget constraint. It should be stressed that the search procedure must find the value of δ for given t (and t_x and t_y), rather than finding the value of t for specified δ. This is because there is not a unique relationship between δ and t. Any value of δ is associated with two income tax rates because, as t increases from zero, the higher rate compensates for the fall in the tax base so that δ can be increased, but beyond some point the negative incentive effect is such that the fall in the tax base dominates and further increases in t involve a lower total revenue and hence lower value of δ.

Some Examples

There is clearly a very wide range of assumptions which may be made using the model presented in section 12.1. For example, the specification of the wage rate distributions requires values of five parameters; this contrasts with only two parameters in the single-period framework. Suppose, however, that the parameter values are as shown in Table 12.1. These assumptions imply a certain amount of regression towards the mean (in wage rates) over time, combined with profiles which are on average quite steep. The regression combined with the random component of changes in relative wage rates implies that the variance of log-wage rates in the second period is 0.546, obtained by substituting in equation (12.7).

Table 12.1   Wage rate parameters

Parameter	Value
$\bar{w}_1$	100
σ_1^2	0.55
σ_ε^2	0.05
b	0.50
g	0.95

Consider the set of taste parameters shown in Table 12.2. The number of parameters to be imposed is very much larger than in the more standard single-period, single-good optimal tax problem where homogeneous preferences are typically assumed. The value of $\rho = 0.75$ implies a fairly high correlation between the coefficients, in the utility function, on leisure and good Y. Hence those who have a relatively strong preference for leisure also have, on average, a strong preference for good Y. Table 12.2 assumes a negative correlation of -0.75 between the coefficient on leisure and the arithmetic mean wage rate (over the two periods) of individuals. Hence those who face a relatively higher average wage rate have, on average, a lower preference for leisure. Higher wage rates will thus tend to be associated with higher working hours (less leisure) and thus higher incomes. The combination of these parameters means also that those with relatively higher incomes will, on average, spend a larger proportion of income on good X relative to good Y. Conversely, the relatively poorer individuals will typically devote a larger proportion of income to good Y.

Table 12.2   Taste parameters

Parameter	Value
$\bar{\gamma}$	0.3
σ_γ^2	0.05
$\bar{\beta}$	0.35
σ_β^2	0.05
ρ	0.75
ρ_w	-0.75
$\bar{\xi}$	0.06
σ_ξ^2	0.003

Given the partial equilibrium nature of the model it is also necessary to impose exogenous prices of the two goods, in addition to the rate of interest. Suppose that $r = 0.05$ and that p_x and p_y are respectively 1.0 and 1.4.

The search for an optimal tax structure requires a three-dimensional search over t_x, t_y and t. For each combination of t_x and t_y, it is possible to search for the value of the income tax rate, t, that maximizes the social welfare function, for a specified value of inequality aversion, ε. This can be achieved by gradually increasing the tax rate, solving for the corresponding value of the transfer payment for which the government's budget constraint is satisfied, and calculating the associated social welfare per person. The calculations are then repeated for variations in t_x and t_y.

One feature of the results is illustrated in Figure 12.1, which shows a three-dimensional diagram with the tax rates t_x and t_y on the base and the maximum value of social welfare, associated with the appropriate income tax rate, shown as the height. The value of inequality aversion used is 0.9. The curvilinear surface is single-peaked and reaches a maximum where $t_x = 0.175$ and $t_y = 0$; the corresponding value of t is 0.495. Hence the optimal tax structure involves a combination of income and consumption taxation, with selectivity such that good Y is not taxed. The result that Y is untaxed in the optimal structure arises from the preference structure of Table 12.2 whereby expenditure on Y forms a larger proportion of the incomes of the relatively poorer individuals. For low rates of tax on good X, t_x, the associated maximum social welfare falls rapidly as t_y is increased. Furthermore, for high t_y, welfare increases rapidly as t_x is increased, but over the range where t_x is high, welfare is not very sensitive to variations in t_y. Indeed, while selectivity in the consumption tax does arise as the optimal structure in this example, a feature of Figure 12.1 is that the three-dimensional surface is relatively flat over a wide range of combinations of t_x and t_y.

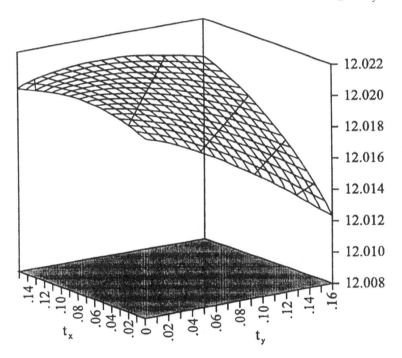

Figure 12.1   Social welfare and consumption taxes

Further insight into the properties of the model may be obtained from Figure 12.2. This shows the variation in social welfare, for the same value of inequality aversion of 0.9, as the income tax rate is increased, for two different consumption tax structures. The upper schedule is for $t_x = 0.3$, $t_y = 0$ while the lower schedule is for $t_x = 0$, $t_y = 0.3$. For each schedule in Figure 12.2, the peak is represented by a single point in the three-dimensional surface of Figure 12.1. From the above discussion it is not surprising that the case of a selective tax on only good X gives a higher social welfare for each income tax rate, though the difference becomes negligible for higher values of t. Not only is the surface in Figure 12.1 quite flat over a wide area, but the schedules in Figure 12.2 are also relatively flat over a wide range of income tax rates. This means that in producing numerical simulation results, it is necessary to use a great deal of accuracy in, for example, solving the government's budget constraint iteratively, and to consider small variations in parameters. The calculations are therefore relatively slow.

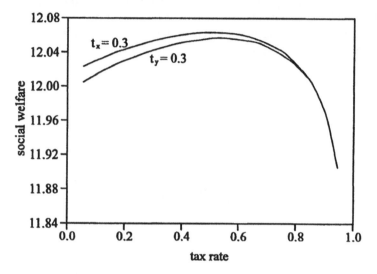

Figure 12.2   Social welfare and income taxation

The familiar relationship between the unconditional transfer payment and the income tax rate is shown, for alternative consumption tax structures, in Figure 12.3. As mentioned earlier, the transfer payment falls after reaching a maximum, so that any value of the transfer is associated with two income tax rates. In the lower schedule $t_x = t_y = 0$, while the middle and upper schedules respectively have selective taxes on good Y and good X of 0.3. The relative positions of these schedules are not surprising given the configuration of parameter values.

The use of the Atkinson measure of inequality implies a trade-off between arithmetic mean utility and its inequality. In the more simple case of a single tax and a single period, the attainable combinations of mean utility and inequality, for a given value of ε, can be plotted as the income tax rate is varied. In the present context, such a relationship exists for each combination of t_x and t_y. Two such curves are shown in Figure 12.4 for just two tax structures. The peak of the three-dimensional surface in Figure 12.1 would actually coincide with a point

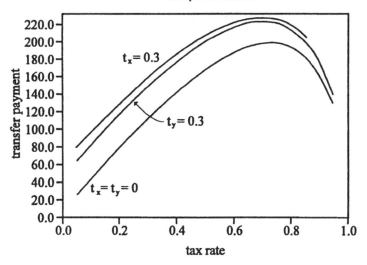

Figure 12.3   The social dividend with alternative tax systems

of tangency of the highest attainable social indifference curve, if all possible profiles (for variations in t_x and t_y) were plotted in a diagram such as Figure 12.4. It can be seen that, although a selective tax on good X, with a zero rate on good Y, is optimal given the assumed distribution of tastes and wage rates, the profile in Figure 12.4 for a selective tax on good X does not totally 'dominate' the profile for a selective tax on good Y (the two curves intersect). The general

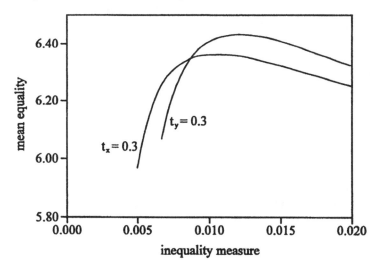

Figure 12.4   Average utility and inequality

shapes of the profiles follow the form that would be expected from the standard results.

The above examples assume significant growth in the average wage rates from the first to the second period, and a rate of interest that is slightly lower than the average time preference rate. This means that the vast majority of individuals borrow in the first period. Hence the interest-income tax has a negligible effect on the results. However, by raising the interest rate and making the growth rate, b, negative a significant number of individuals become lenders and the effect of eliminating the interest-income tax can be examined. With the taste parameters as in Table 12.2, there was little difference between the results, but higher social welfare is achieved with the interest-income tax, which is associated with lower inequality and higher average utility. However, the approach does not allow for any influence of savings on the growth rate, which may be desirable in a more comprehensive analysis.

12.4   A PERIOD OF RETIREMENT

Consider a two-period model in which the second period is a retirement period; this is the model examined at the end of Chapter 7. Suppose that the lifetime utility function can be written in logarithmic form as:

$$U = \alpha \log c_1 + (1 - \alpha) \log h + \alpha\theta \log c_2 \qquad (12.12)$$

Suppose that there is a government pension scheme of the two-tier variety. Individuals whose earnings during the first period are below a basic pension, b, receive only the basic pension. For simplicity, all individuals are regarded as being eligible for the basic pension. Those whose earnings exceed b receive an additional pension equal to a proportion, s, of earnings measured above b. Hence the pension, p, is equal to:

$$p = b \qquad\qquad\qquad \text{for } w(1 - h) \le b \qquad (12.13)$$

$$= b + s\{w(1 - h) - b\} \quad \text{for } w(1 - h) > b \qquad (12.14)$$

Suppose that the pension is financed using a proportional tax or contribution system, where t represents the fixed marginal and average tax rate. The tax system can also be assumed to finance an unconditional lump sum transfer, equal to a, to each individual during the first period; a special case would involve $a = b$. For those whose earnings exceed the basic pension, the lifetime budget constraint can be written as:

$$c_1 + c_2/(1 + r) = a + b(1 - s)/(1 + r) + w(1 - h) \{1 - t + s/(1 + r)\} \quad (12.15)$$

This can be modified for the situation where the individual works but does not qualify for the second-tier pension, by setting $s = 0$. This constraint assumes perfect capital markets and ignores the possibility of interest-income taxation. The latter would reduce the after-tax rate of return for those who lend in the first period to $r(1 - t)$ and introduces a further kink in the budget constraint.

The existence of the two-tier pension scheme means that two types of interior solution must be distinguished. First, for those working but not qualifying for the earnings-related pension, the post-tax wage rate, from (12.15) with $s = 0$, is $w(1 - t)$ while full income, M, is $a + b/(1 + r) + w(1 - t)$. For those who qualify for the earnings-related component, the post-tax wage rate is equal to $w \{1 - t + s/(1 + r)\}$ and full income is $a + b(1 - s)/(1 + r) + w\{1 - t + s/(1 + r)\}$. Consumption in each period may therefore be written as:

$$c_1 = \{\alpha/(1 + \alpha\theta)\}M \quad (12.16)$$

$$c_2 = \{\alpha\theta/(1 + \alpha\theta)\} M(1 + r) \quad (12.17)$$

with the appropriate value of M in each case. If only the basic pension is received, leisure is equal to:

$$h = \frac{\left\{(1-\alpha)/(1+\alpha\theta)\right\}M}{w(1-t)} \quad (12.18)$$

and if the individual qualifies for the second-tier pension, it is:

$$h = \frac{\left\{(1-\alpha)/(1+\alpha\theta)\right\}M}{w\left\{1-t+s/(1+r)\right\}} \quad (12.19)$$

The labour supply incentive provided by the earnings-related pension is reflected in the effective reduction in the marginal tax rate.

Special care must be taken in dealing with corner solutions. The simplest case is where it is not worthwhile supplying any labour if the resulting earnings will only qualify the individual for a basic pension; that is, if $w(1 - h) \leq b$. Appropriate substitution into (12.18) and rearrangement shows that for $h < 1$ the wage must exceed w_L, where:

$$w_L = \frac{(1-\alpha)\{a+b/(1+r)\}}{\alpha(1+\theta)(1-t)} \qquad (12.20)$$

However, the situation is complicated by the fact that the budget constraint is non-convex. This is most easily seen by examining (12.15) for the two cases where $s = 0$ and $s > 0$, as illustrated in Figure 12.5. The effective constraint is the kinked line AEDF. This is very similar to the two-rate single-period tax and

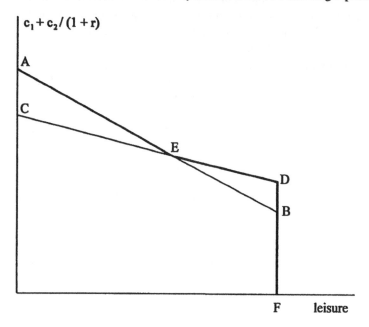

Figure 12.5   An earnings-related pension scheme

transfer scheme examined in Chapter 9. Of the whole range of the constraint, corresponding to the length AED, a part is not relevant because there is some wage rate at which the individual switches, or jumps, from the flatter to the steeper section. This occurs when an indifference curve is tangential to both sections. For a simultaneous tangency along both sections, it is necessary to have, where primes indicate values along the flatter section (flat-rate pension only is received):

$$\left(\frac{c_1}{c_1'}\right)^{\alpha}\left(\frac{c_2}{c_2'}\right)^{\alpha\theta}\left(\frac{h}{h'}\right)^{1-\alpha} = 1 \qquad (12.21)$$

Using the results in (12.16) to (12.19), substitution into (12.21) gives

$$\left(\frac{M}{M'}\right)^{1+\alpha\theta}\left\{\frac{1-t}{1-t+s/(1+r)}\right\}^{1-\alpha} = 1 \qquad (12.22)$$

Where $M' = a + b/(1 + r) + w(1 - t)$ and $M = a + b(1 - s)/(1 + r) + w\{1 - t + s/(1 + r)\}$. Hence $M = kM'$, where:

$$k = \left\{1+\frac{s}{(1-t)(1+r)}\right\}^{(1-\alpha)/(1+\alpha\theta)} \qquad (12.23)$$

It is therefore possible to solve $M = kM'$ to find the wage rate, w_s say, at which the switching between segments occurs, whereby:

$$w_s = \frac{\{a+b/(1+r)\}(k-1)+bs/(1+r)}{(1-t)(1-k)+s/(1+r)} \qquad (12.24)$$

The possibility also arises that, for high tax rates, the value of w_s is less than w_L. This means that the tangency along the flatter range of the budget constraint in Figure 12.5 occurs beyond the relevant range (that is, it occurs where $h > 1$), so that it is never worthwhile working unless the individual qualifies for the earnings-related component of the state pension. In this case it is necessary to obtain the threshold wage, w_m, at which an indifference curve touches the corner at point D and is tangential to the segment AE. At point D, consumption in the two periods, c_1 and c_2, is a and b respectively, with $h = 1$.

Along the segment AE, the values of consumption and leisure are given by (12.16), (12.17) and (12.19), with M defined appropriately. For the tangency and corner to be on the same indifference curve, it can be found that w_m must satisfy:

$$Aw_m^{1-\alpha} - BM^{1+\alpha\theta} = 0 \qquad (12.25)$$

where:

$$A = a^\alpha b^{\alpha\theta}\left(1-t+\frac{s}{1+r}\right)^{1-\alpha} \qquad (12.26)$$

$$B = \frac{\alpha^\alpha (1-\alpha)^{1-\alpha} \{\alpha\theta(1+r)\}^{\alpha\theta}}{(1+\alpha\theta)^{1+\alpha\theta}} \qquad (12.27)$$

$$M = a + \frac{b(1-s)}{1+r} + w_m \left(1 - t + \frac{s}{1+r}\right) \qquad (12.28)$$

The non-linear equation in (12.25) can be solved using Newton's Method, as described in Chapter 5 for the modified minimum income guarantee in the single-period context.

The Government Budget Constraint

Both the income transfer and the state pension must be financed from income taxation. Most state pensions are financed on a pay-as-you-go basis whereby the current pensions are financed from taxes paid by the current labour force. The existence of productivity and population growth gives individuals a higher effective rate of return from membership of the state scheme than the rate of return which could be achieved in the market; this is the basis of the well-known analysis of Aaron (1966). Allowances for population and other changes could easily be made within the framework, but in the present context, where concentration is on distributional comparisons among alternative state pension schemes, it is most appropriate to concentrate on steady-state results in which no inter-cohort redistribution takes place. Kennedy (1990) has argued that the distributional implications of pensions should be examined in the context of a single cohort with deficit neutrality imposed. Thus, any effects of intergenerational transfers should be excluded.

As a single cohort is being considered, the present value of transfers plus pensions must equal the total tax revenue obtained during the working period. Interest-income taxation is excluded and the pension is non-taxable, so there is no government revenue in the second period. As capital markets are assumed to be perfect, the government's discount rate is the same as that at which individuals borrow and lend. The approach also assumes that all individuals live until the end of the second period.

The present value of flat-rate benefits per person in the cohort is $a + b/(1 + r)$. The total earnings-related pensions received during the second period depends on the distribution of earnings, in combination with the pension formula. In principle, it would be possible to suppose that individuals not only face different wage rates, but also have different preferences in terms of their values of α and ξ. However, it would be rather awkward to deal with such a joint distribution and not surprisingly the literature on labour supply typically assumes simply that individuals differ in the wage rate faced. Suppose, then, that the distribution function of w is represented by $F(w)$. Total earnings-related pensions per person are therefore given by:

$$s\int_{w_s}\{w(1-h)-b\}dF(w) \tag{12.29}$$

It is most convenient to use (12.19) to express earnings $w(1-h)$ in terms of w and the parameters of the tax and transfer system, as:

$$w(1-h)=\alpha^*w-\psi \tag{12.30}$$

with:

$$\alpha^*=\alpha(1+\theta)/(1+\alpha\theta) \tag{12.31}$$

and:

$$\psi=\frac{(1-\alpha)\{a+b(1-s)/(1+r)\}}{(1+\alpha\theta)\{1-t+s/(1+r)\}} \tag{12.32}$$

Equation (12.30) gives the familiar-looking result that earnings are a linear function of the wage rate, above a threshold value.

Substituting in (12.29) and rearranging gives total earnings-related pensions per person as the proportional pension rate, s, multiplied by:

$$\alpha^*\bar{w}\{1-F_1(w_s)\}-(\psi+b)\{1-F(w_s)\} \tag{12.33}$$

where $\bar{w}$ is the arithmetic mean value of w and $F_1(w_s)$ denotes the proportion of total income obtained by those with incomes not exceeding w_s; hence F_1 denotes the 'incomplete first moment' distribution function of F.

The final stage involved in specifying the budget constraint is to obtain the income tax base, since the tax system is proportional. For those working in the first period, but earning insufficient to qualify for an earnings-related pension, it is convenient to use (12.33) to write gross earnings as:

$$w(1-h)=\alpha^*w-\psi' \tag{12.34}$$

where ψ' is obtained from the right-hand side of (12.32) simply by setting $s = 0$. The labour supply function, relating $w(1-h)$, or labour measured in 'efficiency units', to the wage rate is therefore the kinked line OABCD shown in Figure 12.6(a). For a wage between w_L and w_s the individual works but does not receive an earnings-related pension. As the wage reaches w_s the individual jumps

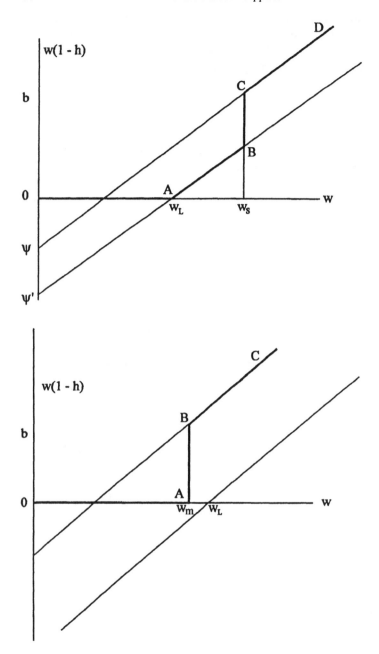

Figure 12.6   Earnings and the earnings-related pension

from B to C and then follows the range CD. Figure 12.6(a) is drawn for $w_s > w_L$, which is the typical situation but, as mentioned above, this inequality can be reversed for very high tax rates. If $w_L > w_s$ then the function is illustrated in Figure 12.6(b) where earnings jump from zero to B at w_m; notice that the earnings corresponding to w_m must exceed the basic pension.

Where $w_s > w_L$, the tax base is therefore equal to the number of individuals in the cohort multiplied by:

$$\int_{w_L}^{w_s} \left(\alpha^* w - \psi' \right) dF(w) + \int_{w_s}^{\infty} \left(\alpha^* w - \psi \right) dF(w) \tag{12.35}$$

This can be rearranged to give:

$$\alpha^* \int_{w_L}^{\infty} w dF(w) - \left\{ \psi' \int_{w_L}^{w_s} dF(w) + \psi \int_{w_s}^{\infty} dF(w) \right\}$$

$$= \alpha^* \overline{w} \{ 1 - F_1(w_L) \} - \psi' \{ F(w_s) - F(w_L) \} - \psi \{ 1 - F(w_s) \} \tag{12.36}$$

The tax rate, t, needed to finance any specified pension scheme, after allowing for labour supply responses, is given by:

$$t = \frac{a + \left[b + s \left[\alpha^* \overline{w} \{ 1 - F_1(w_s) \} - (\psi + b) \{ 1 - F(w_s) \} \right] \right] / (1 + r)}{\alpha^* \overline{w} \{ 1 - F_1(w_L) \} - \psi' \{ F(w_s) - F(w_L) \} - \psi \{ 1 - F(w_s) \}} \tag{12.37}$$

In the case where $w_L > w_s$ then the denominator of (12.37) is changed to:

$$\alpha^* \overline{w} \{ 1 - F_1(w_m) \} - \psi \{ F(w_m) \} \tag{12.38}$$

However, the various terms, such as ψ, ψ', w_s and w_L, all depend on t. The budget constraint can therefore only be solved using numerical methods. It is, however, useful to consider the special case of (12.37) where all individuals qualify for the earnings-related pension; this arises if the minimum wage rate is sufficiently high, given the other parameters. Hence $F(w_L) = F(w_s) = F_1(w_L) = F_1(w_s) = 0$ and the constraint reduces to:

$$t = \frac{a + \left\{ b + s \left(\alpha^* \overline{w} - \psi - b \right) \right\} / (1 + r)}{\alpha^* \overline{w} - \psi} \tag{12.39}$$

This result has a simple interpretation: the required tax rate is the present value of the benefits received by someone with the arithmetic mean wage rate, $\bar{w}$, divided by the corresponding gross earnings. Even this intuitively obvious expression for the tax rate in this special case cannot be solved easily since ψ depends on t.

Tax and Benefit Levels

The procedure described above for solving the government's budget constraint was applied in order to produce the results shown in Figure 12.7. Since the precise units in which incomes and transfers are measured are not relevant, values of μ and σ^2 were set at 1.8 and 0.3 respectively, and the first-period transfer, a, was set at 0.8. In two-period models of this kind it is appropriate to set the rates of interest and time preference quite high (although the absolute values do not affect the comparisons between alternative schemes), and these were set at 0.5 and 0.7 respectively. The value of α was 0.65. It is important to stress that these values were chosen for illustrative purposes only; the comparisons are not affected by specific values.

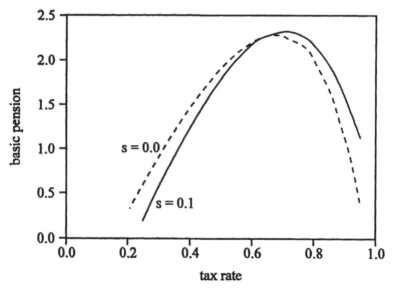

Figure 12.7 The basic pension and tax rates

Figure 12.7 shows how the basic pension can vary as the tax rate is increased, for two alternative values of the proportional pension rate, zero and 0.10. The figure shows that as the tax rate increases, the basic pension ultimately falls because of the decline in the tax base outweighing the rise in *t*. However, because of the labour supply incentive the decline is delayed when there is an earnings-related pension, compared with the flat-rate case. Hence with an earnings-related component, it is possible to obtain a higher basic pension than in a simple flat-rate scheme. Notice that the profiles do not begin at the point $b = a = 0$ because of the existence of the transfer payment during the working period. They would begin at the origin if $a = b$ at all times, but otherwise they have very similar shapes. To extend the tax rate beyond the peak of each profile in Figure 12.7 would involve reducing the income transfer to the poor while also making the relatively rich worse off.

The trade-offs for flat rate and earnings-related schemes are shown in Figure 12.8, using the same parameters as for Figure 12.7. The profiles are for a value of the inequality aversion parameter, ε, of 2 and the multiplicative form of the utility function in (12.12). The vertical axis measures arithmetic mean utility and the horizontal axis measures $I(\varepsilon)$. The indifference curves, representing equal levels of social welfare per person, slope upwards from left to right and higher values of welfare are obtained on indifference curves which are 'higher' when moving from the bottom right to the top left-hand corner of the diagram.

The trade-offs in Figure 12.8 have a number of interesting features. First, for both flat-rate and two-tier schemes, they become very steep so that, beyond a point, attempts to reduce inequality by raising the tax rate (and hence the basic pension) involve large reductions in average utility. Indeed, both profiles are non-concave over a range of values; just as an attempt to increase the basic pension

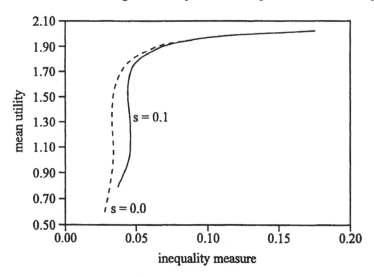

Figure 12.8   Average utility and inequality

by raising the tax rate is eventually self-defeating, inequality also rises slightly over a range.

The second feature of Figure 12.8, and perhaps the most important result, is that the flat-rate pension scheme always dominates the two-tier scheme with an earnings-related component, in that a higher value of social welfare can always be achieved. Despite the labour supply incentive provided by the earnings related pension, the maximum social welfare achievable is less than the maximum attainable with only a flat-rate pension.

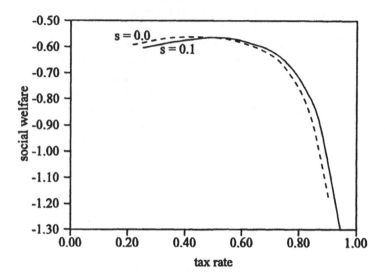

Figure 12.9   Social welfare and the tax rate

It was suggested above that it is appropriate to measure social welfare in terms of individuals' utility levels, given the value placed on leisure in their utility functions. However, it is of interest to consider the implied trade-off between average net lifetime *income* and its inequality, particularly as incomes are the predominant focus of applied studies of inequality. Results are shown in Figure 12.9, again using an inequality aversion parameter of $\varepsilon = 2$. A significant difference compared with the results in Figure 12.8 is that the profiles in Figure 12.9 do not have a 'backward-bending' range. Hence, in this context it is possible for higher tax rates, beyond some value, to reduce the measured inequality of net income while simultaneously increasing the inequality of utility. This contrasts with the single-period results for a linear (negative) income tax, where inequality of net income and utility move in the same direction over the whole range of tax rates. The absence of a backward-bending range in Figure 12.9 should not, however, be thought to suggest that a social welfare function specified in terms of net incomes attains a maximum for a higher tax rate than that at which one in terms of utility reaches a maximum. Indeed, the reverse is true, so that an emphasis on net incomes would produce a tax rate (and basic pension) that is in some sense too low.

It may be noted that the types of trade-off considered are entirely static in that any changes in average lifetime earnings are attributed purely to labour supply effects. There has been much debate on the effects of alternative pension schemes on savings. Aggregate savings in this model include both private savings and public savings measured by the excess of the tax revenue over the amount needed to finance the income transfer, a, given in the first period. For a given basic pension, it has been seen that the positive effect of increasing the proportional rate, s, on labour supply dominates the negative effect of the resulting increase in t, so labour supply increases in aggregate (it does not change for those at the corner solution with $w = w_L$ of course). It is also found that aggregate savings are higher with an earnings-related scheme than with just a flat-rate pension, for given values of b.

APPENDIX 12.1   SOLVING THE TWO-PERIOD MODEL

A solution procedure must be designed to identify which section, or corner, of the non-linear budget constraint of section 12.1 is relevant. The algorithm may be described in terms of a sequence of stages, as follows:

1. First, impose the value of v of $1/\{1 + r(1 - t)\}$, assuming that the individual lends in the first period. Then follow the steps 2–5 below:
2. Check if the individual works in the first period using the following condition, which effectively assumes that the person works in the second period. Letting $k = \gamma/(1 + \theta)$, it can be found that $h_1 < 1$ if:

$$w_1 > \frac{k}{1-k}\left\{vw_2 + \frac{\delta(1+v)}{1-t}\right\} \qquad (12.40)$$

If (12.40) is not satisfied, go to step 4 below. If the condition in (12.40) is satisfied, go to step 3.

3. Check if the individual works in the second period, given that $h_1 < 1$. The condition for $h_2 < 1$ is that:

$$w_2 > \frac{\theta k}{(1-\theta k)v}\left\{w_1 + \frac{\delta(1+v)}{1-t}\right\} \qquad (12.41)$$

The two alternatives are discussed in (a) and (b) below:

(a) If (12.41) is satisfied, then the individual works in both periods and the value of full income, M, representing the maximum present value of income which could be obtained, is given by $M = \delta(1 + v) + (1 - t)(w_1 + vw_2)$. Follow the general rule discussed above for the Cobb–Douglas case to obtain the xs, ys and hs.

Then go to step 5 below.

(b) If (12.41) is not satisfied, it is necessary to check again if the individual works in period 1, given that $h_2 = 1$. This can be found to require the new condition that w_1 must satisfy:

$$w_1 > \frac{\gamma\delta(1+v)}{(1-t)(\alpha+\beta)(1+\theta)} \tag{12.42}$$

If this condition is not satisfied, go to step 4 below. If the inequality in (12.42) is satisfied, it can be concluded that the individual works in the first period, but not in the second. Where $h_2 = 1$ and $h_1 < 1$, full income is $M = \delta(1 + v) + w_1(1 - t)$. Use the standard rules to solve for consumption and leisure.

Then go to step 5 below.

4. It can be concluded that the individual does not work in the first period. It is necessary to check again to find if the individual works in the second period, given that $h_1 = 1$. Redefine k as $\gamma/(\alpha + \beta + \theta)$ and check if the individual works in the second period using the condition that $h_2 < 1$ if:

$$w_2 > \frac{\theta k\delta(1+v)}{v(1-t)(1-\theta k)} \tag{12.43}$$

The two possibilities are considered in (a) and (b) below.

(a) If the condition in (12.43) is satisfied, full income, M, is given by $M = \delta(1 + v) + vw_2(1 - t)$, and consumption and labour supply are found in the usual way.

Then go to step 5 below.

(b) When the inequality in (12.43) is not satisfied, $h_1 = h_2 = 1$, and it can be concluded that the individual never works. The value of full income, M, is equal to $\delta(1 + v)$.

Then go to step 5.

5. On reaching this stage, labour supply and consumption decisions have been solved using the net of tax rate of interest, $r(1 - t)$. This implicitly assumes that the individual lends in the first period. It is therefore necessary to check to find if the individual does in fact lend in the first period, as assumed in step 1 above. If earnings in each period are denoted $y_1 = w_1(1 - h_1)$ and $y_2 = w_2(1 - h_2)$, the individual lends if net income exceeds consumption in the first period, that is if:

$$y_1 (1 - t) + \delta > x_1 p_x' + y_1 p_y' \qquad (12.44)$$

If this condition is satisfied, the solution process is finished. If it is not satisfied, assume that the individual borrows in the first period, so that no interest income is received in the second period. Thus, set $v = 1/(1 + r)$ and repeat steps 2–4 above. After re-solving for the labour supply and consumption plans, check to see if the individual does in fact borrow by reversing the inequality in (12.44). If the person does indeed borrow, stop the procedure. Otherwise the individual is at the corner solution where there is neither borrowing nor lending. This means that each period must be treated separately. For each period, dropping time subscripts, first check to find if the individual works. This requires:

$$w > \frac{\gamma\delta}{(1-\gamma)(1-t)} \qquad (12.45)$$

If (12.45) is satisfied, then set $M = \delta + w(1 - t)$ and solve for consumption; otherwise, $h = 1$.

The procedure is then complete.

13. Voting over tax schedules

The previous two chapters have been concerned with the maximization of a social welfare function, subject to the government's budget constraint, and allowing for varying degrees of inequality aversion. With no inequality aversion, the objective is to maximize total (or average) utility, whereas extreme aversion to inequality leads, in the linear income tax scheme, to the selection of the tax structure corresponding to the maximum attainable value of the social dividend. For intermediate values, a tangency solution between the trade-off relationship between average utility and its equality and a social indifference curve is obtained. This chapter examines an alternative decision rule, the selection of the linear income tax structure preferred by a simple majority of the population. Early treatments of this problem were given by Foley (1967) and Romer (1975).

Majority voting in the case where there are no labour supply responses was examined in Part I. In that framework, each individual wishes to maximize net income, $a + y(1-t)$ for the linear income tax, subject to the linear government budget constraint $a = t\bar{y}$. Each person has linear indifference curves in (a,t) space, and therefore is pushed to a corner solution. Thus, the simple result of majority voting is that all individuals have single-peaked preferences and all those below the arithmetic mean level of earnings prefer a tax rate of unity while all those above $\bar{y}$ prefer a tax rate of zero. (Remember that in a pure transfer scheme, the average tax rate at the arithmetic mean income is zero.) Hence the choice depends simply on the position of the median income, and for a positively skewed distribution the median voter selects the highest marginal rate; for discussion of the feasible range of the rate, see Brunner (1989, pp. 63–7).

This extreme case is not, however, of any practical interest, and this chapter examines the complexities that arise when labour supplies are endogenous. The first implication is that preferences are no longer single-peaked. Section 13.1 examines the treatment of the linear tax in a single-period framework, concentrating on the approach of Roberts (1977), who established a simple condition under which a voting equilibrium exists. Section 13.2 extends the analysis to a two-period framework, and shows that an equilibrium may not exist if there is a tax-free threshold.

13.1 A SINGLE PERIOD

A major complication with endogenous incomes is that preferences may be double-peaked. While an individual is working, there is a range over which reductions in the tax rate are preferred to increases. But when t exceeds a critical level, the individual is pushed to the corner solution where no labour is supplied, and will prefer yet higher tax rates to be imposed on those who are still working. In view of the well-known result that double-peaked preferences can give rise to cyclical voting, it is important to establish whether or not a stable majority exists in this context. This problem has been examined by Roberts (1977), using the following approach.

Preference Orderings

It is convenient to rewrite the individual's utility function in terms of consumption, c, and gross earnings, y, since the latter are determined by the amount of leisure, and hence work, chosen. Using the same notation as in earlier chapters, where $c = a + y(1 - t)$ and $y = w(1 - h)$ for the linear income tax, utility can be written as:

$$U = U(a + y(1 - t), y) \qquad (13.1)$$

The first-order condition for an interior maximum of U is obtained by differentiating U totally with respect to y and is thus given by:

$$(1 - t)U_c + U_y = 0 \qquad (13.2)$$

where U_c and U_y are the appropriate partials. It is the possibility of a corner solution, where (13.2) becomes an inequality, that gives rise to double-peaked preferences.

The effect on utility of a small change in the tax structure can be obtained by totally differentiating (13.1) with respect to a and t, so that:

$$dU = U_c dc + U_y dy \qquad (13.3)$$

Substitution of the total differential, $dc = (\partial c/\partial a)da + (\partial c/\partial t)dt + (\partial c/\partial y)dy$ into (13.3) gives:

$$dU = dy\{(1 - t)U_c + U_y\} + (da - ydt)U_c \qquad (13.4)$$

But from the first-order condition for utility maximization stated in (13.2), the term in curly brackets in (13.4) is zero, so that:

$$dU = (da - ydt)U_c \qquad (13.5)$$

This is Roberts's result (1977, p. 332). The government's budget constraint for a pure transfer system has already been shown to involve the condition that $a = t\bar{y}$, with $\bar{y}$ endogenous and thus a function of t. Differentiating this constraint with respect to t gives:

$$\frac{da}{dt} = \bar{y} + t\frac{d\bar{y}}{dt} \tag{13.6}$$

The second term reflects the effect on aggregate labour supply of the change in the tax rate; this is typically negative and at high values of t it has been seen in Chapter 10 that da/dt itself becomes negative. Dividing (13.5) by dt and using (13.6) to substitute for da/dt gives:

$$\frac{dU}{dt} = \left(\bar{y} + t\frac{d\bar{y}}{dt} - y\right)U_c \tag{13.7}$$

This result shows that dU/dt can be negative for $y < \bar{y}$, where $d\bar{y}/dt$ is negative, so that some individuals with earnings below the arithmetic mean would not vote for an increase in the tax rate.

Hierarchical Adherence

The above framework was used by Roberts (1977) to show that there is a clear set of preferences over tax schedules, giving rise to a majority voting equilibrium in which the median voter dominates. This arises if the ranking of individuals by pre-tax income is not affected by the tax system; this fixed ranking is referred to as *hierarchical adherence*. The result can be seen by considering individuals i and j for whom $y_j \geq y_i$ whatever the tax structure. Person j's change in utility resulting from a revenue-neutral change in t is, from (13.7), given by:

$$\frac{dU_j}{dt} = \left(\bar{y} + t\frac{d\bar{y}}{dt} - y_j\right)U_c^j \tag{13.8}$$

where the superscript on U_c^j is used to refer to person j's utility function. If person i is indifferent to the change in t, then $dU_i/dt = 0$ and from (13.7), this implies that $\bar{y} + td\bar{y}/dt = y_i$. Substituting this result into (13.8) gives:

$$\frac{dU_j}{dt} = \left(y_i - y_j\right)U_c^j \tag{13.9}$$

By assumption, $y_j \geq y_i$, so person j is worse off as a result of a change to which person i is indifferent. If, alternatively, person j is indifferent, then i is better off from an increase in t. So long as the ranking of individuals by income is unchanged, it can also be seen that if an individual prefers a lower to a higher tax rate, all those with a higher income also prefer a lower rate. Furthermore, if an individual prefers a higher rate, all those with a lower income also prefer a higher rate. Hence there is a stable majority associated with the median voter's preferences; the identity of the median voter is unchanged whatever the tax parameters. Roberts (1977) also showed that quasi-transitive choices arise under a broad class of choice mechanisms in addition to majority voting. The argument can be extended to the case of a tax-free threshold with fixed total revenue.

Hierarchical adherence was later referred to by Seade (1982) as 'agent monotonicity' and for further discussion of its role in voting over tax systems, see Brunner (1989, pp. 71–5). With hierarchical adherence there is never an incentive for anyone below the median, whose identity is unchanged, to collude with those above the median, and vice versa. This is a very powerful result. It is therefore necessary to consider whether the assumption of hierarchical adherence is unduly restrictive. If tastes are identical then a sufficient condition for this to hold is that the elasticity of hours supplied is not less than –1. This condition is obviously satisfied in the case of identical Cobb–Douglas preferences, which imply the same linear upward-sloping relationship between y and w for everyone. If all individuals have Cobb–Douglas preferences, the existence of variation in the value of α, the coefficient on consumption, means that the slopes differ. However, all lines, when extended below the horizontal axis, must intersect at the same point, where both y and w are equal to $-a/(1 - t)$. This is illustrated in Figure 13.1 for two individuals. An increase in the tax rate means that the point of intersection moves outwards along the 45° line OE and the slopes remain unchanged. A change in the tax rate cannot therefore produce a change in the ranking of individuals by gross income, whatever the combination of wage rates they face.

It was seen in Chapter 11 that the marginal tax rate that maximizes social welfare, other things remaining equal, increases as the value of the coefficient on consumption increases, when everyone has the same Cobb–Douglas utility function. The same general result applies to the median voter's choice of the marginal tax rate. Whether the median voter's preferred value is above or below the social optimum depends on the degree of inequality aversion of the welfare function. If all individuals have Cobb–Douglas utility functions of the form $c^\alpha h^{1-\alpha}$ where, as in previous chapters, c and h denote consumption and leisure respectively, but differ in their value of α, then the median voter's preferred tax rate depends on the correlation between wages and α. Suppose that they are jointly lognormally distributed as Λ (μ_α, μ_w, σ_α^2, σ_w^2, ρ) with ρ denoting the correlation coefficient, then the distribution of α for a given value

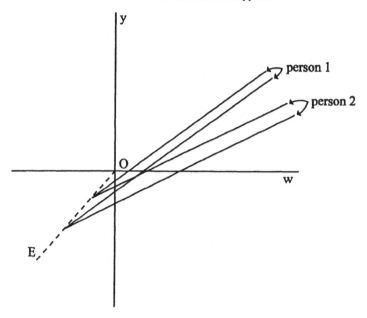

Figure 13.1   Earnings and linear taxation: two individuals

of w is also lognormal with mean of logs given by $\mu_\alpha + \rho(\sigma_\alpha/\sigma_w)(\log w - \mu_w)$ and variance of logarithms equal to $\sigma_\alpha^2(1 - \rho^2)$. This property can be used to simulate a population of individuals. If the variance of logarithms of wages, σ_w^2, is set at 0.5 and the arithmetic mean value of α is 0.7, with a variance of logarithms of 0.10, calculations based on a simulated population show that as ρ varies from -0.75 to $+0.75$, the median voter's preferred value of t increases from 0.15 to 0.55. However, the welfare maximum (for $\varepsilon = 0.5$) remains at $t = 0.30$ in each case.

13.2   A TWO-PERIOD MODEL

This section extends the above treatment to a two-period framework. It is seen that Roberts's result can be applied to the linear income tax in two periods, but breaks down in the case of a system having a tax-free threshold when individuals can shift income between periods.

Income Determination

In the present section the assumption of hierarchical adherence will be preserved by ignoring labour supply decisions and assuming an exogenously given distribution of income-earning ability, y. However, the tax parameters affect individuals' decisions regarding the distribution of taxable income between the two periods, though the ordering of individuals by net lifetime income is preserved. Suppose that individuals must choose between working in both periods and earning y in each period, or investing in higher education and bearing a fixed cost, c, as well as forgoing current earnings of $(1 - \delta)y$, where $0 < \delta < 1$, in return for higher second-period earnings, ky, where $k > 1$. This simple framework has been chosen for purposes of exposition. In general the results obtained below only require that taxable income can be transferred through the lifetime and that individuals of higher income-earning ability face lower costs of transferring income across periods; for a more complex specification, see Creedy (1995c).

Assume also a one-to-one correspondence between utility and post tax income, z, given by $z(\alpha,t,y)$. Therefore, for an equivalent form of the result to hold it is necessary to demonstrate that along indifference curves, $dt/d\alpha\,|_{z_i} \geq dt/d\alpha\,|_{z_j}$ for $i < j$. As pre-tax income is assumed to be monotonically increasing in y this implies:

$$d(dt/d\alpha\,|_z)/dy \leq 0 \qquad (13.10)$$

Thus Roberts's result applies also to this framework if the slope of each individual's indifference curve falls with income-earning ability. The following subsections examine the condition in (13.10) for two types of tax schedule.

The Linear Income Tax

Under the linear income tax uneducated individuals receive a post-tax and transfer income in each period of $a + y(1 - t)$, so that:

$$z_1^u = z_2^u = y + a - yt \qquad (13.11)$$

Net lifetime income, Z^u, is (ignoring discounting) therefore given by:

$$Z^u = 2\{a + y(1 - t)\} \qquad (13.12)$$

Assuming that education expenses are non-deductible, an educated individual receives $z_1^e = \delta y(1 - t) + a - c$ and $z_2^e = ky(1 - t) + a$ in periods 1 and 2 respectively. Net lifetime income is therefore:

$$Z^e = y(\delta + k)(1 - t) + 2a - c \qquad (13.13)$$

Given income-earning ability, y_i, an individual will choose education if $Z^e > Z^u$, that is, if:

$$y_i(1 - t) \{(\delta + k) - 2\} - c > 0 \qquad (13.14)$$

It can be seen from equation (13.14) that for a strictly positive proportion of the population to be educated it is necessary to have $\delta + k > 2$.

Denote by y^* the level of ability above which individuals become educated. Using the above results it is possible to determine the slope of indifference curves in (a, t) space. Assuming that $y > a$, for an uneducated individual, (13.12) shows that:

$$dt/da|_z = 1/y \qquad (13.15)$$

therefore, for $y \leq y^*$:

$$d(dt/da|_z)/dy = -1/y^2 < 0 \qquad (13.16)$$

From (13.13) the slope of an indifference curve for an educated individual is:

$$dt/da|_z = 2/\{y(\delta + k)\} \qquad (13.17)$$

so that, for $y > y^*$:

$$d(dt/da|_z)/dy = -2/y^2(\delta + k) \leq 0 \qquad (13.18)$$

Loosely, (13.16) shows that the marginal tax rate preferred by uneducated individuals falls with ability level. Similarly (13.18) shows that the marginal tax rate preferred by educated individuals also falls with ability level. These results demonstrate that when considering an increase in t and a which leaves utility unchanged, the preferred level of progression falls with ability *within* each sub-group of educated or uneducated individuals. However, for (13.10) to hold it is necessary to demonstrate that indifference curves are downward-sloping over the whole range of y. Since educational choice, determined by (13.14), is a function of the tax rate t it is necessary to consider the preferences of individuals whose educational status changes with changes in the tax structure. This introduces a discontinuity in the schedules at the choice margin, y^*, requiring analysis of a discrete change at that point. Hence $dt/da|_z$ should be as shown in schedule (i) of Figure 13.2. Comparing the left- and right-hand side derivatives at y^*, for (13.10) to hold it is necessary that $\lim_{y \uparrow y^*} dt/da|_z > \lim_{y \downarrow y^*} dt/da|_z$, which from (13.15) and (13.16) implies $1/y > 2/[y(\delta + k)]$ and therefore that $\delta + k > 2$. This must be true from equation (13.14); therefore (13.10) must hold for all y and Roberts's result applies.

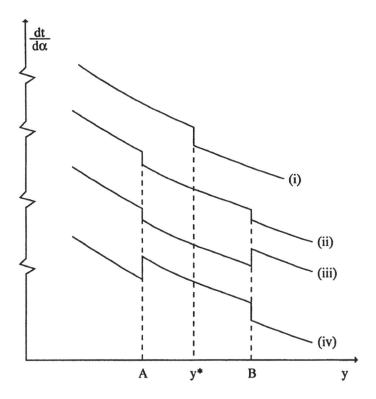

Figure 13.2 Tax preferences in a two-period framework

A Tax-free Threshold

Assume that all individuals are taxed at the rate, t, above an exempted amount, a, which is less than the minimum value of y. Net income for an uneducated individual in each period is therefore:

$$z_1^u = z_2^u = y - (y - a)t \qquad (13.19)$$

If as before the costs are not tax deductible, post-tax income in the first period is $z_1^e = \delta - c\,(\delta y - a)t$, for $\delta y > a$, and $\delta y - c$, for $\delta y < a$. Income in the second period for all educated individuals is $z_2^e = ky - (ky - a)t$.

For an uneducated person, net lifetime income, Z^u, is $2\{y - (y - a)t\}$, so that along an indifference curve:

$$dt/da = t/(y - a) \qquad (13.20)$$

For an educated individual with first-period taxable income below the exemption, lifetime income, Z^e, is $\delta y - c + ky - (ky - a)t$, so that along an indifference curve:

$$dt/da = t/(ky - a) \qquad (13.21)$$

For an educated person with first-period income above the tax free threshold, a, net lifetime income, Z^e is $\delta y - c - (\delta y - a)t + ky - (ky - a)t$, so that along an indifference curve:

$$dt/da = 2t/\{(\delta + k)y - 2a\} \qquad (13.22)$$

Consider the sub-groups in turn. For the uneducated, from (13.20):

$$d(dt/da)/dy = -t/(y - a)^2 < 0 \qquad (13.23)$$

For the educated below the exemption in the first period, from (13.21):

$$d(dt/da)/dy = -kt/(ky - a)^2 < 0 \qquad (13.24)$$

For the educated above the exemption in the first period, from (13.22):

$$d(dt/da)/dy = -2(\delta + k)/\{(\delta + k)y - 2a\}^2 < 0 \qquad (13.25)$$

Consequently condition (13.10) is satisfied within sub-groups but it is again necessary to check the slopes of the function at any discontinuity. In this case there are two points of discontinuity, labelled A and B in Figure 13.2. Point A is the discontinuity due to the educational choice decision and B is that caused by the tax-free threshold. Roberts's result holds for schedule (ii) of Figure 13.2, but it will be violated if either of the situations depicted in schedules (iii) or (iv) of Figure 13.2 occur. For (13.10) to hold at A it is necessary that $\lim_{y \uparrow y^*} dt/da\,|_z > \lim_{y \downarrow y^*} dt/da\,|_z$. From (13.20) and (13.21) this implies $t/(y - a) > t/(ky - a)$ and therefore that $k > 1$, which holds by assumption.

Consider discontinuity B: for (13.10) to hold it is necessary that $\lim_{hy \uparrow a} dt/da\,|_z > \lim_{hy \downarrow a} dt/da\,|_z$. From (13.21) and (13.22) this implies $t/(ky - a) > 2t/(\delta + k)y - 2a$ which requires that $h > k$. This can never be true, thus condition (13.10) is violated. Individuals of higher income-earning ability who are educated and above the threshold in the first period will prefer a tax and threshold combination (a, t) with a higher marginal tax rate than that preferred by someone who is also educated but has marginally lower income-earning ability and is therefore below the threshold in the first period.

This result has a straightforward intuitive explanation. For utility to remain constant, an increase in the threshold requires an increase in t of, say Δt. For individuals who are educated but below the threshold in the first period, an increase in the threshold benefits them only in the second period, by an amount $t\Delta a$. In the second period the effect of a rise in t reduces income by $(ky - a)\Delta t$. In comparison, an individual of slightly higher income-earning ability who is educated, but whose income is above the threshold in both periods, benefits by an amount, $t\Delta a$, in both periods. However, in the first period the tax increase only imposes a cost of $(\delta y - a)\Delta t$, which is smaller than the second period cost of $(ky - a)\Delta t$. Thus for a given increase in the threshold, the higher-ability individual above the threshold obtains twice the benefit, but pays less than twice the cost of the tax change. Thus the individual with higher income-earning ability may favour a higher marginal tax rate and a majority voting equilibrium may not exist.

The condition of hierarchical adherence ensures that, even though individuals have double-peaked preferences over the marginal tax rate, a majority voting equilibrium exists in the single-period framework for both the linear tax and the tax-free threshold. The median voter, that is the individual with the median wage rate, dominates. This convenient result extends to a two-period framework in the case of the linear income tax. However, it does not extend to the case of a tax-free threshold.

PART III

General Equilibrium

14.   Taxation in general equilibrium

The previous two parts of this book have examined tax and transfer systems in a partial equilibrium setting in which taxes do not influence the wage rates faced by individuals, even though labour supplies may be affected. In many contexts this may be a reasonable approximation, given the complexities involved in allowing for a wider range of effects. However, for some purposes a general, rather than partial, equilibrium analysis of the effects of taxes is required. Several large-scale and sophisticated computable general equilibrium models have been constructed for tax analyses, along with the study of many other types of economic policy. Part III of this book aims to provide an elementary introduction to some aspects of the role of taxes in a static general equilibrium framework. It therefore concentrates on the structure of smaller general equilibrium models such as two-sector models. This allows the nature of the interdependencies involved to be more clearly perceived.

Section 14.1 discusses the simple partial equilibrium analysis of tax incidence and refers to some of its limitations in order to motivate the later treatment of general equilibrium. Section 14.2 then presents the basic two-sector general equilibrium model in diagrammatic form. It examines income and consumption taxes using a four-quadrant diagram. The analysis is simplified by the special assumptions that factor supplies are fixed and individuals have identical homothetic preferences. The latter assumption implies that the relationship between the ratio of demands and the price ratio is independent of income. The section also introduces the use of compensating variations as measures of tax burdens. This material provides an introduction to the more formal analysis of Chapter 15.

14.1.   PARTIAL EQUILIBRIUM TAX INCIDENCE

Consider an excise tax imposed on a single good. The first point to stress is that it does not matter whether the tax is collected from buyers or sellers, since the overall result is the same. The equilibrium price before the tax is imposed, p, must satisfy the condition that $D(p) = S(p)$, where D and S are market demand and supply functions respectively. If a tax at the rate t per unit is collected from buyers, the new equilibrium price, p', must satisfy $D(p' + t) = S(p')$. The price, p', is the *tax-exclusive* price of the good. But if the tax is collected from producers, the equilibrium price, p'', must satisfy $D(p'') = S(p'' - t)$. The price,

p'', is the tax-inclusive price of the good. In the first case the net amount paid
per unit by buyers exceeds the price, and in the second case the net amount
received by producers is less than the price paid by consumers. But comparison
of these conditions shows that $p'' = p' + t$, so that the equilibrium quantity, the
tax revenue and the tax-inclusive price paid by consumers is independent of
the administrative process.

The effect of such a tax is shown in Figure 14.1, following the standard diagrammatic treatment that was first produced 150 years ago. Without taxation,
the equilibrium price is p, given by the intersection, at point G, of demand and
supply functions. The imposition of the tax leads to a tax-exclusive price of OC
and a tax-inclusive price of OA, with the difference, AC, being equal to the tax,
t, per unit. The incidence of the tax is typically examined in terms of its effect
on consumers' and producers' surpluses, treating the two 'sides' of the market
as separate groups. The loss of consumers' surplus is measured by the area of
ABGF, while the loss of producers' surplus is measured by the area CBGD.
The relative orders of magnitude are determined by the shapes of the supply
and demand curves. A vertical supply curve or a horizontal demand curve
leads to the burden falling entirely on producers. Conversely, a vertical demand
curve or a horizontal supply curve leads to the burden falling entirely on

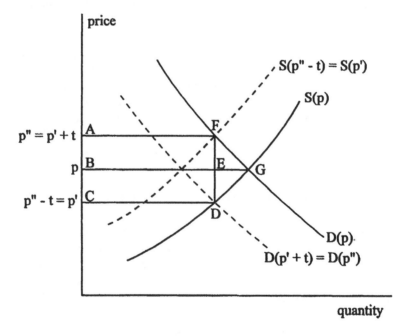

Figure 14.1   Taxation in partial equilibrium

consumers. The general result therefore follows that the burden is borne by the inelastic side of the market.

Figure 14.1 illustrates a further important result. The total tax revenue is equal to the area ACDF (the number of units of the good sold multiplied by the tax per unit). It is therefore clear that if the tax revenue were returned to consumers and producers in full, there would still remain a loss of surplus. The exceptions to this occur where either the supply or demand curve is vertical. This loss, remaining after reimbursing the tax revenue, is a measure of the *excess burden* resulting from the tax; it is given by the size of the area FDG. On the assumption that the curves are approximately linear over the relevant range, the excess burden is measured by one-half of the product of the tax rate and the change in quantity resulting from the tax (from the formula for the area of a triangle).

These results, that the burden of the tax does not typically fall on the side of the market on whom it is imposed for administrative purposes, that the tax is borne in full by the inelastic side of the market, and that there will typically remain an excess burden, are fundamental in public finance analysis. They hold in both partial and general equilibrium contexts.

The Treatment of Small Changes

The above results can be seen more formally by considering the effect of introducing small taxes, so that calculus can be employed. Suppose that the tax is paid to the authorities by consumers, so that the tax-exclusive price, p, must satisfy the condition that:

$$D(p + t) = S(p) \tag{14.1}$$

where p is regarded as a function of t. Differentiating (14.1) with respect to t, where $D' = dD(p + t)/d(p + t)$ and $S' = dS/dp$, gives:

$$D' \frac{d(p+t)}{dt} = S' \frac{dp}{dt}$$

This can be rearranged to get:

$$\left(1 + \frac{dp}{dt}\right) D' - S' \frac{dp}{dt} = 0 \tag{14.2}$$

Hence:

$$\frac{dp}{dt} = \frac{D'}{S' - D'} \tag{14.3}$$

Multiplying numerator and denominator of (14.3) by $p/D = p/S$, and defining the elasticities $\eta_d = (p/D)D'$ and $\eta_s = (p/S)S'$, gives:

$$\frac{dp}{dt} = \frac{\eta_d}{\eta_s - \eta_d} \tag{14.4}$$

Hence if $\eta_d = 0$, the tax-exclusive price is unchanged and consumers bear the full burden of the tax, while if $\eta_s = 0$ the tax-exclusive price falls by the full amount of the tax and the burden is 'shifted' to producers. These results correspond to the earlier diagrammatic argument that the inelastic side of the market bears the burden of the tax.

A similar type of approach has often been applied to general equilibrium analyses of taxation, allowing the relevant equations to be differentiated and manipulated. However, tax changes are typically not small and the imposition of significant tax changes involves the movement to a new equilibrium. It is therefore argued that the nature of the new equilibrium should be the focus of interest.

Problems of Partial Equilibrium Analysis

The most obvious limitation of the partial equilibrium analysis of taxation is that it cannot handle the interdependence among markets. From this point of view it might perhaps be argued that partial analysis should only concentrate on small changes in taxes, so that other effects can more safely be ignored. The partial treatment cannot by its very nature consider the effects on non-taxed industries. Interdependencies can arise from both the product market and the factor market, and the partial treatment is particularly unsuited to go 'behind' the supply and demand curves to examine the effects on factor prices, and hence individuals' incomes and demands.

The treatment of tax revenue is also too simple in partial equilibrium treatments, since the way in which the revenue is ultimately allocated can have important implications for factor and goods markets. Furthermore, the focus on consumers and producers as the two main groups is in some respects rather artificial. A general equilibrium treatment is able to allow for different factor endowments of individuals, and to distinguish their behaviour both as suppliers of factors and demanders of goods. Concentration on individuals as the more appropriate unit of analysis also means that a more satisfactory measure of the nature of the tax burden can be constructed. These aspects will be examined explicitly in the following sections.

14.2 DIAGRAMMATIC TREATMENT OF GENERAL EQUILIBRIUM

The two-good, two-factor, two-person model has its obvious limitations, but it is an extremely useful device for exploring the crucial interdependencies involved. This section presents an elementary diagrammatic representation of the model in order to illustrate some features of taxes in general equilibrium.

The Two-sector Model

The production contract curve lies at the heart of the two-sector model. It is obtained as the locus of points of tangency between isoquants, so that the marginal rates of substitution between factors in production are the same for both goods; this is illustrated in Figure 14.2. Along the contract curve, factors are allocated efficiently both within and between industries. The curve shown in Figure 14.2 displays a situation in which industry X uses capital relatively

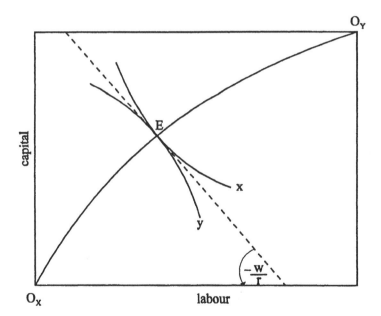

Figure 14.2   The production contract curve

more intensively than industry Y at all output levels along the contract curve. The common tangent associated with each point on the curve gives the ratio of factor prices associated with consistent factor demands in the sense that the respective outputs of X and Y are both produced at minimum costs.

Each point on the production contract curve is associated with an output combination, giving rise to the production possibility curve; this is shown in Figure 14.3. In the absence of taxation the relative price of goods, p_x/p_y, is given by the slope of the production possibility curve. Individuals' incomes are determined by combining their endowments with the factor prices, and combining this information with the goods prices gives the budget constraint facing each individual. General equilibrium requires that the demands of the individuals are consistent with the supplies, as shown in Figure 14.3. In the general equilibrium model only relative prices of factors and goods are determined unless other assumptions are imposed. This is the standard treatment of the two-person, two-good, two-factor model where factor supplies are assumed to be fixed. Allowance for variable factor supplies will be made in Chapter 15.

It is useful to transfer some of the information contained in Figures 14.2 and 14.3, particularly from the production side, into another set of curves. Consider, first, the way in which the factor price ratio varies along the production contract curve, using a simple intuitive argument. Suppose that, starting from point E in Figure 14.2, the output of good X is reduced by moving along the contract curve. By assumption, industry X is relatively capital intensive, so the use of the

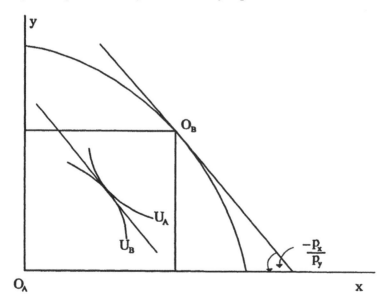

Figure 14.3   General equilibrium

factors in industry Y, released by the contraction of X's output, requires a reduction in the capital rental relative to the wage rate. Hence w/r must increase. Conversely, as the output of good X increases from point E, the wage/rental ratio must fall. The relationship between the factor price ratio and the ratio of X to Y is therefore as shown in Figure 14.4, for different relative factor intensities.

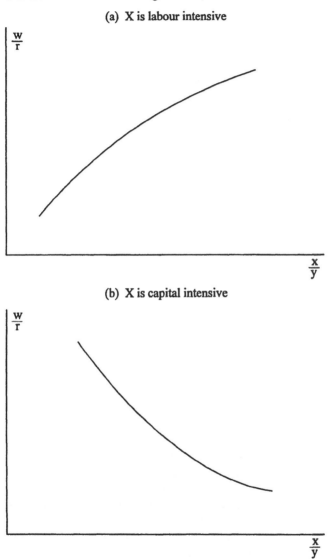

Figure 14.4 *Factor prices and relative outputs*

The relationship between the output ratio X/Y and the relative price ratio p_x/p_y, from the production possibility curve, may be traced as in Figure 14.5. This must be upward-sloping, and may be regarded as a general equilibrium supply curve. Associated with the factor price ratio, from Figure 14.2, and the goods price ratio, from Figure 14.3, there is a further relationship between these variables which may be referred to as a competitive pricing function. This will depend on, among other things, the relative factor intensities. These diagrams are particularly useful in concentrating on relative prices and output levels.

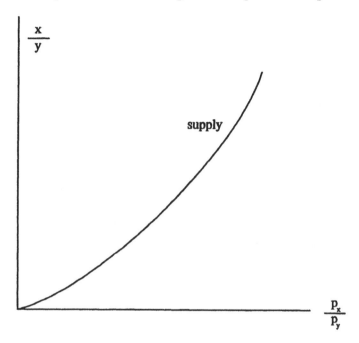

Figure 14.5   The general equilibrium supply function

The diagrams are clearly interrelated, and may usefully be drawn together in a four-quadrant diagram such as that shown in Figure 14.6 for the case where X is labour-intensive. All that is required to complete the model is a general equilibrium aggregate demand curve corresponding to the supply curve shown in the top right-hand segment. The properties of such a demand curve are in general very complex, since the demands of individuals depend on relative prices and their incomes, and the latter depend on endowments and factor prices. There is, however, a particular set of assumptions which enable a very simple form of aggregate demand curve to be used. Suppose that, first, the two individuals have identical tastes so that there is effectively no aggregation problem to deal with. Secondly, assume that utility functions are homothetic; this implies that the ratio of demands for goods X and Y depends only on the ratio of prices and is independent of income. Utility functions such as the Cobb–Douglas and Constant Elasticity of Substitution (CES) have this convenient property. In such a one-person model the demand function may be drawn as a downward sloping curve, as shown in Figure 14.6.

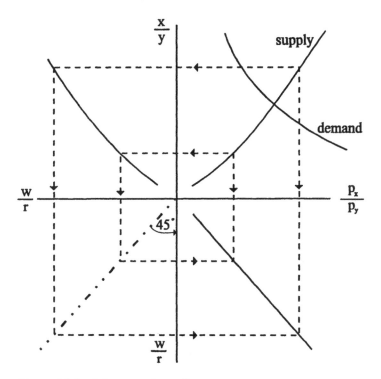

Figure 14.6   A four-quadrant diagram

The model, though highly non-linear, has a unique solution given by the inter-section of the supply and demand curves in Figure 14.6. If, however, the preferences are such that the identical individuals have backward-bending price–consumption curves, then the general equilibrium demand curve may be U-shaped and it is possible that there may be three equilibrium positions.

General Income and Consumption Taxes

The framework illustrated in Figure 14.6 may be used to obtain some insight into the effects of simple tax policies where there are no labour supply responses and the individuals have identical tastes which are also homothetic.

Consider first the use of a consumption tax imposed at the same rate, v, on both goods; the tax-exclusive price of each good is p while the tax-inclusive price is $p(1 + v)$. Suppose in addition that the revenue raised is redistributed to individuals in the form of a social dividend. Hence the government does not spend the revenue directly on the two goods. The fact that the tax rate is the same for each good means that the relative price of goods is unchanged, so that the supply curve in Figure 14.6 remains unchanged. Similarly, there is no reason why the relationship between x/y and w/r, and between w/r and p_x/p_y, should change. The assumption of homothetic identical preferences implies that, even though there may be a change in the distribution of income as a result of the tax and transfer scheme, the general equilibrium demand curve also remains unchanged. Remember that the framework considered here assumes fixed factor supplies; allowance for the consumption of leisure would imply that there is an untaxed good and therefore a distortion introduced into the model. This type of general consumption tax therefore has no effect on any of the curves in Figure 14.6; relative factor and goods prices and outputs are the same. There is only a change in the distribution of goods between the two individuals. (Remember that the analysis is entirely static, so that any possible implications for saving behaviour are ignored.)

Suppose that, instead of a consumption tax, an income tax is imposed at a fixed marginal and average rate and that incomes from wages and capital are taxed at the same proportional rate. Again, assume that a simple transfer system operates in which all the tax revenue is shared equally between the two individuals. Such an income tax does not give rise to any distortions so again none of the curves in Figure 14.6 is shifted in any way. The tax only has a redistributive impact. This result holds irrespective of the nature of the production functions and utility functions, so long as the latter are identical and homothetic.

A Selective Tax

The general income and consumption taxes considered in the previous section have only a redistributive effect, given the assumption of identical tastes, no labour supply responses and the use of a social dividend, because they involve no distortions. The effect of a selective tax on one good, say good X, is more complex and depends on the relative factor intensities. If industry X is relatively labour-intensive, then the transfer of resources to industry Y is unambiguously associated with a reduction in the wage/rental ratio. However, if X is relatively capital-intensive, the movement along the production contract curve is associated with a relatively higher demand for labour.

The possibilities are shown in Figures 14.7 and 14.8, for the cases where X is labour- and capital-intensive respectively. The selective tax on X means that

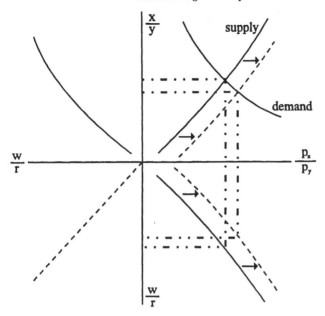

Figure 14.7 A selective tax on labour-intensive good

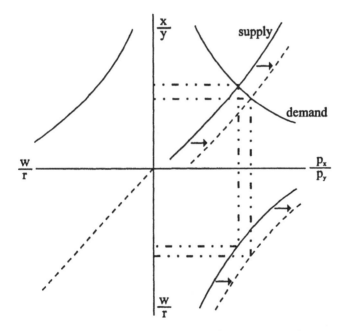

Figure 14.8 A selective tax on capital-intensive good

a given ratio x/y is associated with a higher price ratio p_x/p_y, therefore shifting the supply curve to the right. Factor market pricing is not affected, so the curve in the bottom right-hand quadrant must also shift outwards to the right. In Figure 14.7 this can only lead to a reduction in the ratio, w/r. The precise extent of the fall in the wage relative to the capital rental will depend on the substitution elasticities. In Figure 14.8 the outward shift in the two curves, in the case where X is relatively capital-intensive, gives rise to an increase in the ratio of w to r.

Measuring Tax Burdens

The above diagrammatic analysis may be regarded as giving some information about the extent to which different factors bear the burden of any given tax structure. A reduction in w/r is said to be associated with the result that labour bears a greater share of the tax than capital. However, even in the simple case of identical homothetic tastes and a social dividend, the diagrammatic approach does not contain any information about the distribution of income. It therefore says nothing about the extent to which the burden is borne by different *individuals*.

In the simple partial equilibrium framework, the burden of the tax was considered in terms of its effect on consumers' and producers' surpluses, and it was seen that the total loss typically exceeds the amount of revenue raised, leading to a deadweight loss. Many analyses of taxation (particularly of partial factor taxes) in a general equilibrium context have also been concerned to examine the burdens borne by such groups as 'workers' and 'capitalists'. They have therefore concentrated on the implications of tax changes for the ratio of the wage to the capital rental. However, taxes ultimately fall on individuals, and it is often desirable to measure their effects on those individuals.

A more appropriate concept of the burden at the individual level is that of the compensating variation. This provides a money measure of the impact of price changes on the individual (bearing in mind that, depending on how the government uses the revenue and on individual endowments, some individuals will gain from a tax change). The compensating variation is a measure of the amount of money which needs to be given to a loser (or taken from a gainer) in order to restore the individual to the same level of utility as that experienced before the price change.

The compensating variation for each individual is most easily evaluated using the concept of the expenditure function. This expresses the minimum expenditure required to attain a given utility level, as a function of utility and commodity prices. The expenditure function can be written as $E(U,p)$, where U is utility and p is the price vector. If subscripts 0 and 1 indicate the levels before and after a change in the tax structure, the compensating variation for an individual is given as:

$$E(U_0, p_1) - E(U_0, p_0) \qquad (14.5)$$

The second term in (14.5) is the actual level of expenditure before the tax change. The compensating variations, reflecting the price changes, can then usefully be compared with the changes in the net income of each individual. Expenditure functions will be examined in more detail in the next chapter in the context of explicit assumptions about the form of the direct utility function.

This chapter has presented a diagrammatic model of a basic general equilibrium model. The special assumptions of fixed labour supplies and identical homothetic preferences of individuals were made. It was shown that a general consumption tax is equivalent to an income tax (imposed equally on labour and rental income) and both structures have no effect on outputs and relative prices of goods and factors. The tax structure will involve redistribution between individuals, depending on their endowments, but this cannot be examined using the diagrams. A selective tax on one of the goods increases the relative price of the taxed good and, if the good is relatively labour intensive, reduces the wage/rental ratio. The assumptions used are clearly very strong, and it is desirable to relax them. Further progress in examining the implications of tax changes in general equilibrium requires the use of a formal mathematical model. This is the subject of the following chapter.

15. A two-sector model

The diagrammatic approach used in the previous chapter cannot be adapted to deal with less simple assumptions, particularly concerning different tastes and endogenous labour supplies. Further progress requires the production of a formal model. One approach is to write down the cost functions for each industry, from which the factor demands may be obtained. The assumption of competitive markets gives the equality of goods prices and marginal costs, and the factor demands must be consistent with full employment conditions. The model is completed by writing the expenditure functions, setting the price to be used as numeraire, and imposing equilibrium in goods markets. Comparative static exercises may be carried out by appropriate differentiation; see Atkinson and Stiglitz (1980). However, the limitation of the analysis to small changes in the tax system is a high cost to pay for tractability of comparative static exercises.

The discussion in this chapter therefore considers a two-sector model which may be used to examine alternative tax structures by using numerical analyses of the change in the equilibrium when the tax structure changes. Section 15.1 presents the production components of the model. The efficient allocation of factor supplies is considered, and the implied factor price ratio and goods price ratio are derived. The way in which the prices feed into individuals' demands is examined in section 15.2, along with the procedure used to solve the model. Taxes are introduced into the model in section 15.3, and alternative tax structures are discussed in section 15.4. For simplicity, the analysis uses Cobb–Douglas production and utility functions. However, Appendix 15.1 presents results for the case of constant elasticity of substitution (CES) functions.

15.1   PRODUCTION

The static two-sector model presented below involves the production of two goods, X and Y, where amounts produced and consumed of these goods are denoted by the lower-case letters x and y. The unit prices of the goods are denoted p_x and p_y. The two individuals are labelled A and B. Inputs of labour and capital services are denoted L and K respectively, and it is assumed throughout that units are such that the total amount of capital in the economy is one unit. Labour supplies are allowed to be endogenous, and the total supply of labour is written as L_T. Labour and capital are homogeneous, with the wage rate and rental per unit denoted w and r respectively.

Cobb–Douglas Production Functions

Suppose that both goods are produced under constant returns to scale Cobb–Douglas conditions, so that in general the production functions can be written as:

$$x = A_x L^{\alpha_x} K^{1-\alpha_x} \tag{15.1}$$

$$y = A_y L^{\alpha_y} K^{1-\alpha_y} \tag{15.2}$$

The total supply of labour is L_T, and the fixed supply of capital services is normalized to unity, so that $0 \le x \le A_x L_T^{\alpha_x}$ and $0 \le y \le A_y L_T^{\alpha_y}$. The marginal products in industry X are:

$$-\frac{dK}{dL} = \frac{\partial x/\partial L}{\partial x/\partial K} = \frac{\alpha_x}{1-\alpha_x}\frac{K}{L} \tag{15.3}$$

Hence the marginal rate of substitution of labour for capital, $-dK/dL$, is given by:

$$-\frac{dK}{dL} = \frac{\partial x/\partial L}{\partial x/\partial K} = \frac{\alpha_x}{1-\alpha_x}\frac{K}{L} \tag{15.4}$$

Similar results apply to industry Y, although if K and L units of capital and labour are used in industry X, then $1 - K$ and $L_T - L$ are available for use in Y. The production contract curve is given by equating the marginal rates of substitution, so that:

$$\frac{\alpha_x}{1-\alpha_x}\frac{K}{L} = \frac{\alpha_y}{1-\alpha_y}\frac{(1-K)}{(L_T - L)} \tag{15.5}$$

Hence the equation of the contract curve is obtained by solving (15.5) for K in terms of L, as:

$$K = \{1 + \delta(L_T/L - 1)\}^{-1} \tag{15.6}$$

with:

$$\delta = \frac{\alpha_x(1-\alpha_y)}{\alpha_y(1-\alpha_x)}$$

The Factor Price Ratio

For any given input of labour in industry X, the corresponding input of capital can be obtained directly from the contract curve in (15.6). The factor price ratio w/r is equal to the corresponding marginal rate of substitution at the relevant point on the contract curve. Since isoquants are tangential along the contract curve, only one industry needs to be considered. Substitute for K in (15.4), using (15.6), and equate the result to w/r, giving:

$$\frac{w}{r} = \frac{\alpha_x}{1-\alpha_x} \frac{\left\{1+\delta(L_T/L-1)\right\}^{-1}}{L}$$

$$= \frac{\alpha_x}{1-\alpha_x}\left\{L(1-\delta)+\delta L_T\right\}^{-1} \qquad (15.7)$$

The Goods Price Ratio

The goods price ratio, p_x/p_y is given from the slope, dy/dx, of the production possibility curve at the appropriate point. Hence:

$$\frac{p_x}{p_y} = -\frac{dy}{dx} \qquad (15.8)$$

However, it is not possible to derive the equation of the production possibility curve explicitly, so the following indirect method must be used to obtain the slope. For any given amount of labour used in industry X, the corresponding amount of capital, K(L), is given from the equation of the production contract curve in (15.6). Appropriate substitutions into the production functions (15.1) and (15.2) therefore give the corresponding outputs of X and Y as:

$$x = A_x L^{\alpha_x} K(L)^{1-\alpha_x} \qquad (15.9)$$

$$y = A_y (1-L)^{\alpha_y} \{1-K(L)\}^{1-\alpha_y} \qquad (15.10)$$

In the simple case where $\alpha_x = \alpha_y$ and labour supply is fixed at $L_T = 1$, then substitution into the contract curve of (15.6) gives $\delta = 1$ and $K = L$. Substituting into (15.9) and (15.10) gives two linear equations in L so that it is possible to eliminate L and express y as a linear function of x, with slope given by $-A_y/A_x$. In the more general case, the slope of the production possibility curve can be obtained using:

$$\frac{dy}{dx} = \frac{dy/dL}{dx/dL} \tag{15.11}$$

The terms on the right hand side of (15.11) are obtained from (15.9) and (15.10), with K(L) given by (15.6). It can be shown that:

$$\frac{dx}{dL} = -\frac{x}{L}\left\{\alpha_x + \delta(1-\alpha_x)L_T\frac{K}{L}\right\} \tag{15.12}$$

$$\frac{dy}{dL} = -\frac{y}{L_T - L}\left\{\alpha_y + \delta(1-\alpha_y)L_T\left(\frac{L_T - L}{1-K}\right)\left(\frac{K}{L}\right)^2\right\} \tag{15.13}$$

The term in (15.13) must be negative since y falls as L, the input of labour into industry X, increases. This involves a movement along the contract curve.

15.2   DEMAND AND LABOUR SUPPLY

The Determination of Incomes

The results of the previous section have shown how, starting with a specified amount of labour used in the production of good X, the resulting outputs of X and Y along with the factor and goods price ratios may be obtained, assuming that resources are used efficiently. There is insufficient information to determine absolute price levels, so it is necessary to normalize the price of one of the goods. Alternative ways of 'closing' the model may be used, but they are not considered here. Suppose that $p_x = 1$, so the corresponding price of good Y is immediately given as $-dx/dy$, from (15.8). The wage and capital rental can be obtained by imposing the adding-up requirement that the total value of output is equal to the total value of factor incomes. This gives:

$$wL_T + r = x + yp_y \qquad (15.14)$$

which can be rearranged to solve for r as:

$$r = \frac{x + yp_y}{1 + (w/r)L_T} \qquad (15.15)$$

Hence, having obtained w/r from section 15.2, the absolute values of w and r can be obtained.

To determine individuals' demands and labour supplies, an assumption regarding individuals' endowments of capital is required. Suppose that person A holds a proportion, k, of the capital services available, so that person B holds $1 - k$. The non-labour incomes of A and B are therefore kr and $(1 - k)r$ respectively. With this information it is possible to calculate the full incomes, M_A and M_B, of the two individuals, defined as the maximum income that could be obtained (that is, if the individuals consume no leisure). With an assumption about tastes, the demands and labour supplies of each individual can be evaluated, resulting from individual utility maximization. The approach is to consider leisure as another good whose price is the wage rate per unit. The analysis of consumption and labour supply discussed in Chapter 9 is therefore directly applicable in the present context. It is only necessary to extend the treatment to include two goods, as follows.

Cobb–Douglas Preferences

Consider a single individual choosing consumption levels of the two goods, x and y, along with leisure, h. The individual's total endowment of time is normalized to unity, so h may be regarded as the proportion of time spent in leisure. The utility function is written as a three-good Cobb–Douglas function:

$$U = U(x,y,h) = x^\theta y^\beta h^\gamma \qquad (15.16)$$

It is convenient to impose the relation $\gamma = 1 - \theta - \beta$. If π represents non-wage income, obtained from the individual's endowment of capital, then utility in (15.16) is maximized subject to the constraint that:

$$\pi + w(1 - h) = p_x x + p_y y \qquad (15.17)$$

Form the Lagrangean:

$$\Omega = U + \lambda\{\pi + w(1 - h) - xp_x - yp_y\} \qquad (15.18)$$

The first-order conditions, obtained by differentiating Ω with respect to x, y and h, and setting the results equal to zero, are therefore:

$$\theta U = \lambda x p_x, \ \beta U = \lambda y p_y \text{ and } \gamma U = \lambda h w \qquad (15.19)$$

Adding these three conditions gives $(\theta + \beta + \gamma)U = \lambda(x p_x + y p_y + wh)$, and re-arranging the budget constraint in (15.17) to get $\pi + w = p_x x + p_y y + wh$, it can be seen that the Lagrangean multiplier is $\lambda = U/(\pi + w)$. As in Chapter 9, it is useful to define $M = \pi + w$ as the maximum amount of income the individual could obtain with the given wage rate; this concept is referred to as *full income*. Substituting for $\lambda = U/M$ into the above first-order conditions gives:

$$x = \theta M/p_x \qquad (15.20)$$

$$y = \beta M/p_y \qquad (15.21)$$

$$h = \gamma M/w \qquad (15.22)$$

Notice that if the individual has no non-wage income, the consumption of leisure, and therefore supply of labour, is independent of the wage rate. The individual works (that is, $h < 1$) only if $w > \gamma\pi/(1 - \gamma)$. These results reflect the standard Cobb–Douglas properties; expenditure is a fixed proportion of full income, Engel curves are straight lines and demand curves are rectangular hyperbolas. By dividing (15.20) by (15.21) it can be found that the ratio x/y is inversely proportional to p_x/p_y, but does not depend on M. This is the homothetic property discussed in Chapter 14.

Expenditure Functions

It was suggested in Chapter 14 that the calculation of tax burdens in terms of compensating variations is most conveniently carried out using the expenditure function. This function, $E(U, p)$, denotes the minimum expenditure, at the prices, p, required to attain the utility level, U. In the present context, since the demands have already been obtained from the direct utility function, the expenditure function can be obtained using the indirect utility function, V, where utility is expressed as a function of prices and full income, as $V(p, M)$. For example, substituting for x, y, and h from (15.20) to (15.22), into the utility function of (15.16) gives:

$$V(p, M) = U = \left(\frac{\theta M}{p_x}\right)^\theta \left\{\frac{\beta M}{p_y}\right\}^\beta \left(\frac{\gamma M}{w}\right)^\gamma \qquad (15.23)$$

Solving (15.23) for M gives:

$$M = E(U, p) = U\left\{ \left(\frac{p_x}{\theta}\right)^\theta \left\{\frac{p_y}{\beta}\right\}^\beta \left(\frac{w}{\gamma}\right)^\gamma \right\} \qquad (15.24)$$

The appropriate compensating variations can be found using the expression (14.5) given in Chapter 14.

General Equilibrium

The previous discussion has followed the path of starting from a particular value of total labour supply, L_T, and an amount of labour used in the production of good X. Assuming that factors are used efficiently, the allocation of capital to industry X and hence the outputs of both X and Y can be obtained, along with the implied factor price ratio. The implied opportunity cost ratio, and hence goods price ratio, is then obtained from the slope of the production possibility curve. Setting the price of good X to unity and using the adding-up requirement enables the absolute values of the price of good Y, along with the capital rental and wage rate, to be determined. The factor and goods prices, combined with assumptions about the preferences of each individual, are then used to derive the labour supplies and demands for the two goods. A situation of general equilibrium only exists if the resulting total labour supply is equal to the initial assumed value, L_T, and if the demands for X and Y correspond to the supplies: the labour and goods markets must each be in equilibrium.

One approach to the examination of a general equilibrium would be to write down the equilibrium conditions for two of the three markets (since equilibrium in two markets implies equilibrium in the third) in terms of supply being equal to demand. This would produce a set of simultaneous equations with as many equations as there are endogenous variables. But the resulting equations are highly non-linear, so they must be solved using an iterative numerical procedure.

Consider, for example, the case where individuals' labour supplies are fixed, with person A holding L_A units and person B holding $L_T - L_A$ units of labour. It has already been assumed that A holds k units of capital, while B holds the remaining $1 - k$ units. It is therefore only necessary to consider the market for one good, say X. Given that p_x has been set to unity, the equilibrium condition in this market can be written as:

$$A_x L_x^{\alpha_x} K^{1-\alpha_x} = \theta_A M_A + \theta_B M_B \qquad (15.25)$$

where as before the θs are coefficients on good X in the utility functions and the Ms are incomes given by:

$$M_A = rk + wL_A \text{ and } M_B = (1 - k)r + (L_T - L_A)w \qquad (15.26)$$

In considering (15.25) it must be remembered that K must satisfy the equation of the production contract curve given by (15.6); the ratio w/r is given by (15.4); p_y is given by combining (15.12) and (15.13); and the absolute values of r and w are obtained using (15.15), where the output of good Y is taken from (15.9). It would be possible, but rather cumbersome, to make the appropriate substitutions into (15.25) in order to obtain an equation in only L, the amount of labour used in industry X. The resulting equation would be highly non-linear, and would require numerical methods for its solution. However, the following iterative procedure is equivalent to solving such an equation.

For the fixed labour supply case, the above results can be used to construct an iterative procedure for solving the model. Starting from an arbitrary input of labour into industry X, the associated supply and demand for good X can be obtained by following the various stages set out above. If there is an excess supply of good X, then a slightly lower input of labour in industry X is used, and the process repeated. This process will converge to an equilibrium in the market for X, and hence also in that for good Y. The same kind of procedure can be used for solving the model where labour supplies are endogenous, but it is rather longer since two markets have to be considered. A two-stage iterative process can be used, as follows. Starting with an arbitrary total amount of labour, the previous procedure can be used until equilibrium in the market for, say, good X is obtained. At this point the assumed total amount of labour may be compared with the total supply generated as a result of the factor and goods prices associated with equilibrium in the market for X. If there is an excess supply of labour, the total amount assumed in the first stage is increased slightly and the process is repeated. Convergence is reached when there is simultaneously equilibrium in the labour market and the market for good X. The production and utility functions used here are sufficient to guarantee that this type of adjustment process is stable; that is, it will converge to an equilibrium which, in addition, is unique.

Consider, for example, the simple case where labour supplies are fixed and production and utility functions are Cobb–Douglas. Suppose that $A_x = A_y = 1$, $\alpha_x = 0.3$ and $\alpha_y = 0.7$, so that industry Y is labour-intensive. Assume that A holds all the labour (one unit) and B holds all the capital, and that $\theta_A = 0.3$ with $\theta_B = 0.6$. In this example the 'capitalist' has a relatively strong preference for the capital-intensive good, X. If there are no taxes, it can be found that equilibrium occurs where $x = 0.491$ and $y = 0.594$, giving a wage rate and capital rental of 0.578 and 0.528 respectively, and the price of good Y is 1.040.

15.3.   TAXES IN THE BASIC MODEL

The previous two sections have ignored taxation, although this was done only to simplify the various expressions. Before introducing taxes, it is necessary to distinguish the types of comparison which may be made using this type of model. Within the general equilibrium framework it is necessary to be explicit about the way in which the tax revenue is used. The following discussion will assume that all of the tax revenue is redistributed to individuals in the form of a transfer payment. An alternative would be to suppose that the government spends the revenue on the two goods, according to an assumed utility function. The above models do not have financial assets, so governments cannot be assumed to borrow from individuals. Comparisons of tax structures in which the total tax revenue is constant are referred to as *differential incidence* studies. Alternatively, *balanced budget incidence* studies allow total tax revenue to change. Examples of each type will be given below.

The Introduction of Taxes

A wide variety of tax systems may be examined in the general equilibrium framework, but for simplicity suppose that a proportional income tax is applied to wage and property incomes at the rates t_w and t_π respectively. Furthermore, indirect taxes may be applied to the tax-exclusive prices of the goods at the proportional rates v_x and v_y; the tax-inclusive prices are thus $p_x(1 + v_x)$ and $p_y(1 + v_y)$. Producers respond to the tax-exclusive prices of goods, while consumers respond to tax-inclusive prices. However, firms respond to tax-inclusive factor prices while individuals, in their labour supply decisions, respond to the net wage rate. Hence in the approach described above, which at each iteration determines factor prices and goods prices for a particular allocation of labour to one industry, the resulting price ratios can be interpreted as those which are relevant from the firm's point of view.

Total tax revenue, R, is given by:

$$R = t_w w L_T + r t_\pi + x v_x + y p_y v_y \qquad (15.27)$$

In determining absolute values of w, r and p_y, for $p_x = 1$, the additivity condition is:

$$w(1 - t_w) L_T + r(1 - t_\pi) + R = x(1 + v_x) + y p_y(1 + v_y) \qquad (15.28)$$

On substituting for R, it is found that the previous relationship, in (15.14), is unchanged. Hence, the component of the model where allowance must be made for taxation involves the demands and labour supplies, not the factor prices and tax-exclusive goods prices.

If, as mentioned earlier, the tax revenue is redistributed to individuals in the form of an unconditional transfer payment or social dividend, T, each individual receives:

$$T = R/2 \qquad (15.29)$$

Consider person A, whose endowment of capital has been assumed to be k units, and who (like person B) has been assumed to be endowed with one unit of time. Person A's full income, M_A, is given by:

$$M_A = rk(1 - t_\pi) + T + w(1 - t_w) \qquad (15.30)$$

The results in section 15.2 may be adapted by the appropriate alteration of the full income, M, and by writing $w(1 - t_w)$, that is the net of tax wage rate, instead of w, and writing $p_x(1 + v_x)$ and $p_y(1 + v_y)$ instead of p_x and p_y. Care must also be taken to modify the conditions under which labour supply is non-zero. The modification of the expenditure functions in (15.23) and (15.24) is achieved in a similar way.

Consider again the example given at the end of section 15.2, and introduce a selective tax on good X at the rate of 0.25, with the revenue being used to finance a social dividend paid to both individuals. The tax implies a reduction in the equilibrium output of good X to 0.434, with that of good Y increasing to 0.648. The increase in the output of the labour-intensive good leads to a higher wage rate of 0.619, with the capital rental falling to 0.513. The tax inclusive price of good X becomes 1.25, and the price of good Y has also risen to 1.078. The tax revenue finances a dividend of 0.054. The fact that the selective tax raises the wage rate and is imposed on the good for which person A, the 'worker', has a relatively lower preference, means that A is unequivocally better off from the tax change. The price change, compared with the no-tax situation, produces a compensating variation for A and B respectively of 0.057 and 0.085. However, the increase in their net (nominal) incomes are 0.095 and 0.039, so that A's increase in income exceeds the compensating variation, while the opposite is true of B. The tax change has in this case produced an increase in the income of the richer person, so any inequality averse welfare function judges the tax to produce a reduction in social welfare. This example is considerably simplified by the assumption of a fixed labour supply, but further comparisons are made below.

Some Comparisons

Consider the use of selective taxes in the case where labour supplies are endogenous. Suppose that production functions have values of A and α of 1 and 0.3 in the production of X, and 1 and 0.70 respectively in the production of Y. Suppose tastes are identical, with $\theta = 0.2$ and $\beta = 0.6$ (thus $\gamma = 0.2$), and to avoid any redistributive effects assume that the capital is equally divided between A and B. It is known from the discussion in Chapter 14 that, with endogenous labour supplies, a uniform consumption tax is no longer equivalent (in its effects on output and prices) to a uniform income tax. However, consider the balanced budget incidence comparisons shown in Table 15.1, which considers alternative combinations of t_w and t_π, with $v_x = v_y = 0$ in all cases.

Table 15.1   Income taxes with endogenous labour

Case	t_w	t_π	w/r	ΣU	T
1	0.3	0.3	1.1986	0.7042	1.193
2	0.2	0.2	1.1432	0.7084	0.130
3	0.3	0	1.1986	0.7042	0.115
4	0.2	0	1.1432	0.7084	0.078
5	0.3	0.2	1.1986	0.7042	0.167
6	0.2	0.3	1.1432	0.7084	0.156

Note: Production and utility functions are given in the text.

The value of tax revenue is different in all six cases of Table 15.1, but for given t_w, the value of the wage/rental ratio (along with total utility) is independent of the value of t_π. These results therefore show that the tax on the capital rental is in a sense fully borne by capital, since the wage rate is unaltered by the tax. The result established in Chapter 14 for the partial equilibrium framework, that the tax is borne by the inelastic side of the market (or fully shifted by the elastic side), therefore also holds in the general equilibrium framework. This important result also holds if individuals have different utility functions. The full impact of the selective tax will, however, depend on the precise ownership structure and structure of preferences.

15.4   ALTERNATIVE TAX STRUCTURES

One important issue in public finance concerns the optimal combination of direct and indirect taxes, and the question of whether or not indirect taxes should be imposed at a uniform rate. This is essentially a 'second-best' problem; since it is not possible to tax individuals' *endowments*, the question is whether other distortions should be eliminated. This is not the place to review the extensive and complex literature, but some results, far from straightforward to derive, can be summarized fairly easily. The framework usually considered is one in which individuals have identical preferences and face the same prices for goods and services but differ in the wage rate they face. The distribution of wage rates is taken as being exogenously given in a static model. With a linear income tax, a uniform system of indirect taxes is optimal if Engel curves are linear and the marginal rate of substitution between goods is independent of leisure. With non-linear income taxation, uniformity does not require linear Engel curves. The argument for uniformity therefore depends fundamentally on the existence of an optimal (second-best) income tax and transfer system applied to all individuals and on the structure of preferences.

A further implication of these results is worth stressing. With non-linear taxation, if these strong conditions hold there is in fact no role for indirect taxation since a uniform indirect tax is equivalent to a tax on income. If, for dynamic reasons, it is desired to offer a stimulus to saving, then debate will focus on the role of interest-income taxation. Alternatively, with linear taxation, it is simplest to have just uniform indirect taxes and lump sum grants, so that there is no need to observe individuals' incomes, as required by an income tax.

This section provides an illustration of the use of selective taxation in the general equilibrium model. It is intended simply to illustrate the role of selectivity, without suggesting that it is meant to be realistic. The parameter values used for the production and utility functions are given in Table 15.2 (for each production function $A_x = A_y = 1$). It can be seen that good X is assumed to be relatively labour intensive. The individuals have different preferences; person A is assumed to prefer good Y, while person B prefers good X. Both individuals are assumed to have an endowment of one unit of labour time, while person B is assumed to hold all the capital (which is normalized to be one unit).

Table 15.2   Parameter values

Utility functions		
	θ	β
Person A	0.2	0.6
Person B	0.5	0.2
Production functions		
	α	
Good X	0.7	
Good Y	0.3	

General equilibrium

The assumption about endowments means that person B is the richest individual and also supplies less labour than person A. Any selective tax structure which imposes an indirect tax on only good X is likely to favour person A, the poorest individual, since this individual is assumed to have a stronger preference for good Y. However, the assumption that good X is labour-intensive does not operate in A's favour, since all A's income is obtained from wages (and the transfer payment), and such a selective tax will reduce the wage rate. The labour supply of both individuals is thus expected to fall, although in some cases person B may be at a corner solution where no labour is supplied. Hence the net impact on person A is ambiguous.

The effect on social welfare of any tax policy will depend also on the nature of the social welfare function used, defined in terms of individual utilities, particularly the implied trade-off between total utility and its distribution. It is appropriate in this context to specify social welfare as a function of individuals' utilities, given the endogeneity of labour supplies. The examples use the well-known iso-elastic social welfare function, W, such that $W = (U_A^{1-\varepsilon} + U_B^{1-\varepsilon})/(1-\varepsilon)$, where the parameter ε measures inequality aversion. The examples are given for the fairly high value of $\varepsilon = 1.8$.

· The assumption that individuals have different tastes ensures that the optimal tax structure (that is, the structure which maximizes W) will involve some selectivity. If $v_x = v_y = 0$, it can be found that W is maximized with $t = 0.41$, giving $W = -6.0960$. When both indirect tax rates are set at 0.05, the value of t which maximizes W is reduced to 0.38, but the maximum value itself is unchanged. When, however, $v_x = 0.05$ and $v_y = 0$, W increases to -6.09099, for a tax rate, t, of 0.39. This increase in social welfare is associated with a reduction in total utility, though with $\varepsilon = 1.8$ this is more than compensated by the reduction in inequality. Finding the optimal structure requires, of course, an extensive numerical search procedure over values of t, v_x and v_y.

Instead of calculating the optimal structure, which must, from the above argument, involve selective indirect taxation, it is of interest to consider an example of a tax reform. Suppose there is a change in the tax mix starting from a position in which only an income tax operates. Results are shown in Table 15.3, starting from the case where $t = 3$ and $v_x = v_y = 0$ shown in the first row. The table shows that this tax system finances a transfer payment to each individual of 0.162.

Table 15.3   Alternative tax structures

t	v_x	v_y	Transfer	W
0.3	0	0	0.162	−6.1166
0.2	0.141	0.141	0.162	−6.1171
0.2	0.303	0	0.162	−6.1016

In making a change in the tax mix, an assumption of revenue neutrality (that is, an unchanged total tax revenue) is not necessarily appropriate since there will also be concern over the real level of the transfer. The tax mix changes considered here maintain a fixed real social dividend. The direct tax rate is first reduced to 0.2 and an iterative search procedure is used to find the value of $v_x = v_y$ for which the real value of the transfer payment is unchanged. This common rate is found to be 0.141, giving a value of W of −6.1171. Hence the uniform indirect tax reduces the value of the social welfare function. The final row of Table 15.3 sets the value of t at 0.2, but searches for the value of v_x, with $v_y = 0$, for which the real transfer is unchanged. The value of W is higher than in the previous two tax structures. In each case, however, total utility is lower than when only an income tax is used. Furthermore, it is found that an inequality aversion parameter of $\varepsilon = 1.2$ is not sufficient for the benefit of the inequality reduction to outweigh the reduction in total utility.

This chapter has presented a formal two-sector general equilibrium model allowing for variable labour supplies, income (wage and rental) tax and commodity taxes, and has shown how it can be solved using a two-stage iterative procedure. The model was used to illustrate a range of tax policies. The convenient results generated by the special assumptions of Chapter 14 no longer hold. However, the partial equilibrium result that a tax is borne by the inelastic side of the market was found to hold also in the general equilibrium framework.

APPENDIX 15.1   CES FUNCTIONS

This appendix repeats the formal analysis of sections 15.1 and 15.2, using the more complex case of constant elasticity of substitution (CES) functions.

CES Production Functions

If, instead of the constant unit elasticity of substitution between factors displayed by Cobb–Douglas functions, the elasticities are non-unit but constant, then production functions take the form:

$$x = A_x (L^{-\rho_x} + \alpha_x K^{-\rho_x})^{-1/\rho_x} \qquad (15.31)$$

$$y = A_y (L^{-\rho_y} + \alpha_y K^{-\rho_y})^{-1/\rho_y} \qquad (15.32)$$

with $\rho_x, \rho_y > -1$; $\alpha_x, \alpha_y < 1$. The elasticities of substitution are given by $\sigma_x = 1/(1 + \rho_x)$ and $\sigma_y = 1/(1 + \rho_y)$. The marginal products are given by:

$$\frac{\partial x}{\partial L} = \frac{xL^{-\rho_x}}{L\left(L^{-\rho_x} + \alpha_x K^{-\rho_x}\right)} = \left(\frac{x}{L}\right)^{1+\rho_x} \tag{15.33}$$

$$\frac{\partial x}{\partial K} = \alpha_x \left(\frac{x}{K}\right)^{1+\rho_x} \tag{15.34}$$

Hence the marginal rate of substitution in industry X is given by:

$$-\frac{dK}{dL} = \frac{1}{\alpha_x}\left(\frac{K}{L}\right)^{1+\rho_x} \tag{15.35}$$

If L and K units are used in industry X, then $L_T - L$ and $1 - K$ are available for Y, so that in the production of Y:

$$-\frac{dK}{dL} = \frac{1}{\alpha_y}\left(\frac{1-K}{L_T - L}\right)^{1+\rho_y} \tag{15.36}$$

The production contract curve is given by equating (15.35) and (15.36) but (with $\rho_x \neq \rho_y$) the resulting equation can not be solved explicitly for K in terms of L. In numerical work it is therefore necessary to solve for K, given L, using an iterative search procedure. A simple approach is to use Newton's Method, as follows. Write the contract curve as $F(K) = 0$, where:

$$F(K) = \frac{1}{\alpha_x}\left(\frac{K}{L}\right)^{1+\rho_x} - \frac{1}{\alpha_y}\left(\frac{1-K}{L_T - L}\right)^{1+\rho_y} \tag{15.37}$$

Starting with a trial value of K, K_0, for a given value of L, a new value, K_1, is obtained using:

$$K_1 = K_0 - F(K_0)/F'(K_0) \tag{15.38}$$

This approach is based on the use of the approximation of the function by its tangent at a point. The process in (15.38) is repeated until $K_1 \approx K_0$. The derivative $F'(K)$ is given by:

$$F'(K) = \frac{dF}{dK} = \frac{1+\rho_x}{\alpha_x L}\left(\frac{K}{L}\right)^{\rho_x} + \frac{1+\rho_y}{\alpha_y(L_T - L)}\left(\frac{1-K}{L_T - L}\right)^{\rho_y} \quad (15.39)$$

In the CES case, w/r can be found by appropriate substitution into (15.35), where K is given as the root of $F(K) = 0$ using the iterative method described earlier.

The approach to finding the price ratio for the CES case follows that used for Cobb–Douglas functions, except that the contract curve is not explicitly available. First, it is necessary to obtain expressions for dx/dL and dy/dK. After appropriate substitution into (15.31) and (15.32), it can be found that:

$$\frac{dx}{dL} = x^{1+\rho_x}\left\{L^{-1-\rho_x} + \alpha_x K(L)^{-1-\rho_x}\frac{dK}{dL}\right\} \quad (15.40)$$

$$\frac{dy}{dL} = -y^{1+\rho_y}\left\{(L_T - L)^{-1-\rho_y} + \alpha_y\{1 - K(L)\}^{-1-\rho_y}\frac{dK}{dL}\right\} \quad (15.41)$$

The term dK/dL refers to the slope of the production contract curve. This can be obtained by implicit differentiation, using $F(K)$ as given by (15.37), whence:

$$\frac{dK}{dL} = -\frac{dF/dL}{dF/dK} \quad (15.42)$$

The term dF/dK has already been given in (15.39), and:

$$\frac{dF}{dL} = -\frac{1+\rho_x}{\alpha_x L}\left(\frac{K}{L}\right)^{1+\rho_x} - \frac{1+\rho_y}{\alpha_y(L_T - L)}\left(\frac{1-K}{L_T - L}\right)^{1+\rho_y} \quad (15.43)$$

remembering that K is a function of L, as before, so that once the root of $F(K) = 0$ has been found numerically, the goods price ratio can be obtained directly using the above results, and appropriate substitution into (15.14) and (15.15).

CES Preferences

Consider first the general case of the CES utility function with k goods, such that:

$$U = \left(\sum_{i=1}^{k} \beta_i x_i^{-\rho} \right)^{-1/\rho} \tag{15.44}$$

with $\beta_i > 0$, $\rho > -1$, and $\sigma = 1/(1 + \rho)$ is the elasticity of substitution between any pair of goods. Utility is maximized subject to the budget constraint:

$$M = \sum_{i=1}^{k} x_i p_i \tag{15.45}$$

Form the Lagrangean:

$$\Omega = U + \lambda \left(M - \sum_{i=1}^{k} x_i p_i \right) \tag{15.46}$$

The first-order conditions are thus:

$$\frac{\partial \Omega}{\partial x_i} = \left(\sum_{i=1}^{k} \beta_i x_i^{-\rho} \right)^{-(1+\rho)/\rho} \beta_i x_i^{-(1+\rho)} - \lambda p_i = 0 \tag{15.47}$$

for $i = 1, ..., k$. Taking the first-order conditions for goods i and j therefore gives:

$$\frac{p_j}{p_i} = \frac{\beta_j x_j^{-(1+\rho)}}{\beta_i x_i^{-(1+\rho)}}$$

which can be rearranged to give:

$$x_i = \left(\frac{\beta_i p_j}{\beta_j p_i} \right)^{\sigma} x_j \tag{15.48}$$

Multiply (15.48) by p_i and add over all i so that:

$$\sum_i p_i x_i = M = x_j \sum_i p_i \left(\frac{\beta_i p_j}{\beta_j p_i}\right)^\sigma$$

which gives:

$$x_j = M\left(\frac{\beta_j}{p_j}\right)^\sigma \left[\sum_{i=1}^k p_i \left(\frac{\beta_i}{p_i}\right)^\sigma\right]^{-1} \tag{15.49}$$

To apply these results to the case of two goods plus leisure, it is necessary to set $M = \pi + w$, and note that the price of leisure is w. Substitute the demands in (15.49) into the direct utility function to get the indirect utility function, V, as:

$$V(p, M) = \left[\sum_i \beta_i \left\{\psi M\left(\frac{\beta_i}{p_i}\right)^\sigma\right\}^{-\rho}\right]^{-1/\rho} \tag{15.54}$$

Solving this for M gives the expenditure function as:

$$M = E(U, p) = U\psi^{-1}\left[\sum_i \beta_i \left(\frac{\beta_i}{p_i}\right)^{-\rho\sigma}\right]^{1/\rho} \tag{15.55}$$

from which the compensating variations can be obtained.

16. Income distribution in general equilibrium

This chapter explores the relationship between the factor and personal income distributions within a general equilibrium framework. The effects on the distributions of changes in the tax structure are also examined. The main objective is to try to understand the main relationships involved. The general equilibrium model is modified so that it contains many individuals. Preferences are heterogeneous and labour supplies are allowed to vary. Hence the personal distribution of income arises from differential responses to factor and goods prices, which are affected by the tax structure.

Several general equilibrium models have been produced in order to examine the impact of various tax changes, but these models do not generate the personal distributions that are of interest here; examples include those in the tradition of Harberger (see McClure, 1975) and Shoven and Whalley (1973). There are also tax models which have been designed to exploit details on households provided by household expenditure surveys, but these do not allow for labour supply or other general equilibrium effects of tax changes; see, for example, Atkinson and Sutherland (1988). These studies are quite separate from the literature concerned with optimal income and commodity taxation, discussed in Part II, where tax rates are chosen to maximize a social welfare function subject to a government budget constraint being satisfied. Individuals are simultaneously regarded as maximizing utility subject to a constraint which itself depends on the tax structure imposed by the government. The interdependencies involved in such a 'dual decision' problem, combined with the corner solutions arising from non-linear budget constraints facing individuals, make the first-order conditions complex in structure. The studies of this kind nearly all impose a fixed distribution of wage rates, from which random drawings are made to produce a simulated population. They typically assume that all individuals have the same tastes.

The present chapter departs from the optimal tax literature in the following important ways. First, there is a need in both approaches to model heterogeneity. A desirable feature of the models would be heterogeneity in both preferences and abilities. However, in the standard optimal tax framework it is more tractable to assume common preferences with a fixed distribution of abilities. In the general equilibrium framework used here the introduction of a large variety of types of labour would place emphasis on their role in production. Instead, emphasis is placed on heterogeneity in consumption and leisure choices. There is a single wage corresponding to homogeneous labour in a two-factor general equilibrium model. However, individuals have different preferences in that, while they are all assumed to have the same type of utility function, they have different parameter values. The joint distribution of parameter values therefore plays a significant role in generating the endogenous distribution of income.

Section 16.1 briefly describes the main elements of the general equilibrium model. Section 16.2 introduces a linear income tax and explores the relationship between the various distributions. Section 16.3 examines the trade-off between equity and efficiency implied by the use of a social welfare function, for comparison with the typical partial equilibrium results.

16.1 THE MODEL

The framework of analysis is the two-sector model described in Chapter 15. This has two goods and two factors of production, where the total amount of capital services is fixed but labour supplies are endogenous. The following two subsections briefly describe the production and demand components of the model and the final subsection presents the specification of heterogeneity. This approach avoids any linearization, so the model is capable of handling a wide range of tax rates.

Production Functions

The production functions are assumed to be of the constant returns to scale, constant elasticity of substitution (CES) form. Hence, if L and K respectively denote inputs of labour and capital services, the outputs, x and y, in industries producing goods X and Y are given by:

$$x = A_x(L^{-\rho_x} + \alpha_x K^{-\rho_x})^{-1/\rho_x} \tag{16.1}$$

$$y = A_y(L^{-\rho_y} + \alpha_y K^{-\rho_y})^{-1/\rho_y} \tag{16.2}$$

with $\rho_x, \rho_y > -1$, $\alpha_x, \alpha_y < 1$. The elasticities of substitution are $\eta_x = 1/(1 + \rho_x)$ and $\eta_y = 1/(1 + \rho_y)$. The special case of $\eta_x = \eta_y = 1$ gives the Cobb–Douglas form. The assumed parameter values for the production functions are given in Table 16.1.

The table does not give values of the efficiency parameters A_x and A_y in the production functions. For convenience these were determined to ensure that the maximum possible amount of each good that could be produced is set to one unit if half the total available labour supply is available, combined with all the capital. This normalization is obviously arbitrary, but the absolute values are not of importance here.

Table 16.1   Parameter values of production functions

α_x	η_x	α_y	η_y
0.03	0.7	0.04	0.5

Demand and Labour Supply

Each individual is assumed to have a CES utility function defined over goods X and Y and leisure. Each person has an endowment of one unit of time, and devotes a proportion, h, to leisure and $1 - h$ to work. Then:

$$U = (\theta x^{-\delta} + \beta y^{-\delta} + \gamma h^{-\delta})^{-1/\delta} \tag{16.3}$$

with $\theta, \beta, \gamma > 0$, and $\sigma = 1/(1 + \delta)$ is the elasticity of substitution between all pairs of goods. Furthermore, without loss of generality $\gamma = 1 - \theta - \beta$.

Heterogeneous Preferences

As stated above, this chapter examines the implications for income distribution of heterogeneous labour supply responses to prices and the wage rate. It is therefore necessary to specify the joint distribution of the taste parameters θ, β, γ and σ (remembering that $\theta + \beta + \gamma = 1$). Since it is not possible to draw on empirical results, the approach taken is to use fairly simple assumptions involving a small number of parameters and a flexible functional form. Given that all the parameters must be strictly positive, the lognormal distribution was used as this is only defined for positive variables. First, it is assumed that the elasticity of substitution is distributed independently of the other parameters, with mean and variance of logarithms respectively of μ_σ and s_σ^2. Thus σ is $\Lambda(\mu_\sigma, s_\sigma^2)$ and given a random $N(0,1)$ variate, v say, the corresponding value of α is obtained using:

$$\sigma = \exp(\mu_\sigma + v s_\sigma) \tag{16.4}$$

The other parameters are a little more awkward, and there are only two degrees of freedom in setting the three values for each individual. The procedure adopted was to assume that β and γ are jointly lognormally distributed as $\Lambda(\mu_\beta, \mu_\gamma, s_\beta^2, s_\gamma^2, \phi)$ where ϕ is the correlation coefficient between the logarithms of β and γ. A value of γ was obtained using:

$$\gamma = \exp(\mu_\gamma + vs_\gamma) \qquad (16.5)$$

and then the corresponding value of β was obtained using the conditional distribution of β for given γ:

$$\beta = \exp\{\mu_\beta + \phi(s_\beta/s_\gamma)(\log \gamma - \mu_\gamma) + vs_\beta\sqrt{(1 - \phi^2)}\} \qquad (16.6)$$

where the values of v in (16.5) and (16.6) are independent random observations from $N(0, 1)$. The corresponding value of θ is obtained using $\theta = 1 - \beta - \gamma$. This means that the distribution of θ is not itself lognormal since the product, not the sum, of lognormals is lognormal. Furthermore, care must be taken to ensure that all θ values are positive; if a value turns out to be negative, it is simply rejected and the procedure started again. Parameter values are shown in Table 16.2. These were used to generate the distributions for 100 individuals.

Table 16.2   Preferences of workers

μ_σ	s_σ^2	μ_γ	s_γ^2	μ_β	s_β^2	ϕ
1.2	0.1	0.4	0.2	0.2	0.1	0.9

The Allocation of Capital

A decision must be made about the endowment of capital, and it is assumed that the majority of individuals hold no capital. The assumption is made that there is just one 'capitalist' who owns all the capital (normalized to one unit) and has preferences which may be distinctly different from those of the 'workers'. The capitalist is assumed to be ineligible for the social dividend, discussed below. It is assumed that for the capitalist, γ, β and σ take the values 0.5, 0.3 and 0.5 respectively.

Linear Taxation

The presentation of the model has so far ignored income and commodity taxation. It is possible to examine a wide range of tax systems, but for simplicity this chapter uses a linear tax structure. Suppose that a proportional income tax is applied to wage and property incomes at the rates t_w and t_r. Furthermore, indirect taxes may be applied to the tax-exclusive prices of the goods at the proportional rates t_x and t_y; the tax-inclusive prices are thus $p_x(1 + t_x)$ and $p_y(1 + t_y)$. Producers respond to tax-exclusive prices of goods, while consumers respond to tax-inclusive prices. However, producers respond to tax-inclusive factor prices while individuals, in their labour supply decisions, respond to the net wage and net property income. Thus the prices determined above can simply be regarded as those relevant to producers. Total tax revenue, R, is equal to:

$$R = t_w w L_T + r t_r + x p_x t_x + y p_y t_y \tag{16.7}$$

It is necessary to make an assumption about the allocation of tax revenue. It would be possible to assume that the government consumes some of the revenue in some specified way, but the following exploration considers a 'pure' transfer system in which all revenue is redistributed to individuals in the form of an unconditional transfer payment, or social dividend, T.

An Example

The basic model described above is capable of being used to examine a wide range of situations. For presentation purposes, attention is restricted to a small range of alternatives. In order to obtain comparisons with the partial equilibrium optimal tax literature, the following comparisons consider the use of only a wage tax. As the wage tax increases, labour supply falls and more people are at the corner solution where they do not work at all. The higher tax rate is able to finance a higher social dividend until the reduction in the tax base outweighs the effect of the higher rate. The relationship between the social dividend and the tax rate displays the shape familiar from the partial equilibrium literature.

The effects on relative goods prices, and relative and absolute outputs, as t_w increases, are shown in Figure 16.1. By assumption, workers on average have stronger preferences for good X than the capitalist, and it is assumed to be relatively more labour-intensive in production. As the wage tax increases, the relative price of good X rises, and this is associated with a fall in the relative output of good X; this is shown in Figure 16.1(a). The movement is not along a fixed production possibility curve because of the reduction in labour supply as t_w increases; this is considered in more detail below. The absolute outputs both decline as shown in Figure 16.1(b). The variation in relative outputs reflects neither a demand nor a supply curve, but reflects a changing equilibrium.

16.2 TAXATION AND DISTRIBUTION

The Factor Distribution

The fall in the relative output of the labour-intensive good would, in a model having fixed factor supplies, usually imply a fall in the wage relative to the capital rental. But in the present model the supply of labour falls in response to the higher wage tax; this is shown in Figure 16.2(a). Since the supply of capital is

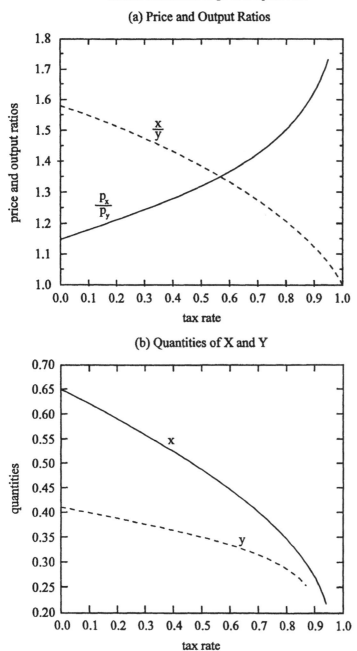

Figure 16.1   Price and output ratios

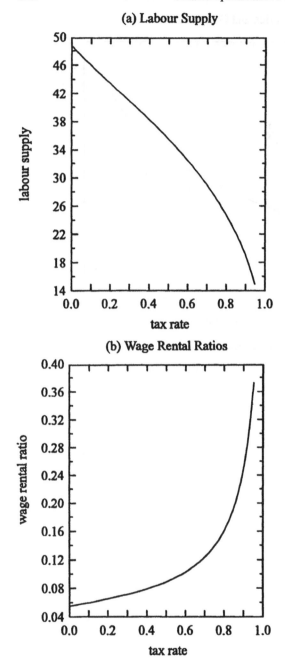

Figure 16.2   Taxes and the factor distribution

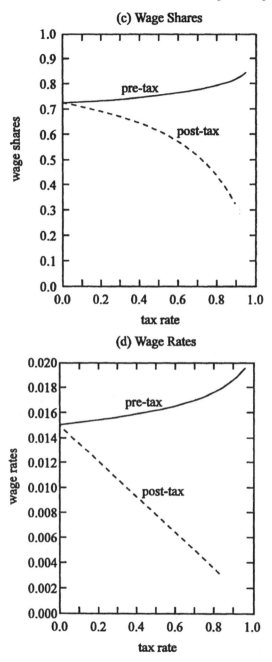

Figure 16.2   Taxes and the factor distribution

fixed, the effect on the wage/rental ratio is not obvious. The implications in the present example are illustrated in Figure 16.2(b), where the wage to rental ratio is seen to increase. The wage increases relative to the capital rental as production of the labour-intensive good falls, because the relative fall in the demand for labour is outweighed by the reduction in the supply of labour induced by the tax rate rise. The increase in the wage tax rate therefore leads to an increase in the pre-tax share of wages in total income. This is shown in Figure 16.2(c). However, the increase in the pre-tax share is associated with a reduction in the post-tax share of wages. The change in the factor distribution, before taxation, is relatively small, given the large variation in the wage tax rate and the associated changes in the goods price ratio and the relative output of the two goods. Despite the fact that the gross wage rate rises as a result of the tax rate increase, the net-of-tax wage rate falls so labour supply decreases. This property is illustrated in Figure 16.2(d). This reduction in labour supply modifies the effect of the rise in w on the share of wages in total income.

The Personal Distribution

The increase in the wage tax rate is associated with a higher social dividend until the tax base falls relatively more rapidly. The increasing importance of this social dividend means that the inequality of net income falls as the tax rate increases, and there are more people who do not participate in the labour market as t_w increases. It would be possible to examine the extent to which the distribution can be approximated by various functional forms. But this would be of little value; the form depends on the distribution of preferences for which there is virtually no information. It also depends very much on the tax structure; for example, the introduction of a higher rate of tax above some specified gross income would lead to a different distribution affected by the bunching of individuals at another kink in the budget constraint. However, it is useful to consider the behaviour of summary measures of inequality, and for this purpose various values of Atkinson's measure of inequality were obtained. The use of this measure requires the assignment of a value to the inequality aversion parameter, ε, and it is most appropriate to consider a range of values. Figure 16.3(a) shows the inequality of net income for two values of ε as the tax rate, t_w, increases. It can be seen that, in each case, the inequality of net income is sensitive to variations in the tax rate.

Profiles of the inequality of gross income are not shown because the Atkinson measure cannot be calculated where there are zero values. However, in cases where all workers are employed for a range of lower tax rates, the inequality of gross income is found to increase with t_w. This is consistent with the results obtained in the standard partial equilibrium framework. Figure 16.3(b) shows

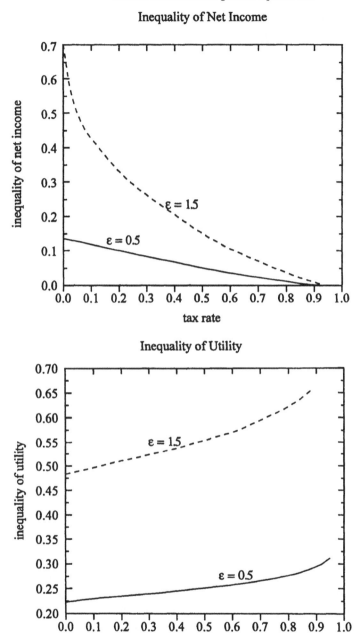

Figure 16.3   Inequality and taxes

the profile of the inequality of utility, where it is seen to increase slightly as t_w increases. This result is at first sight a little surprising, and is not typically found in the standard treatment of taxation with endogenous labour supplies using a fixed distribution of wage rates. It therefore warrants further investigation and is considered in the following subsection.

Income and Utility

In examining the possible variations in the inequality of gross and net income and utility, it is most convenient to use the special case where the elasticity of substitution is unity, that is, the Cobb–Douglas form. Consider also, for simplicity, the case of a single good with price normalized to unity. Hence the individual is considered to maximize utility, $U = c^\alpha h^{1-\alpha}$, and faces a 'full income', M, of $T + w(1 - t)$ where T is the value of the social dividend, as above. The interior solutions are given by:

$$h = \frac{(1-\alpha)M}{(1-t)w} \tag{16.8}$$

$$c = \alpha M \tag{16.9}$$

Using (16.8) the gross earnings, y, are given by:

$$y = w(1 - h) = \alpha w - \psi \tag{16.10}$$

with:

$$\psi = \frac{T(1-\alpha)}{1-t} \tag{16.11}$$

Equation (16.10) gives the familiar result that the relationship between y and w is a straight line over the range of w for which $h < 1$ inclined at a slope of α. With heterogeneous tastes, these lines have different slopes but, if extended into the negative range, all lines will meet at a single point – since the value of w for which $y = w$ is $-T/(1 - t)$ and is the same for each individual.

Examples are shown in Figure 16.4 for two individuals. For a given combination of T and t, the lines emanate from point I in the negative orthant. For a higher value of t, T will typically also increase and the common point moves out to I'. For a given wage rate of w, the figure shows persons 1 and 2 earning

y_1 and y_2 respectively. It has been seen that in the general equilibrium context an increase in t is accompanied by an increase in the wage rate. Figure 16.4 shows that when t increases and the wage increases to w', the earnings y'_1 and y'_2 display more inequality, however measured, than y_1 and y_2. Thus it is not difficult to show that an increase in the tax rate, accompanied by an increase in the wage rate, can lead to an increase in the dispersion of gross income, although the progressivity of the tax system produces a reduction in the inequality of net income.

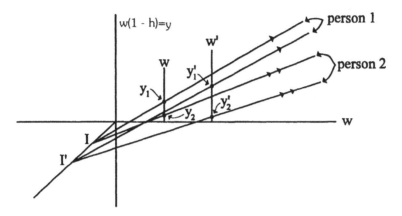

Figure 16.4   Earnings and the wage rate: two individuals

Consider, however, the effect on utility of each person. Given the Cobb–Douglas specification of the utility function, utility can be expressed in terms of w, t and so on, as follows:

$$U = \{\alpha\{w(1-t)+T\}\}^\alpha \left[\frac{(1-\alpha)\{w(1-t)+T\}}{w(1-t)} \right]^{1-\alpha} \qquad (16.12)$$

$$= \alpha^\alpha(1-\alpha)^{1-\alpha}\{w(1-t)\}^\alpha\{1+T/(1-t)w\}$$

This result holds only for interior solutions. Hence for two individuals with taste parameters α_1 and α_2, and assuming as above that they face the same wage rate at all times, the ratio of utilities is:

$$\frac{U_1}{U_2} = \{w(1-t)\}^{\alpha_1-\alpha_2} \left[\frac{\alpha_1^{\alpha_1}(1-\alpha_1)^{1-\alpha_1}}{\alpha_2^{\alpha_2}(1-\alpha_2)^{1-\alpha_2}} \right] \qquad (16.13)$$

Equation (16.12) shows that utility falls as α increases, for given values of the other variables. The person with the stronger preference for consumption of goods must give up relatively more leisure (since both individuals face the same budget constraint, having the same value of full income), and has a lower utility as a result. Thus if $\alpha_1 > \alpha_2$, it follows that $U_1 < U_2$ and the ratio U_1/U_2 is less than one. Equation (16.13) shows that, for $\alpha_1 > \alpha_2$, the ratio of utilities increases as $w(1 - t)$, the net-of-tax wage rate, increases. Thus, if an increase in the tax rate results in an increase in the wage rate (in the general equilibrium context), such that the net wage nevertheless falls, then the ratio U_1/U_2 falls. Hence, starting from $U_1/U_2 < 1$, the ratio falls yet further and the dispersion of utility increases. The requirement that the net-of-tax wage rate falls, despite the rise in the pre-tax wage rate, is indeed met in the examples shown above; see Figure 16.2(d).

16.3   A SOCIAL WELFARE FUNCTION

As seen in Part II, the optimal tax literature considers the maximization of a social welfare function, specified in terms of individual utilities using the well-known iso-elastic form of social welfare function:

$$W = \frac{1}{1-\varepsilon}\sum_{i=1}^{N} U_i^{1-\varepsilon} \qquad (16.14)$$

It is possible to express social welfare in terms of arithmetic mean utility and its inequality, as measured by the Atkinson measure $I(\varepsilon)$, as follows:

$$\frac{W}{N} = \frac{\left[\overline{U}\{1 - I(\varepsilon)\}\right]^{1-\varepsilon}}{1-\varepsilon} \qquad (16.15)$$

This formulation represents an explicit trade-off between equity, reflected by $1 - I(\varepsilon)$, and efficiency, reflected by $\overline{U}$. It shows the extent to which the social welfare function (16.14) is prepared to 'purchase' more equality with a reduction in total utility, or vice versa. The terms on which such a decision can be made, that is, the relationship between $\overline{U}$ and $I(\varepsilon)$ generated by the general equilibrium model, can only be obtained numerically. It has been seen that the inequality of utility actually increases as t_w increases. However, total utility initially increases before eventually falling. This generates the relationships shown in Figure 16.5(a) and 16.5(b). The downward-sloping section for each value of ε, which involves a reduction in total utility along with an increase in equality, is

utility and inequality ($\varepsilon = 0.5$)

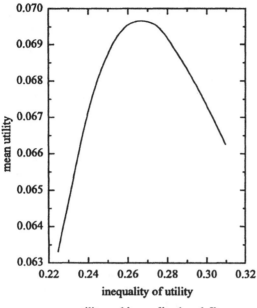

utility and inequality ($\varepsilon = 1.5$)

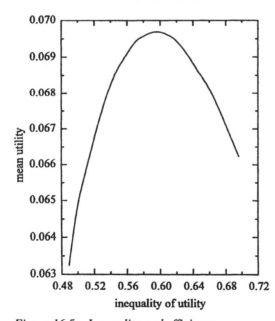

Figure 16.5   Inequality and efficiency

not a relevant range from the point of view of social decision-taking. The social indifference curves are upward-sloping and there is a point of tangency which corresponds to the optimal. The present context is one in which extra total utility is purchased at a cost in terms of an increase in inequality. This contrasts with the partial equilibrium framework in which both total utility and its inequality fall as the tax rate is increased.

Several sensitivity analyses were also carried out in order to ensure that the major results are robust with respect to changes in parameter values. It was found that, as selected parameter values were varied, all the relevant variables considered above changed monotonically. Changes in the correlation coefficient between taste parameters β and γ have very little effect on the results, but this is not surprising given the restriction on the sum of θ, β and γ. There is therefore little danger that the results examined above are unrepresentative. More interesting results concern the elasticities of substitution in both production and consumption. As the average value of the elasticity of substitution in consumption is increased, the wage/rental ratio and wage share are found to increase slightly, while the inequality of net income falls very slightly. However, the inequality of utility increases more rapidly. When the elasticities of substitution in production are increased, there is little effect on the inequality of either net income or utility, although the wage share increases relatively rapidly for values less than unity, and more slowly thereafter. The factor distribution is thus seen to respond more to production elasticities, while the personal distribution responds relatively more to consumption elasticities. For further details see Creedy and Lim (1995).

Within the model there is much scope for many analyses of alternative tax policies and their influence on factor and personal distributions. The present chapter has explored only a limited range of policies. Furthermore, it is not clear at this stage to what extent the major results are model-specific. But in view of the fact that separate areas of distributional analyses are usually considered in isolation, it can be argued that the present exercise provides some initial insights into the relevant interdependencies.

References

Aaron, H. (1966) The social insurance paradox. *Canadian Journal of Economics*, 32, 371–9.

Aitchison, J. and Brown, J.A.C. (1957) *The Lognormal Distribution*. Cambridge: Cambridge University Press.

Alt, J. (1988) Uncertain tax policies, individual behaviour and welfare. *American Economic Review*, 78, pp. 237–45.

Amiel, Y. and Cowell, F.A. (1992) Measurement of inequality: experimental test by questionnaire. *Journal of Public Economics*, 47, pp. 3–26.

Amiel, Y. and Creedy, J. (1994) Measuring inequality aversion. University of Melbourne Department of Economics Research Paper, 400.

Atkinson, A.B. (1970) On the measurement of inequality. *Journal of Economic Theory*, 2, pp. 244–63.

Atkinson, A.B. (1975) *The Economics of Inequality*. Oxford: Oxford University Press.

Atkinson, A.B. (1983) *Social Justice and Public Policy*. London: Harvester.

Atkinson, A.B. (1987a) On the measurement of poverty. *Econometrica*, 55, pp. 749–64.

Atkinson, A.B. (1987b). Income maintenance and social insurance. In *Handbook of Public Economics,* vol. II, ed. A.J. Auerbach and M. Feldstein, New York: North-Holland, pp. 779–908.

Atkinson, A.B. (1992) Measuring inequality and differing social judgements. In *Research on Economic Inequality*, vol. 3, ed. T.M Smeeding, Greenwich: JAI Press, pp. 29–56.

Atkinson, A.B. (ed.) (1973) *Wealth, Income and Inequality*. Harmondsworth, Middx: Penguin.

Atkinson, A.B. and Stiglitz, J.E. (1980) *Lectures in Public Economics*. New York: McGraw-Hill.

Atkinson, A.B. and Sutherland, H. (1988) *Tax-Benefit Models*. London: STICERD.

Auerbach, A.J. (1987) The theory of excess burden and optimal taxation. In *Handbook of Public Economics*, vol. I, ed. A. J. Auerbach and M. Feldstein, Amsterdam: North-Holland, pp. 61–80.

Auerbach, A.J. and Kotlikoff, L. (1987) *Dynamic Fiscal Policy*. Cambridge: Cambridge University Press.

Australian Treasury (1985) *Reform of the Australian Tax System*, Draft White Paper.

Barlow, R. and Sparks, G. (1964) A note on progression and leisure. *American Economic Review*, 54, pp. 372–7.

Barzel, Y. and McDonald, R.J. (1973) Assets, subsistence and the supply curve of labour. *American Economic Review*, 63, pp. 621–33.

Beckerman, W. (1979a) The impact of income maintenance programmes on poverty in Britain. *Economic Journal*, 89, pp. 261–79.

Beckerman, W. (1979b) *Poverty and the Impact of Income Maintenance Programmes in Four Developed Countries*. Geneva: International Labour Office.

Besley, T. (1990) Means testing versus universal provision in poverty alleviation programmes. *Economica*, 57, pp. 119–29.

Blinder, A. (1978) On making the tradeoff between equality and efficiency operational. Paper presented at the Meetings of the Allied Social Science Associations, Chicago, Ill.

Bosworth, B., Burtless, G. and J. Sabelhaus (1991) The decline in saving: evidence from household surveys. *Brookings Papers on Economic Activity*, 1, pp. 183–241.

Breit, W. (1974) Income redistribution and efficiency norms. In *Redistribution Through Public Choice*, ed. H.M. Hochman and G.E. Peterson, New York: Columbia University Press, pp. 3–21.

Brunner, J.K. (1989) *Theory of Equitable Taxation*. Berlin: Springer-Verlag.

Cameron, L. and Creedy, J. (1994) Taxation and the redistribution of lifetime income. In *Taxation, Poverty and Income Distribution*, ed. J. Creedy, Aldershot, Hants.: Edward Elgar, pp. 140–62.

Cameron, L. and Creedy, J. (1995) Indirect tax exemptions and the distribution of lifetime income: a simulation analysis. *Economic Record*, 71, pp. 77–87.

Casperson E. and Metcalf, G. (1993) Is a value added tax progressive? Annual versus lifetime incidence studies. National Bureau of Economic Research, Working Paper no. 4387.

Chatterji, M. (1979) A note on progressive taxes and the supply of labour. *Journal of Public Economics*, 12, pp. 215–20.

Christiansen, V. and Jansen, E.S. (1978) Implicit social preferences in the Norwegian system of social preferences. *Journal of Public Economics*, 10, pp. 217–45.

Coulter, F.A.E., Cowell, F.A. and Jenkins, S.P. (1994) Equivalence scale relativities and the extent of inequality and poverty. In *Taxation, Poverty and Income Distribution*, ed. J. Creedy, Aldershot, Hants.: Edward Elgar, pp. 87–103.

Cowell, F.A. (1981) Income maintenance schemes under wage-rate uncertainty. *American Economic Review*, 71, pp. 692–703.

Creedy, J. (1978) Negative income taxes and income redistribution. *Oxford Bulletin of Economics and Statistics*, 40, pp. 363–9.

Creedy, J. (1979) Income averaging and progressive taxation. *Journal of Public Economics*, 12, 387–97.

Creedy, J. (1982a) Some analytics of income tax/transfer schemes. *Journal of Economic Studies*, 9, no. 3, pp. 30–9.

Creedy, J. (1982b) *State Pensions in Britain*, Cambridge: Cambridge University Press.

Creedy, J. (1985) *Dynamics of Income Distribution*. Oxford: Basil Blackwell.

Creedy, J. (1992a) *Demand and Exchange in Economic Analysis: A History from Cournot to Marshall*. Aldershot, Hants.: Edward Elgar.

Creedy, J. (1992b) *Income, Inequality and the Life Cycle*. Aldershot, Hants.: Edward Elgar.

Creedy, J. (1992c) Revenue and progressivity neutral changes in the tax mix. *Australian Economic Review*, 2, pp. 31–8.

Creedy, J. (1993a) The role of selectivity in consumption taxes: should consumption taxes be uniform? *Economic Analysis and Policy*, 23, no. 1, pp. 1–13.

Creedy, J. (1993b) Taxation in general equilibrium: an introduction. *Hacienda Publica Espanola*, 127, no. 4, pp. 61–82.

Creedy, J. (1994a) Taxes and transfers with endogenous earnings: some basic analytics. *Bulletin of Economic Research*, 46, pp. 97–130.

Creedy, J. (1994b) Two-tier state pensions: labour supply and income distribution. *Manchester School*, LXII, no. 2, pp. 167–83.

Creedy, J. (1995a) Taxes and transfers: target efficiency and social welfare. *Economica* (forthcoming).

Creedy, J. (1995b) Taxes, transfers and income distribution: some computer programs. University of Melbourne Department of Economics Research Paper, no 456.

Creedy, J. (1995c) *The Economics of Higher Education*. Aldershot, Hants: Edward Elgar.

Creedy, J. and Disney, R. (1989) The new pension scheme in Britain. In *The Economics of Social Security*, ed. by A. Dilnot and I. Walker, Oxford: Oxford University Press, pp. 224–38.

Creedy, J. and Disney, R. (1992) Financing pensions in alternative pay-as-you-go pension schemes. *Bulletin of Economic Research*, 44, pp. 39–53.

Creedy, J. and Francois, P. (1993) Voting over income tax progression in a two-period model. *Journal of Public Economics*, 50, pp. 291–8.

Creedy, J. and Gemmell, N. (1982) The built-in flexibility of progressive income taxes: a simple model. *Public Finance*, 37, no. 2, pp. 361–71.

Creedy, J. and Gemmell, N. (1984) Income redistribution through taxes and transfers in Britain. *Scottish Journal of Political Economy*, 31, pp. 44–59.

Creedy, J. and Lim. G. (1995) Factor and personal income distribution and taxation in general equilibrium. *Journal of Income Distribution*, 4, pp. 51–77.

Creedy, J. and McDonald, I.M. (1992) Income tax changes and trade union wage demands. *Australian Economic Papers*, 31, pp. 47–57.

Creedy, J. and Morgan, M. (1993) Pension and tax structures in an ageing population. *Journal of Economic Studies*, 19, pp. 50–65.

Creedy, J., Disney, R. and Whitehouse, E. (1993) The earnings-related state pension: indexation and lifetime redistribution in the UK. *Review of Income and Wealth*, 39, pp. 257–78.

Dagum, C. (1990) On the relationship between income inequality measures and social welfare functions. *Journal of Econometrics*, 43, pp. 91–102.

Dalton, H. (1954) *Principles of Public Finance*. London: Routledge & Kegan Paul.

Davies, J., St-Hilaire, F. and Whalley, J. (1984) Some calculations of lifetime tax incidence. *American Economic Review*, 74, pp. 633–49.

Diamond, P.A. and McFadden, D.L. (1974) Some uses of the expenditure function in public finance. *Journal of Public Economics*, 3, pp. 3–21.

Diamond, P.A. (1977). A framework for social security analysis. *Journal of Public Economics*, 8, pp. 275–98.

Dixit, A.K. and Sandmo, A. (1977) Some simplified formulae for optimal income taxation. *Scandinavian Journal of Economics*, 79, pp. 417–23.

Edgeworth, F.Y. (1925) *Papers Relating to Political Economy*. London: Macmillan.

Foley, D.K. (1967) Resource allocation and the public sector. *Yale Economic Essays*, 7, pp. 45–98.

Foster, J., Greer, J. and Thorbecke, E. (1984) A class of decomposable poverty measures. *Econometrica*, 52, pp. 761–2.

Fullerton, D. and Rogers, D.L. (1993) *Who Bears the Lifetime Tax Burden?* Washington, D.C.: Brookings Institution.

Gemmell, N. (1985a) The incidence of government expenditure and redistribution in the United Kingdom. *Economica*, 52, pp. 335–44.

Gemmell, N. (1985b) Tax revenue shares and income growth. *Public Finance*, 40, pp. 137–45

Gevers, L., Glejser, H. and Rouyer, J. (1979) Professed inequality aversion and its error component. *Scandinavian Journal of Economics*, 81, pp. 238–43.

Gini, C. (1912) *Variabilita e Mutabilita*. Bologna.

Glejser, J., Gevers, L., Lambot, Ph. and Morales, J.A. (1977) Inequality aversion among students. *European Economic Review*, 10, pp. 173–88.

Graaf, J. de V. (1977) Equity and efficiency as components of the general welfare. *South African Journal of Economics*, 45, pp. 362–75.

Gruen, F.H. (1985) Australian government policy on retirement incomes. *Economic Record*, 61, pp. 213–21.

Hanoch, G. and Honig, M. (1978) The labor supply curve under income maintenance programs. *Journal of Public Economics*, 9, pp. 1–16.

Harberger, A.C. (1962) The incidence of the corporation income tax. *Journal of Political Economy*, 70, pp. 215–40.

Harding, A. (1994) Lifetime vs annual income distribution in Australia. In *Taxation, Poverty and Income Distribution*, ed. J. Creedy, Aldershot, Hants.: Edward Elgar, pp. 104–39.

Harding, A. and Mitchell, D. (1992) The efficiency and effectiveness of the tax-transfer system in the 1980s. *Australian Tax Forum*, 9, pp. 277–304.

Heady, C. (1993) Optimal taxation as a guide to tax policy: a survey. *Fiscal Studies*, 14, pp. 15–41

Hemming, R. (1980) Income tax progression and labour supply. *Journal of Public Economics*, 14, pp. 95–100.

Hersoug, T. (1984) Union wage response to tax changes. *Oxford Economic Papers*, 36, pp. 37–51.

Ihori, T. (1987) The optimal linear income tax: a diagrammatic analysis. *Journal of Public Economics*, 34, pp. 379–90.

Ippolito, R.A. (1985) Income taxation and lifetime labour supply. *Journal of Public Economics*, 26, pp. 327–47.

Jacobsson, U. (1976) On the measurement of the degree of progression. *Journal of Political Economy*, 5, pp 161–8.

Jenkins, S. (1988) Calculating income distribution indices from micro-data. *National Tax Journal*, XLI, pp. 139–42.

Jenkins, S. and Millar, J. (1989) Income risk and income maintenance: implications for incentives to work. In *The Economics of Social Security*, ed. A.W. Dilnot and I. Walker, Oxford: Oxford University Press, pp. 136–52.

Jones, R.W. (1965) The structure of simple general equilibrium models. *Journal of Political Economy*, 79, pp. 437–59.

Kakwani, N.C. (1977) Measurement of tax progressivity: an international comparison. *Economic Journal*, 87, pp. 71–80.

Kakwani, N. C. (1980) *Income Inequality and Poverty: Methods of Estimation and Policy Applications*. Oxford: Oxford University Press.

Kakwani, N.C. (1984) On the measurement of tax progressivity and redistribution effect of taxes with applications to horizontal and vertical equity. *Advances in Econometrics*, 3, pp. 149–68.

Kanbur, R. and Tuomala, M. (1994) Inherent inequality and the optimal graduation of marginal tax rates. *Scandinavian Journal of Economics*, 96, pp. 275–82.

Kay, J.A. (1990) Consumption and income taxation: horizontal equity and life cycle issues. In *Heidelberg Congress on Taxing Consumption*, ed. M. Rose, Berlin: Springer-Verlag, pp. 84–108.

Kay J.A. and Morris, C.N. (1979) Direct and indirect taxes: some effects of the 1979 Budget. *Fiscal Studies*, 1, pp. 1–10.

Kennedy, B.R. (1990) Financial consistency in longitudinal microsimulation: homemaker pensions re-examined. *Review of Income and Wealth*, 36, pp. 215–22.

Kesselman, J.R. and Garfinkel, I. (1978) Professor Friedman, meet lady Rhys-Williams: NIT vs CIT. *Journal of Public Economics*, 10, pp. 179–216.

King, M.A. (1980) Savings and taxation. In *Public Policy and the Price System*, ed. G.A. Hughes and G.M. Heal, London: Allen & Unwin, pp. 1–35.

Kotlikoff, L.J. and Summers, L.H. (1987) Tax incidence. In *Handbook of Public Economics*, vol. II, ed. A.J. Auerbach and M. Feldstein, Amsterdam: North-Holland, pp. 1043–92.

Lambert, P.J. (1985a) On the redistributive effect of taxes and benefits. *Scottish Journal of Political Economy*, 32, pp. 39–54.

Lambert, P.J. (1985b) Endogenizing the income distribution: the redistributive effect, and Laffer effects, of a progressive tax-benefit system. *European Journal of Political Economy*, 1, pp. 3–20.

Lambert, P.J. (1988) Okun's Bucket: a leak and two splashes. *Journal of Economic Studies*, 15, pp. 71–8.

Lambert, P.J. (1990) The equity–efficiency trade-off: Breit reconsidered. *Oxford Economic Papers*, 42, pp. 91–104.

Lambert, P. J. (1993a) *The Distribution and Redistribution of Income*. Manchester: Manchester University Press.

Lambert, P.J. (1993b) Evaluating impact effects of tax reforms. *Journal of Economic Surveys*, 7, pp. 205–42.

McLure, C.E. (1975) General equilibrium incidence analysis: the Harberger model after ten years. *Journal of Public Economics*, 4, pp. 125–61.

Mieszkowski, P.M. (1969) Tax incidence theory: the effects of taxes on the distribution of income. *Journal of Economic Literature*, 7, pp. 1103–24.

Mirrlees, J.A. (1976) Optimal tax theory: a synthesis. *Journal of Public Economics*, 6, pp. 327–58.

Mirrlees, J.A. (1990) Taxing uncertain incomes. *Oxford Economic Papers*, 42, pp. 34–45.

Mitchell, D. (1991) *Income Transfers in Ten Welfare States*. Newcastle: Avebury.

Muliere, P. and Scarsini, M. (1989) A note on stochastic dominance and inequality measures. *Journal of Economic Theory*, 49, pp. 314–23.

Musgrave, R.A. and Thin, T. (1948) Income tax progression, 1929–48. *Journal of Political Economy*, 56, pp. 498–514.

Nordhaus, W. (1973) The effects of inflation on the distribution of economic welfare. *Journal of Money, Credit and Banking*, 5, pp. 465–508.

Okun, A.M. (1975) *Equality and Efficiency: The Big Trade-off.* Washington, D.C.: The Brookings Institution.

Oswald, A.J. (1983) Altruism, jealousy and the theory of optimal non-linear taxation. *Journal of Public Economics*, 20, pp. 77–87.

Plotnick, R. (1981) A measure of horizontal inequity. *Review of Economics and Statistics*, 63, pp. 283–8.

Poterba, J.M. (1989) Lifetime incidence and the distributional burden of excise taxes. *American Economic Review*, 79, pp. 325–30.

Press, W.H., Flannery, B.P., Teukolsky, S.A. and Vetterling, W.T. (1986) *Numerical Recipes.* Cambridge: Cambridge University Press.

Robbins, L. (1930) On the elasticity of demand for income in terms of effort. *Economica*, 10, pp. 123–9.

Roberts, K.W.S. (1977) Voting over income tax schedules. *Journal of Public Economics*, 8, pp. 329–40.

Romer, T. (1975) Individual welfare, majority voting and the properties of a linear income tax. *Journal of Public Economics*, 4, pp. 163–85.

Sadka, E., Garfinkel, I. and Moreland, K. (1982) Income testing and social welfare: an optimal tax-transfer model. In *Income Tested Transfer Programs: The Case For and Against*, ed. I. Garfinkel, New York: Academic Press, pp. 291–313.

Sandmo, A. (1983) Progressive taxation, redistribution and labour supply. *Scandinavian Journal of Economics*, 85, pp. 311–23.

Scarf, H.E. with Hansen, T. (1973) *The Computation of Economic Equilibria.* New Haven, Conn.: Yale University Press.

Seade, J. (1982) On the sign of the optimum marginal income tax. *Review of Economic Studies*, 49, pp. 637–43.

Sen, A. (1973) *On Economic Equality.* Oxford: Clarendon Press.

Shapley, L.S. and Shubik, M. (1977) An example of a trading economy with three competitive equilibria. *Journal of Political Economy*, 85, pp. 873–5.

Shiller, R.J., Boycko, M. and Korobov, V. (1991) Popular attitudes towards free markets: the Soviet Union and the US compared. *American Economic Review*, 81, pp. 385–400.

Shorrocks, A.F. (1983) Ranking income distributions. *Economica*, 50, pp. 1–17.

Shoven, J.B. and Whalley, J. (1973) General equilibrium with taxes: a computational procedure and an existence proof. *Review of Economic Studies*, 60, pp. 475–90.

Stern, N.H. (1977) Welfare weights and the elasticity of the marginal valuation of income. In *Studies in Modern Economic Analysis*, ed. M. Artis and R. Nobay, Oxford: Basil Blackwell.

Stern, N.H. (1976) On the specification of models of optimum income taxation. *Journal of Public Economics*, 6, pp. 123–62.

Suits, D. (1977) Measurement of tax progressivity. *American Economic Review*, 67, pp. 747–52.

Waterson, M. (1985) On progressive taxation and risk taking. *Oxford Economic Papers*, 37, pp. 510–19.

Wells, P. (1955) General equilibrium analysis of excise taxes. *American Economic Review*, 45, pp. 345–59.

Williams, R. (1980) Structural change and private consumption: evidence from the 1974–75 Household Expenditure Survey, *Economic Record*, 56, pp. 54–68.

Yitzhaki, S. (1983) On an extension of the Gini index. *International Economic Review*, 24, pp. 617–28.

Zabalza, A. (1983) The CES utility function, non-linear budget constraints and labour supply: results on female participation and hours. *Economic Journal*, 93, pp. 312–30.

Index

Printed and bound by CPI Group (UK) Ltd, Croydon, CR0 4YY

23/04/2025

14661001-0004